PHENOMENAL

Triumphant!

SUPERNATURAL

BIGGEST

WEIRD WIZARDRY

AND

Astonishing

MIGHTY

BEST

Thrilling

MARVEL
OF
THE CENTURY

AILBLAZING

AMAZING

NDING

Extraordina

SENSATIONAL!

ING

COLOSSAL

ENORMOUS

NG

SPIRITE

NEVER BEFORE
SEEN

DARING

UNIQUE

FEARLES

MAGNIFICENT

WONDROUS

Miraculou

THE
DREAM
MACHINE

ABSOLUTEL

INSPIRING

WONDROUS

ORIGINAL

CURIOUS

Perilou

W.C. COUP'S NEW UNITE

THREE TIMES LARGER THAN EVER. EXHIB

LU LU THE **FLYING ARTIST.** POSITIVELY THE ONLY FLYING MAN IN THE WORLD, HIS FIRST APPEARANCE IN AMERICA.

WILL APPEAR AT EVERY PERFORMANCE IN HIS GREAT

MONSTER SHOWS.

D IN 3 RINGS AT SAME TIME. - COMBINED WITH

NUBIVAGIAN DART THROUGH THE AIR LIKE A BIRD FLYING ENTIRELY ACROSS THE MAMMOTH PAVILION

101 RANCH MIDWAY
NEWARK. N.J.
—1930—

Edited by
NOEL DANIEL

THE CIRCUS

1870s – 1950s

With essays and captions by
DOMINIQUE JANDO

additional essays by
LINDA GRANFIELD

and historical consultation by
FRED DAHLINGER, JR.

TASCHEN

HONG KONG KÖLN LONDON LOS ANGELES MADRID PARIS TOKYO

The Birth of American Popular Culture

Just a few generations ago, at the end of the 19th century, giant circuses crisscrossed the country on the new transcontinental railroads, attracting millions of viewers each year. The wild success of these circuses was unique among all other forms of entertainment, giving rise to the American pop culture we know today. In scope and ambition, the circus invented the rules of engagement for today's global entertainment industry: launching sensational press campaigns, employing global talent scouts, and bringing entertainment directly to audiences through the latest technology. The circus was the Super Bowl, the Olympics, and the Hollywood blockbuster all in one, brought right to your backyard.

But the circus is as much about the poetry of its performers as it is about its supersized proportions. Long before the Beat poets made "on the road" a generation's rallying cry, circus performers personified the romance of the open road and the grit of individualism. For over two years, I set out on a journey to uncover the inside stories of the American circus, retracing its yearly coast-to-coast circuit of bombast and flare. I studied archives across the United States, looking for clues that would help me understand the performers' fierce individualism, their love of the transient life, and their inexhaustible drive to entertain.

The images in this book capture the entrepreneurial audacity for which the circus became famous, and also the remarkable personalities and energy of its performers. Making this book I discovered that what happened behind the scenes of the circus was just as exciting as the performances. Ultimately, from 40 sources I gathered 30,000 images, and from those chose the 900 that best give insight into the circus as a world unto itself, a living organism with its own rules and way of life. These images represent the stories of those who lived and loved the circus and who endeavored to make the impossible possible. Most of the images have never been published, and many have never been seen, including those from 100-year-old performers' photo albums, and rare Kodak slides from the 1940s and '50s. The best images of the circus phenomenon aren't static relics of a forgotten era. They are very much alive with the color, energy, and power to entertain now as they had years ago.

Many archivists, private collectors, curators, librarians, historians, and circus fans have supported me during the making of this book. Every image here has survived 50 to 100 years because of the care of a single person and their belief in the circus' vital and important legacy. It is because of their efforts to preserve these artifacts that circus history remains accessible to us. I, like all readers of this book, am indebted to their desire to preserve the tenacity of the human spirit that is the circus.

Noel Daniel, Los Angeles, 2008

CONTENTS

SOMETHING WICKED THIS WAY COMES

Linda Granfield

SOMETHING WICKED THIS WAY COMES

Linda Granfield

By 1900 the circus dominated American popular culture. Circuses companies crisscrossing America that year entertained millions of the 76 million people living in the United States at the time. From May to October each year, tens of thousands of eye-popping circus posters were emblazoned on sheds and billboards as far as one could see. Enormous crowds gathered to watch elaborate circus parades move through city centers to announce the day's show, with some parades attracting as many as 150 thousand spectators in one afternoon. Few could resist the parade's exotic animals, the band's thunderous music, the shimmering spangles on the pretty women who were poised high atop elephants. By 1905 during the height of the circus' golden age, there were nearly 100 circuses and menageries, each playing to mesmerized audiences of between several hundred to over 20,000 a day all over the country. Well before the advent of film, radio, and television, the circus was the largest entertainment industry the world had ever seen.

opposite
1945 When the circus came to town, it unveiled its **odd people, amazing wild beasts, and extraordinary performers,** putting an indelible mark on each place it visited.

page 21
1954 ***Star aerialist Pinito Del Oro*** epitomizes the lure of the circus: an exciting world of fantasy where remarkable people perform daring feats with grace and gusto. Before the era of mass media, going to the circus was the ultimate escape and a unifying source of popular culture for a very diverse America, regardless of the viewers' social standing, ethnic origins, or whether they lived in the city or country.

The circus had been creeping into American culture for over a century during a period of rapid geographical expansion in the United States. Between 1804 and 1806 the legendary explorers Meriwether Lewis and William Clark traveled to the Pacific Coast and back, and the pioneers and frontiersmen who followed the explorers pushed past the Mississippi River to settle new towns that quickly grew into cities. In the years since the first American circus performed in 1793, the U.S. population grew from four to 23 million by 1850, and 31 states and five territories stretched coast to coast. The young nation was constantly expanding, and propelling that growth were the homesteaders who moved West. Among those visionaries were circus owners who eagerly took their shows to new audiences via the dusty, rutted pathways and wagon trails through the wilderness. Before circuses moved by rail, performers and their gear were loaded onto horse-drawn wagons that took to the dirt roads for months on end. By the 1870s these wagon trains included as many as 100 vehicles.

A City on the Move

In farming communities and small cities, the circus generally stayed one day only, an invigorating pace permitted by the use of the highly mobile canvas tent. This was long enough to perform two shows, which virtually everyone in the community attended. The greens and golds of grain fields were dotted with bold red-and-blue circus posters that seemed to magically appear as the circus advance man, and later whole crews, moved ahead of the circus. Entire communities adapted to the arrival of the circus. Businesses closed and school lessons were suspended so all could partake in the spectacle, a welcome diversion in what was an otherwise isolated environment. After the show, all gear, performers, and animals were packed up and moved to a new venue for yet another day and night of entertainment in towns surrounded by woods or prairie.

Western rivers such as the Mississippi and Ohio provided new highways for the circus, starting in the 1840s. These "boat shows" traveled by flatboats or steam-driven paddle wheelers, and once set up on shore could seat thousands of people under the big top. What had been routes of exploration for centuries had become part of an entertainment highway. After the Civil War (1861–65), westward settlement and the industrialization of the East Coast and Midwest meant more communities, factories, job opportunities, and increased profits for captains of industry like Andrew Carnegie and John D. Rockefeller, of steel and oil fame respectively. The drudgery of factory life, with its long hours and poor working environments, coupled with crowded and

1939 This map from the 1939 Ringling Bros. and Barnum & Bailey route book shows the distance traveled by the circus train in a seven-month season. It traveled *coast to coast, north to south,* and with a few excursions into Canada. Before film, no other form of live entertainment was able to match the circus in national exposure.

MAP OF THE 1939 COAST-TO-COAST TOUR OF THE RINGLING BROS AND BARNUM & BAILEY COMBINED SHOWS

top
1945 *Clown Felix Adler*, left, and friend were among the unusual creatures the circus presented. They were living overstatements of human foibles and ridiculousness, characters that could be laughed at openly.

1924 *One hundred double-length cars* on three special trains were required to transport the more than 1,000 artists and personnel, hundreds of animals, and a giant city of white canvas and red wagons. The circus burst into town one morning and was gone 24 hours later.

below, left and right
1944 and 1911 Weeks before its arrival, circus advance men *plastered colorful posters on every available surface.* Everyone knew of the circus' arrival, and no one wanted to miss it. Indeed, in many remote places, it was the most exciting day of the year.

top performance. With these new developments, the circus was becoming big business in the world of popular entertainment.

Barnum's understanding of the public's desire for all things unusual and captivating had been what initially compelled him to leave his general store business, develop a museum, then the circus with Coup and Castello in 1872, and finally in 1881 the new Barnum & London circus with James A. Bailey and James L. Hutchinson, which ultimately became the famous Barnum & Bailey circus. With its elaborate spectacles and ambitious goal of reaching hundreds of thousands of spectators in a single seven-month season, Barnum & Bailey, along with the equally resplendent and massive Adam Forepaugh circus, made audiences gape in awe at a grandeur and size never seen before in a traveling show and made small circus owners look on in envy.

By 1880 the new communication lines stretching across the 38 American states and nine territories meant new and sophisticated platforms for planning extensive circus routes. Circus schedules could be more rapidly drawn up or changed, and newspaper reporters could file stories for the press by telegraph and telephone. Life was moving more swiftly. The frontier was considered closed by the late 1800s as the railroad and the communities that sprung up around it flourished. The national

unsanitary conditions in the growing tenements of American cities made going to see the circus an exciting, welcome respite, if the few coins needed to buy a ticket could be pulled together.

The Greatest Show on Earth

The completion of the first transcontinental railroad tracks, which stretched across the United States by 1869, meant that the new "iron horse" could move larger circuses greater distances faster, and the development of local rail lines enabled circuses to reach more and larger audiences. Circus owners quickly took advantage of this speedier service to access all corners of the new American territories. Tons of equipment could be moved more rapidly than ever before with the help of ramps and other logistical innovations, albeit still with exhaustive effort, so the circus could travel through the night to deliver its magic to the next day's site. It was in 1872 that P. T. Barnum, Dan Castello, and W. C. Coup's circus, which they called the Greatest Show on Earth, dramatically changed the way circuses moved by rail. Their ambitious idea was to transport an entire circus by train along a preplanned route—the big top show, menagerie, sideshow, parade—where previous railroad shows had moved only the big

1941 At long last on a beautiful summer morning, the circus has rolled into town and made its home on an empty lot. An *army of workers* unloads the red wagons and erects acres of canvas tents. Circus Day has arrived.

below
1940s *Watching the tents go up* was part of the excitement on Circus Day, and many got up early to witness the spectacular speed with which the circus was erected.

opposite
1946 "The Big Top isn't just an inanimate, mobile structure in which to seat the audience, but *a living thing of vital canvas, rope and wood* that is breathed to life each day…that is the secret of the circus." (Ringling Bros. and Barnum & Bailey route book, 1941)

population was growing by leaps and bounds, adding 12 million souls in the last decade of the 19th century alone.

World's Largest Mobilization of Talent

Mergers meant larger circuses now traveled in dozens of railway cars, reaching 100 cars in 1922. The typical single performance ring under the big top grew to two rings and finally to a stunning three rings, four stages, and a hippodrome track all under one tent. By 1911 over 20 circuses traveled by rail, delivering entertainment to Americans all over the country. But with the circus boom that had begun in the 1870s came fierce competition for every circus to be the biggest and the most successful. One circus might arrive in town to find that the advance men for another operation had pasted over their posters with advertisements for their own show. The pressure for each to surpass the other also led to ambitious investments in American and international circus performers.

To this day business entrepreneurs around the world study Barnum's 1858 lecture "The Art of Money Getting." In it he espouses his take on financial success: "In the United States, where we have more land than people," declared Barnum, "it is not at all difficult for persons in good health to make money." Section headings of his lecture, such as "Whatever You Do, Do It With All Your Might," "Read the Newspapers," and a key factor in Barnum's success, "Advertise Your Business," continue to inspire today's entrepreneurs. Advertising, in fact, was a paramount issue. Circus owners were famous for coming up with eye-catching promotional glitz and ballyhoo to promote their operations and compete with other attractions for the same few coins that people could spare for leisure activities. More than a quarter of a circus' budget might be spent on marketing and advertising alone, collectively more than any other entertainment business at the time. But competition for the working American's spare change was fierce. There were flourishing vaudeville and variety shows that featured some of the same types of performers as the circus such as acrobats, mentalists, magicians, and animal acts. At the same time, burlesque shows, while less numerous, offered primarily male audiences a more titillating entertainment that featured women more scantily clad than the spangled ladies of the circus.

By the early 1900s nickelodeon theaters were taking off, and by the 1920s commercially viable silent film had arrived. A wane in circus audiences that had begun to be felt around 1905 became more evident as circus bands and calliopes were exchanged for the pianist's musical accompaniment of mute film stars on-screen. Films offered a new and exciting make-believe world, and circuses, with their live acts in real time, found themselves having to compete with movies for their audiences. The quest to increase audiences in light of the new forms of entertainment resulted in breathtaking new acts, and the circus star system, which had always been a part of the circus world, began to display new and glamorous Hollywood-style promotional tactics. The women, in particular, were photographed and promoted as starlets. Famous aerialist Bird Millman sang and danced on the tightwire as camera bulbs flashed. Lillian Leitzel, "the Queen of Aerial Gymnasts," allowed photographers into her private railroad quarters to show how she lived when she wasn't performing high above the ring. Gossip columnists who followed silent screen stars wanted the latest scoop on the handsome and fearless circus performers too. When the great trapeze artist Alfredo Codona performed one of the first triple-back somersaults off the flying trapeze, he made the news. When the lovely bareback rider Harriet Hodgini ran away

from the circus for love, she made the news. The colorful and bohemian lifestyles of both circus and film stars sold newspapers and tickets.

With the advent of World War I (1914–18), thousands of able-bodied men enlisted for military service. Thousands more went to work in the many businesses that manufactured products for the war effort. Suddenly there were fewer men to fill the jobs on circus lots. The men who remained were too old for military service and less physically able to take on heavy work. Everyone who remained on the circus lot, including young women, persevered as the rest of the home-front forces did, and waited for the war to end and the men to come back to life under the big top.

The end of the war, however, brought the American circus, and the rest of the world, another horror: the Spanish flu pandemic. Millions died. The numbers attending the circus dwindled further as people focused on the horrors at hand. In addition, some former circus employees, now veterans, were unable to return to work for they

were now disabled casualties of war. It became too difficult for many of the circuses to continue. New survival strategies were considered, and out of the wartime chaos was born a new show: the Ringling Bros. and Barnum & Bailey circus, which staged its first joint circus in 1919 and was an attempt to reinvigorate audiences that had been in decline since 1905. For a nation traumatized by war and sickness, the new venture, jam-packed with all the charismatic stars, dramatic music, incredible thrills, and pageantry of two-shows-in-one, was a much needed jolt of excitement that had been, and could be, a part of life.

But times were changing. As communities expanded and distances grew between parade sites and show lots, circus parades through towns disappeared. At the same time, more than half a million of Henry Ford's Model T cars clogged the nation's expanding roads. The Roaring Twenties had arrived. Hemlines rose, women finally got the right to vote, and silent film performers like Charlie Chaplin, Buster Keaton

1940s A cathedral of wonders, the big top was the heart of the circus. Human and animal performers from all over the world performed there *daily for more than 20,000 people* between two shows. In its golden age at the turn of the century, the American circus was the world's largest entertainment industry.

The Barnum & Bailey Greatest Show on Earth

SECTION 4. PERFORMING WILD BEAST DIVISION OF THE **NEW MILLION DOLLAR FREE STREET PARADE.** OPEN DENS AND CARVED ELEGANT CHARIOTS CONTAINING THE FINEST SPECIMENS OF *LIONS, TIGERS, WOLVES, BEARS, PANTHERS, LEOPARDS AND HYENAS* WITH DARING TRAINERS IN EACH DEN. EXHIBITING MORE MENAGERIE FEATURES FREE, THAN OTHERS CHARGE TO SEE.

THE WORLD'S GRANDEST, LARGEST, BEST, AMUSEMENT INSTITUTION.

(a former circus clown), and W. C. Fields (a former juggler) moved into the film world. Another circus rival was now found in the home, where wooden cabinet and tabletop radios had pride of place in American living rooms in the 1920s and 1930s. This audible entertainment, which included comics (radio "clowns") and the news, was long term for anyone who could afford the price of the wood-paneled box and the electricity it required.

Like other companies, circuses were hit hard by the stock market crash of 1929. Suddenly, circus seasons were shorter. Circus employees were laid off, and the lines of townspeople wanting jobs as temporary roustabouts grew. There simply wasn't enough money to operate as before. The Great Depression was upon the country, and any leisure activities were infrequent and expensive. The golden age "boom" of the circus was long over. The Depression had brought bust for many companies, and the circus was not spared. The saying may have been "Buddy, can you spare a dime?" but you needed 50 cents for an adult circus ticket and half that for a child's. The choice between food and fun was abundantly clear.

The Show Must Go On

American circus owners had to develop new ways to lure audiences away from their living rooms and onto the midway. Urban sprawl continued to devour acreage used for circus lots. Among the federal Works Progress Administration projects was road building, and truck circuses took advantage of the newly paved routes to bring the circus into the smallest communities. Nevertheless, some circuses closed down for good. It can be argued that circus performers were quite capable of surviving the Depression given that many of them had owned only what they traveled with and knew how to live frugally. They were creative, inventive people who could do much with little. This ability was something millions of unemployed Americans had to cruelly learn during the Depression years.

During World War II (1939–45), once again men, including circus performers, enlisted and women carried on the home front. Despite fuel rationing the federal government permitted circus trains to operate, and shows were once again raising morale. During this time other art forms interpreted the circus theme. The Disney

top
1890s Before the first performance, the circus gave a ***free street parade.*** The long procession of gilded wagons, wild animals, horses, performers, and elephants usually left the circus lot by 9 a.m.

1902 In Corsicana, Texas, on October 9, no one would have missed the Ringling Bros. street parade. In the circus' golden era, ***tens of thousands would line the streets*** to see the strange colors, sounds, smells, and imagery of this exuberant national phenomenon.

opposite
1955 Circus people appeared ***both glamorous and alien.*** They looked, dressed, and acted like no one in their community and took risks in their performances that would often not be tolerated elsewhere, embodying an altogether different kind of physical daring.

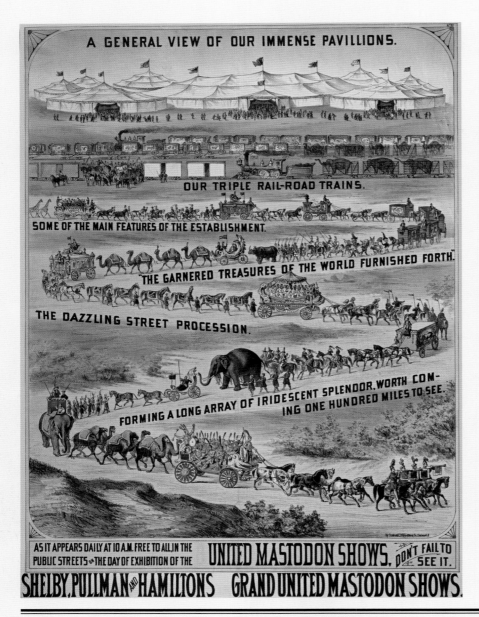

A GENERAL VIEW OF OUR IMMENSE PAVILLIONS.

OUR TRIPLE RAIL-ROAD TRAINS.

SOME OF THE MAIN FEATURES OF THE ESTABLISHMENT.

"THE GARNERED TREASURES OF THE WORLD FURNISHED FORTH."

THE DAZZLING STREET PROCESSION.

FORMING A LONG ARRAY OF IRIDESCENT SPLENDOR. WORTH COMING ONE HUNDRED MILES TO SEE.

AS IT APPEARS DAILY AT 10 A.M. FREE TO ALL IN THE PUBLIC STREETS ON THE DAY OF EXHIBITION OF THE UNITED MASTODON SHOWS. DON'T FAIL TO SEE IT.

SHELBY, PULLMAN AND HAMILTONS GRAND UNITED MASTODON SHOWS.

1881 This circus poster depicts the arrival of the circus trains, the vast city of canvas going up, and the *thunderous free street parade*, all part of the excitement, and helpful in enticing townspeople to buy tickets to the big top performance.

below
1930s On Circus Day, *businesses closed and schools were let out*. In the early days of the circus before it traveled by train, the gigantic procession of horse-drawn wagons, performers, noisy bandwagons, and animals marked the arrival of the circus in town. Later, a street parade would take place after the circus trains arrived, the parade wagons unloaded, and the tents erected.

opposite
1909 "In those days...all the glamour, the excitement, the music and the thrill of the cry, *'Here comes the circus parade'*, were too much for me and it left me eye-popped and open-mouthed with amazement, awe and envy." (Clark Gable, "Circus Day Dreams", Ringling Bros. and Barnum & Bailey program, 1951)

opposite below
1945 The practice of doubling equipment and performers was born of pure necessity. These *ornate, gilded wagons* were used to transport baggage and props during the setup but were also used in the circus parades and spectacles.

pages 32–33
1879 By the late 19th century, the transcontinental railroads had fully developed and communities had mushroomed along its tracks. The *railroad circus business boomed* and ever larger circuses sprung up from mergers. Pullman cars and Palace horsecars became the circus community's home for the seven-month duration of the season.

pages 34–35
1953 "The Circus has become *an American institution* and is part of every kid's growing up...to all of us the dream of pink lemonade, the big circus parade, the elephants, tigers and clowns has been part of growing up." (Burt Lancaster, "A First of May Guy," Ringling Bros. and Barnum & Bailey program, 1951)

pages 36–37
1931 This is *a "straw house" matinee* (a full house, in reference to the days when straw was put on the ground to seat the overflow of spectators) under this giant 14,000-seat big top. Latecomers are still pouring in, while the opening parade, known as the grand entry, has already begun.

PARADE OF BARNUM & BAILEY SHOW SHELDON, IA,

animated film *Dumbo* (1941) showcased circus life just as the United States entered the war. The story of the big-eared elephant and the depiction of the roustabouts on the lot brought the circus into the venues of its competitor, the movie theater, although the film actually indicted the circus and marginalized it. A year later, in an effort to involve leading designers and choreographers, John Ringling North hired famed choreographer George Balanchine to create an elephant ballet for Ringling Bros. and Barnum & Bailey, incorporating music by renowned composer Igor Stravinsky. Those who had sniffed at the circus as lowbrow suddenly saw it as being culturally significant. Other important designers brought onboard the circus around this time were Hollywood and Broadway costume designers Miles White and Billy Livingston.

News of the Allied forces' D-Day invasion of France on June 6, 1944, filled the pages of the world's newspapers. One month later, however, another event took over the headlines. Nearly 7,000 were attending a Ringling Bros. and Barnum & Bailey show in Hartford, Connecticut, watching the famous Wallenda family build their human pyramid on the high wire. Suddenly, there was fire, and the waterproof coating of the big top canvas added fuel to the growing flames. In a matter of minutes, 168 were dead in what was the worst disaster in the history of the circus around the world.

A Page From Yesterday

Understandably, people were afraid to go to circus tent shows after the Hartford fire, even though new regulations prevented the use of the same flammable waterproofing sealant that had caused the devastation. By the next year, the Greatest Show on Earth was once again performing in tents that were now fireproofed. Slowly the public returned to the big top. The war was coming to an end, but so was the long life of the circus under canvas. As veterans returned home, cities and suburban subdivisions grew. Television provided more immediate entertainment in the comfort of the living room; there was no need to travel to an outlying field. A turn of a plastic knob brought images of both real and imagined worlds into one's very home.

It became more expensive for circus owners to maintain their shows. The labor force that was once available was now protected by unions that demanded higher wages for circus employees. By 1956 it was fiscally impossible to cart a huge circus around America by rail. Both of the two remaining big top circuses that

traveled by train abandoned the railroad and started traveling by truck, one going indoors, the other remaining under the tent. The 17 remaining motorized circuses appeared under tents, while other troupes played in open-air stadiums or indoor sports arenas. Nevertheless, the glory days of the big tent show that moved by rail were over.

The circus had riveted the imagination of millions and thrived at a time when people lived very differently from how they do today. Access to live entertainment was easier, concerns for animal management were different, and there was less competition for one's leisure time. The circus declined for a number of reasons, among them changing entertainment technology and the ever-increasing competition for new audiences. Yet the American circus has not disappeared. Circus arts are taught in training schools, and circus history continues to inspire new performance art, pop culture and music, literature, fine art, and theater. An apt reflection of the inventiveness and energy of the human spirit, the circus stands as a vital foundation of American popular culture.

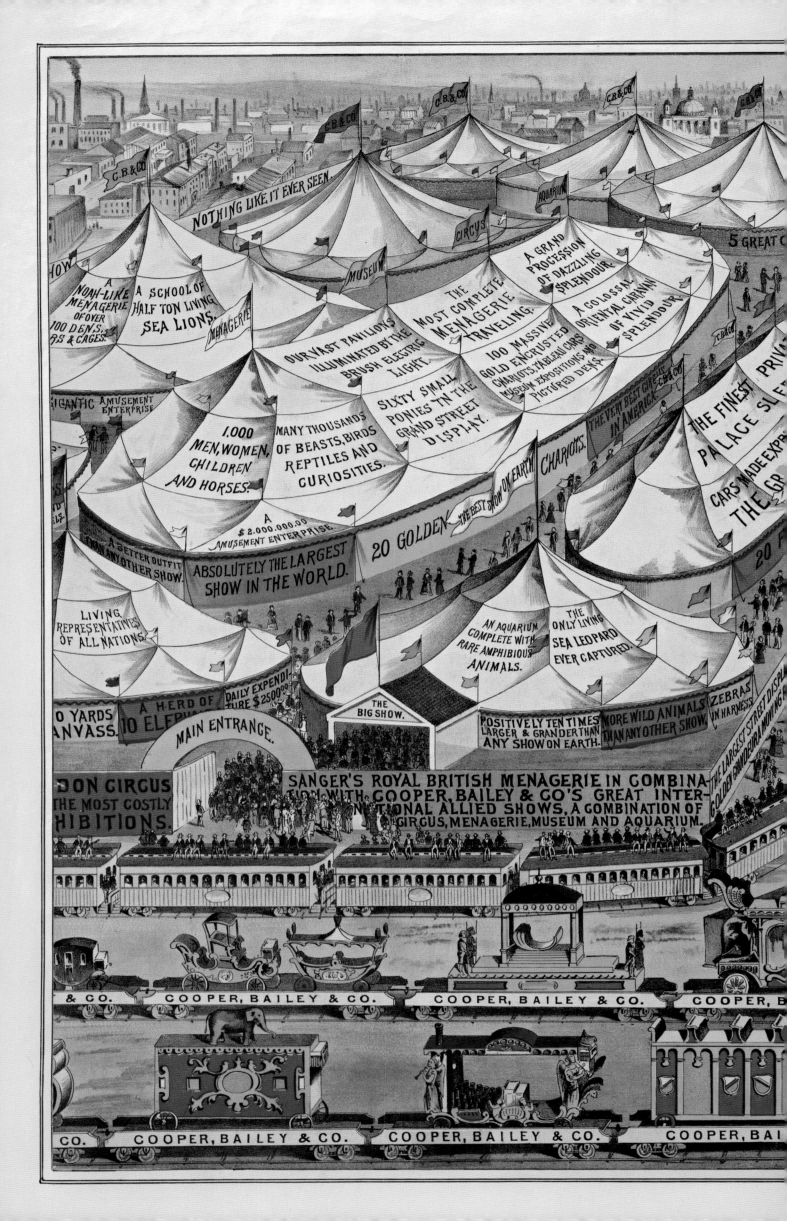

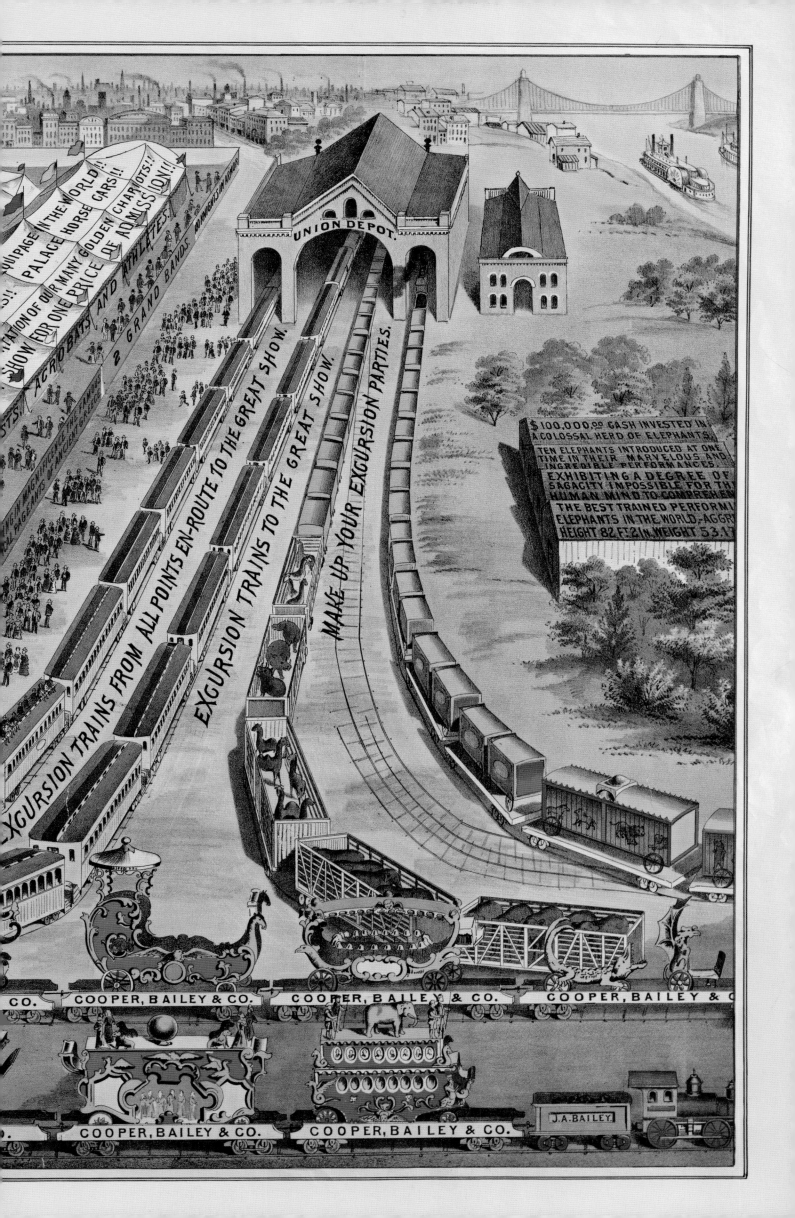

WORLDWIDE ROOTS

OF

CIRCUS INVENTION, PERFORMANCE, AND PLAY

Dominique Jando

WORLDWIDE ROOTS OF CIRCUS INVENTION, PERFORMANCE, AND PLAY

Dominique Jando

Many components of the modern circus run deep in the history of popular entertainment. One can argue that the first caveman who ever balanced a club on his nose to elicit the admiration of his friends (or hit himself on the head to make them laugh) was, in effect, sowing the seeds of what would later become the circus. The first known depictions of performing acrobats and jugglers appeared some 5,000 years ago in Egypt in the Early Dynastic Period (circa 3000 B.C.). The Egyptians developed a strong tradition of acrobatic and juggling arts and later taught these arts to the Greeks, who in turn taught the Romans. The Romans spread them throughout their vast empire through the itinerant troupes of performers called *funambuli*, literally meaning "ropewalkers," after the most spectacular attraction they offered. The rise of these itinerant troupes, with their regional networks and constant travel, would ultimately enable the performing arts to be passed on through the centuries, setting the stage for the circus to be born.

opposite
1880s Chinese acrobats and jugglers first appeared more than 2,000 years ago in the Han Dynasty. European travelers who saw them reported their extraordinary feats in illustrations like this one. As far-fetched as this spectacle looks, it was a close approximation of actual acts.

page 39
ca. 1585 The 16th-century painting *A Young Daughter of the Picts,* attributed to Jacques Le Moyne de Morgues, shows a woman whose skin is covered with floral illustrations. She is reminiscent of the tattooed people Western explorers were encountering in their seafaring exploits.

The performances of early itinerant entertainers often had religious undertones. Most of their routines had developed in communal rituals in which the remarkable physical skills of a few individuals were used to create easily accessible metaphors for overcoming life's hardships. These rituals generally celebrated mankind's sheer capacity for survival. In China, for example, acrobats, magicians, and jugglers first appeared in the harvest celebrations of the Han Dynasty 2,000 years ago. During the long, idle winter months, some peasants and craftsmen used their free time to develop their acrobatic, balancing, or juggling skills, improving their status within the community by becoming performers in these celebratory rituals. They practiced their stunts with everyday objects available to them on the farm or in their houses: cups, saucers, plates, ladders, fork, tables, chairs, etc. In time, these ordinary items would develop into specialized performing props. Western entertainers followed a similar path. For instance, the priests of Cybele, the mother goddess worshipped in Asia Minor, traveled to Rome from Athens, from village to village, displaying trained lions and leopards along with juggling and magic performances. These performances were intended to spread the cults of Dionysus, the orgiastic god of fertility who became the Roman god Bacchus, and Serapis, a Greco-Egyptian deity of the underworld.

The Devil Loves to Dance

But this collusion between religion and entertainment would eventually create suspicion and antagonism between performers and those in positions of religious power. The entertainers, knowing their "powers" were far from magical, soon realized that audiences enjoyed their performances for what they were—entertainment—despite the symbolism, metaphors, or "miracles" religious authorities wanted to attach to them. Thus, the performers embraced their power to entertain and began working for themselves. It became apparent to audiences that these exceptional skills didn't come from divine empowerment. The entertainers were simply human, and their talents the result of hard work and remarkable abilities. Feeling threatened, religious powers retaliated by accusing the entertainers, who had severed their art from religious ceremonies, of using witchcraft to accomplish their extraordinary feats. Relations between religious powers and performers would thereafter be uneasy for centuries.

Traveling entertainers found their professional identity during the Middle Ages, when they began to perform in the giant fairs that had spread all over Europe and Asia. Held annually, these fairs were immense regional markets that served as global trading places for the merchants who gathered there from every corner of the known world. Fairs were an open window on a universe of foreign and exotic people and were a focal point for intercultural exchanges. Merchants welcomed the traveling entertainers, whose amazing feats attracted larger crowds to the fairs. There, acrobats, jugglers, and animal trainers from the world over could compare their various skills, exchange techniques and ideas (or steal them), and take advantage of the unique artistic cross-pollination these gatherings offered them.

At the fairs, traveling acrobats, jugglers, and ropedancers also met entertainers of different genres, with whom they would join forces, centuries later, under the white tops of the American circus. First were the animal exhibitors who showed strange and exotic creatures in their wooden booths and canvas enclosures—such as a rhinoceros, an elephant, or a roaring tiger kept in a cage—to crowds of awestruck, and slightly frightened, onlookers. Later, in the 19th century, these exhibitors would work with the itinerant animal trainers, and together develop the traveling menagerie. Another group was that of human and animal freaks of nature, who were sometimes exhibited not much differently than wild beasts. They would eventually become the main draw of P. T. Barnum's American Museum in New York and ultimately populate the uniquely American circus sideshow.

Traveling entertainers also acquired the name *saltimbanchi*, an Italian locution that means "those who jump on to the bank" (or bench)—the elementary stage they erected by putting planks between a couple of barrels or sawhorses. These "banks" were also used as counters by the moneylenders who worked at these fairs. Consequently, moneylenders became known as bankers, and in England traveling entertainers became known as mountebanks, a literal translation of the Italian word. Mountebank, however, acquired a pejorative meaning when some entertainers began working for quacks, medicine men, and tooth pullers, who also conducted their business "on the bank." For these con men, jugglers, acrobats, and magicians were efficient crowd gatherers, even performing a "miracle" or two when needed. Some entertainers eventually embraced the jobs of the crooks that employed them. In time, mountebank became the name for a quack as well as an entertainer, giving the latter a bad name.

The Rise of Performing Dynasties

The fact that that word *saltimbanchi* defined traveling entertainers suggests the Italian ancestry of many of them. Indeed, Italian acrobats were in the vast majority, and they were celebrated all over Europe. The first acrobatic treatise was published in French in 1599 by one of them, Arcangelo Tuccaro, who was also the "personal

opposite

1806 Although there is no direct connection between the modern circus and Roman circuses, the modern circus borrowed the chariot race from the ancient games. Chariot races, like the one in this *reproduction of a first-century A.D. mosaic* from Lugdunum (present-day Lyon), became a staple of the American circus in the late 19th and early 20th centuries.

ca. 1580 These muscle men were *early jugglers* who manipulated objects like heavy stones and bronze balls. In the 19th century, circus jugglers often used heavy objects like cannonballs. By the 20th century, modern jugglers stunned audiences with their fast-paced juggling using light clubs, rings, and balls.

below

1612 *Antiquae urbis splendor* by Giacomo Lauro includes depictions of Roman amphitheaters such as *Rome's Coliseum* from the first-century A.D. Modern circuses resemble the Coliseum in their shape and in their use of wild animals, but modern circus animals are trained to perform, not fight deadly battles.

ca. 1900 When international commerce and colonialism developed in the 19th century, European and American circuses scouted far and wide for new talent. The **Asian acrobatic arts** they discovered and the performers they brought back with them became popular additions to their shows.

trainer" of king Charles IX and later Henri IV of France. Later many circus names would denote these Italian origins: Chiarini, Franconi, Truzzi, Ciniselli, Ferroni, Caroli, Fratellini, Cristiani, Rastelli, to cite a few legendary circus dynasties. Today, in North America and Europe, practically every circus family of old stock, whatever its name, has some Italian blood.

The community of itinerant entertainers formed a world of their own, with its own rules and traditions. They also protected each other, which was vital when traveling between tightly knit, sedentary communities. They were foreign intruders whose "unearthly" talents were sometimes perceived as disturbing and dangerous—possibly even the work of Satan—and they were often the object of harassment and persecution. Nonetheless, their free, itinerant lifestyle attracted other migrant people. Many Gypsies and Jews joined their ranks and created their own performing dynasties. For all the importance of these itinerant entertainers in the establishment of the modern circus, however, these acrobats, jugglers, and animal trainers didn't originate it. This would be the work of another community of traveling performers, the English trick riders, who were extremely popular in Europe during the second half of the 18th century.

By the 18th century, Britain had asserted itself as an effective constitutional monarchy, the first of its kind in Europe. This development facilitated the rise of a rich, entrepreneurial middle class and weakened the spending power of the nobility with two notable side effects: the end of extravagant courtly entertainments and the subsequent birth of commercial theater. One court entertainment that fell victim to these social changes was the spectacular equestrian carousel, a lavish piece of pageantry in which hosts of handsomely attired riders exhibited their skills and paraded on their horses in intricate ensemble patterns that were true equestrian ballets. The disappearance of these pageants produced another remarkable side effect, summarized by the 20th-century popular entertainment historian, Maurice Willson Disher: "When a curb was put on the spending powers of kings, [carousels] gave way before the 18th century to riding-schools, built by the nobility for the exercise of horsemanship and arms. These, in turn, suffered from the pinch of economy, and riding-masters had to turn showmen."

Ill-tempered, Flamboyant, but Extremely Talented

Roman "circuses" such as the Circus Maximus are often thought to have been the origin of the modern circus, but this is a popular myth. In 1768 a former military instructor, Sergeant-Major Philip Astley, began exhibiting his equestrian prowess on the outskirts of London on the South Bank near Westminster Bridge. He performed in a circular arena (as was customary with many trick riders), which was called "circle," or "circus," a Latin word used to describe any circular area such as London's famous traffic roundabout, Piccadilly Circus. Six-feet-tall (a giant for his time), Astley was overbearing, ill-tempered, grandiloquent, flamboyant, and, above all, extremely talented. He also had a keen sense of showmanship coupled with sharp business acumen. Astley's first summer season in London proved extremely profitable, and this led him to secure a lease on a nearby empty lot at the foot of Westminster Bridge, where he built his Astley's Riding School. It was an open-air structure with a 65-feet-circular arena surrounded with boxes for the spectators, who were protected from London's notorious weather by a roof. His shows attracted large crowds of horse enthusiasts (and there were many since the horse was man's most vital partner), but Astley's repertoire was not inexhaustible and he knew that his audience's interest would eventually wear down.

First Ever Circus Is Born

In 1770 Astley decided to expand his reach and lure the popular segment of the London audience to his equestrian shows. To do this he hired the drawing muscle of London theaters: acrobats, ropedancers, and jugglers. Legitimate theaters used

opposite
ca. 1860 *Exotic animals like elephants and tigers* were exhibited in traveling menageries in Japan starting in the 19th century, just as they were in Europe and America. In America these traveling menageries would later merge with the circus. Wild animals were an awesome sight and illustrated the reach of the trade routes expanding worldwide.

ca. 1827 *Indian jugglers* in Europe were part
of the cross-pollination of circus arts among
traveling entertainers. Other itinerant performers
included the Roma, commonly known as Gypsies, from India and Jews from across Europe.

these performers as entertainment between the various plays in their programs. In a
similar fashion, Astley began having them perform between his displays of horsemanship, adding variety to his performances. And taking his cue from London's commercial theaters, he ended his shows with a pantomime, a farcical play that included
such well-liked traditional characters as "Harlequin" and "Columbine," as well as
"Clown"—a comic stage character that had originated in the Elizabethan theater.
Henceforth, the circus as we know it, with its panoply of multiple performers inter-
mixed with athletic acts involving horses and other animals, was born.

Astley had struck gold. In 1779 he rebuilt his Astley's Riding School with a roof
and renamed it Astley's Amphitheatre. The ring had shrunk to a diameter of about
42 feet—quickly becoming the standard for all circus rings—and a small stage had
been added beside it for the presentation of pantomimes and acrobatic acts. Astley's
success increased, and competition came quickly, first by one of his former trick riders, Charles Hughes. In 1782, in association with the well-known composer and
librettist Charles Dibdin, Hughes built a luxurious amphitheater on Blackfriars Road,
not far from Astley's showplace, which Dibdin pompously named Royal Circus
Equestrian and Philharmonic Academy. It would be known more simply as Hughes's
Royal Circus—the first time that the word "circus" was used to identify a modern
place of performance. With its lavish decoration and furnishings, and its vast theater
stage behind the equestrian ring, the Royal Circus would be the model for all circus
buildings in Europe and the Americas until the end of the 19th century. (Circus shows
then, and in major European cities today, were given in purpose-built buildings.) Even
Astley would rebuild his amphitheater in 1794 on the model of the Royal Circus.

As a purely visual form of entertainment unhindered by language barriers, the
circus quickly spread all over the Western world. Astley, who had opened other circuses
in the British Isles, eventually established the first Parisian circus on the Boulevard du
Temple (the famous "Boulevard du Crime") in 1783, and it was a French equestrian,
Jacques Tourniaire, who introduced the circus in 1825 to Russia. Eastern and Northern

Europe also had a strong equestrian tradition that was influenced by the Spanish
riding masters who had come to Germanic Europe during Charles V's Holy Roman
Empire. The epicenter of this tradition was Vienna, the capital of Austria (which still
houses the world-famous Spanish Riding School), where Juan Porté opened a circus in
1780. Another Spanish riding master, Pierre Mahyeu taught horsemanship to Northern Europe's first great circus directors, Christophe de Bach (who in 1808 founded the
Circus Gymnasticus in Vienna's illustrious park, the Prater) and Rudolf Brilloff. One
of Brilloff's pupils and performers, Jakob Ernst Renz, would establish himself in
Berlin and become Germany's greatest circus director. And so the rapid healthy
growth of circus enterprises went on and on.

When the French Revolution in 1789 forced Astley to flee Paris, his
Amphithéâtre Anglais was taken over by an Italian equestrian, Antonio Franconi, who
renamed it Cirque Olympique. The name Franconi became synonymous with the
Parisian circus for more than a century, and the Franconi family would have a significant, albeit indirect, influence on the evolution of the American circus. In 1835
Laurent and Henri Franconi, son and grandson of Antonio Franconi, created a new
place of entertainment they called l'Hippodrome de l'Étoile. Hippodromes were a
sidebar in circus history, a large open-air arena devoted to equestrian arts and lavish
spectacles, including dramatic staged chariot races. When the Hippodrome de l'Étoile,
the first Parisian hippodrome, was erected in the shadow of the Arc de Triomphe, its
owners proclaimed that it would be to Paris what the Circus Maximus once was to
Rome, planting the seeds of the legend of a connection between modern and Roman
circuses. Hippodromes became very popular and flourished all over Europe. In 1853
the American circus entrepreneur Seth B. Howes and his partners, Richard Sands,
John J. Nathans, and Avery Smith, erected Franconi's Hippodrome in New York City,
luring into the combine an obscure son of Henri Franconi, Henri Narcisse Franconi,
to give the operation an air of legitimacy. This hippodrome disappeared in 1856,
but other showmen revived the concept in the 1870s, including, most notably, P. T.

opposite
ca. 1860 *Chinese ropedancers and balancers*
and their Western counterparts performed acts
that were often similar. To American or European circus audiences, however, the Chinese
performers' costumes, style of performing, and
music dramatically set them apart from their
Western colleagues.

Le Meravigliose Forze dei Nicolotti nella Città di Venezia.

Barnum, W. C. Coup, and Dan Castello in 1874, with their P. T. Barnum's Great Roman Hippodrome on Madison Avenue and 26th Street. The show, with a hippodrome track and extended performing area (which would eventually be filled with multiple rings), was the harbinger of a unique style of presentation that American circuses would eventually make their hallmark.

The New World Hungry for Entertainment

But it was a pupil of Charles Hughes, the English equestrian John Bill Ricketts, who established the first American circus. Ricketts was by all accounts an extremely talented performer who had just created his own company in Britain when the French Revolution (1789–99) started. As England and the rest of Europe prepared for war, Ricketts decided it would be best for him to try his luck elsewhere, and he set out for the newly formed United States of America. An astute entrepreneur, Ricketts followed the path of Philip Astley: He first opened a simple riding school in Philadelphia, which at the time was the capital of the United States, in the fall of 1792. Once his reputation as a riding master was well established, he opened his first circus at the corner of Market Street and 12th Street on April 3, 1793. It was a roofless affair—simply a ring surrounded by box seats, behind which there was standing room—and the performance was of a purely equestrian nature. But success came immediately in a capital hungry for entertainment, and Ricketts quickly brought over from Europe some members of his former English company, including the acrobat and ropedancer Spinacuta and his wife, a multitalented performer, along with his young brother Francis, and the clown McDonald.

As Ricketts's success grew, more of his British performers would rejoin him. In August he moved to New York City where he opened a similar arena on Greenwich Street. Ricketts would eventually build permanent circuses in Philadelphia, New York, and Boston, and in Quebec and Montreal in Canada, as well as in several other cities along the East Coast—although there his structures were often hastily built for the

engagement, and most of them didn't last. Ricketts's circuses were designed on the model of the Royal Circus (but not with the same luxury of details), including a ring and a stage, and the composition of his shows was very similar to those of Astley and Hughes. But in December 1799 Ricketts's Pantheon, the circus and home base he had built in Philadelphia at Chestnut Street and Sixth Street, was destroyed by fire. After a false start trying to resurrect his business, he set sail to Jamaica, where he had many relatives, but his ship was captured by Caribbean pirates. He eventually managed to recoup his losses in Guadeloupe and then decided to sail back to England. His story, unfortunately, ended there.

Circuses in the United States became increasingly popular. Like their European counterparts, circus pioneers in America built temporary or permanent circuses wherever they needed to perform. But the country was rapidly expanding, and they had to reach communities that were evermore scattered and distant. Traveling quickly and lightly became an important issue to these peripatetic American circus managers. In 1825 Joshua Purdy Brown decided to present his show under a canvas tent, which he called a "pavilion," instead of using the temporary wooden constructions that were popular with traveling circuses. Tents were cheaper, lighter, faster to erect and to take down, easy to transport, and, of course, they lasted the entire circus season. More important, they allowed the circus to visit communities of lesser populations, where it could play for one day only, and to adjust to the ever-changing demographics of a land in constant expansion.

Thus, the American circus entered a new era. It was mainly an itinerant enterprise, developing efficient traveling techniques over time that enabled it to move swiftly across the country and offer daily performances. The circus' unique ability to reach an audience wherever one was to be found, even in hard to reach and less populated areas of the United States, helped it become the most popular form of entertainment America had ever known.

L. Giarré inc:

Vari giuochi de Messicani

The Surprizing
by, the Grand Turk
He has perform'd n
Theatre Royal Cov
now at the Ne

Printed & Sold by R. Sayer opposite

10. *Astu qui satagunt validum illaqueare Leonem,*
Tædam alacres læua; dextra, quo auertere poſsint

A facie flammam, gestant scutum: Leo flammæ
Aspectum fugitans prætenta in retia currit.

VI.

Scènes exécutées par Mr. Martin.

Repos sur le Lion.

Délivrance de ses enfans des Boas Constricters.

Repos sur la Lionne.

Mr. Martin vainqueur du Lion.

Mr. Martin, le lion Néron et le tigre Atir.

Combat du Lion.

L'Hyène mouchetée.

Mr. Martin défendu par ses Lions contre les attaques des Indiens.

Mr. Martin reprenant la pâture du Lion d'entre ses griffes.

Mr. Martin et le tigre Atir.

Le Gladiateur et le Boa Constricter.

Exercices du Lion Cobourg.

pages 52–53
ca. 1580 The *capture of wild animals for exhibition* existed long before the circus was invented in 1770. By the 19th century, interest in wild animals grew to extraordinary proportions with the expansion of European colonial empires, which fueled the trading and training of ever more exotic wild animals.

ca. 1831–33 In 1831 French **big-cat trainer Henri Martin** starred in the pantomime *Les lions de Mysore* at the Cirque Olympique in Paris and became an instant sensation. In 1819 Martin had been the first wild-animal trainer to interact with his animals instead of fight them.

opposite
ca. 1760 These elegant visitors to a French menagerie illustrate famous fabulist Jean de La Fontaine's **"The Monkey and the Leopard."** In this fable, the leopard is admired for his beauty, while the ugly monkey, not pictured, is a smart, agile performer. The idea that wild animals such as leopards could also perform was utterly foreign at the time.

MR GRIMALDI as CLOWN,

In the Popular new Pantomine of

MOTHER GOOSE.

opposite
1807 *Joseph Grimaldi's greatest role* was as Clown in the pantomime *Harlequin and Mother Goose* at London's Theatre Royal in Covent Garden. Elizabethan theater clowns like Grimaldi were heir to medieval court jesters and remained popular characters until the mid-19th century, punctuating theater performances with comic interludes.

right
1810s *Monsieur Louis* was one of the many British theater clowns who tried to emulate the success of Joseph Grimaldi. In the late 1700s and early 1800s, clowns in the theater attracted audiences, and Philip Astley, the inventor of the first circus in 1770, added clowns to his equestrian performances to enhance their appeal.

MONS. LOUIS AS CLOWN.

London Published by J. REDINGTON, 73 Hoxton Street, Formerly called 208 Hoxton Old Town.

MR GRIMALDI, as Clown.

left
ca. 1870 *American stage clown Tony Denier* made his mark performing *Humpty Dumpty*, the first American pantomime. Like Grimaldi, Denier was a traditional theater clown. When clowns were added to the first circuses 100 years earlier, they were hired from the theater.

center
1822 The *clown costume worn by Joseph Grimaldi* originated from the medieval jester's costume, which was a caricature of the court servant. In Europe the ensemble became extravagantly ornate; in America it was simplified as clowning shifted from oral comedy to physical gags under the big top.

1808 *British illustrator Thomas Rowlandson* captures an equestrian performance inside the newly revamped Astley's Amphitheatre. Visible are features common to most American and European circus buildings through the mid-1800s: a ring for equestrian acts and a stage for acrobats and pantomimes. Astley's remained a London landmark until it was demolished in 1893.

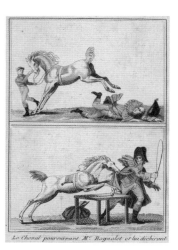

1817 These advertising cards show the ***diverse repertoire of the famous Franconi family:*** from equestrian pantomimes, top row, left and center; to comic scenes, top row, right; to equestrian stunts, bottom row, left and center. Eventually they tried their hand at wild animals. Coco the stag, bottom row, far right, was the first of their nonequine stars. Audiences knew that a horse could be trained, but to see a wild stag perform tricks was an awesome sight.

opposite, top and bottom
early 19th century The ***Franconis were a pioneering equestrian family*** of Italian origin who reigned over the French circus for more than a century. Like all early circus riders, the Franconis were celebrities and attracted a fashionable crowd well versed in equestrian arts. Until the end of the 19th century, the horse was man's most vital partner, and trick riders such as the Franconis developed circus acts around the immense popularity of their equestrian abilities.

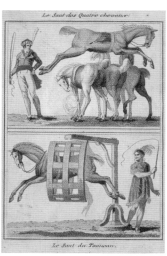

Exercice de Franconi.
N.º 1.

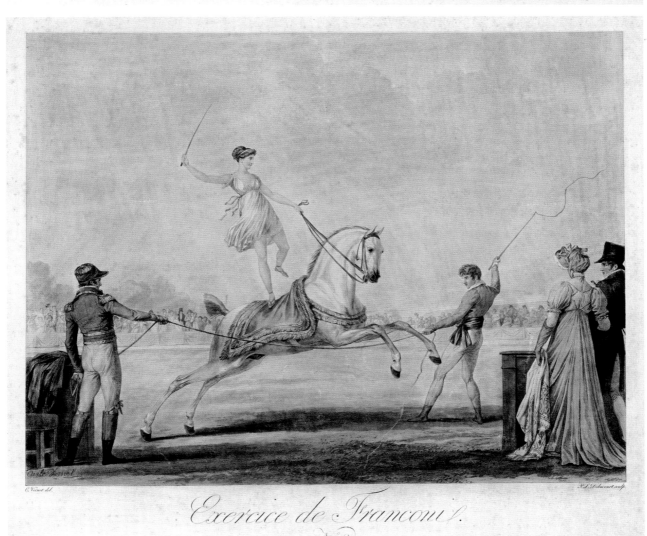

Exercice de Franconi.
N.º 2.

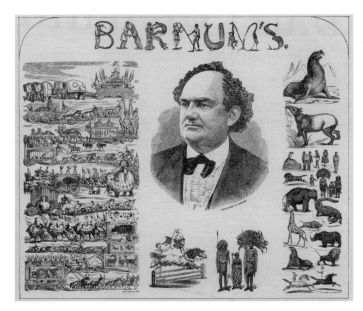

1873 Even before becoming a circus owner in 1871, *P. T. Barnum acquired fortune and fame* by brilliantly promoting attractions such as Swedish opera singer Jenny Lind and the celebrated midget Tom Thumb. Barnum was one of the most famous Americans of the 19th century, and his name and likeness were staples of his circus advertising. Over time, Barnum became synonymous with the circus.

opposite
1879 In 1871 at the age of 61, P. T. Barnum entered the circus business. Two years later, he came up with the now famous circus name *The Greatest Show on Earth.* Barnum's keen sense of what sells and his unique promotional tactics and showmanship helped make the American circus the largest and most popular form of entertainment the world had ever known.

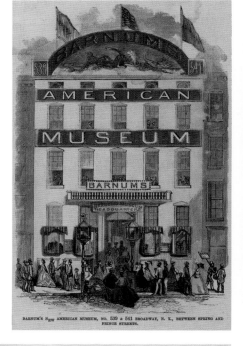

BARNUM'S NEW AMERICAN MUSEUM, NO. 539 & 541 BROADWAY, N. Y., BETWEEN SPRING AND PRINCE STREETS.

pages 62–63
1855 Before the three-ring circus was introduced in 1881, the American circus was still mostly one ring. But it was already acquiring *a style all its own: spectacular, energetic, and grandiose.* The circus was on the verge of becoming "bigger and better than ever," the famous tagline used by the American circus as it entered its golden age in the 1870s.

below and right
1879 and 1856 Barnum ran his *American Museum,* right, on Broadway in New York from 1841 to 1865. It was a mixture of pseudoscientific exhibitions, human and animal oddities, popular theater, and vaudeville, and was visited by 38 million people. Even as a circus owner in the 1870s, he never forgot his wildly popular museum. He even envisioned *reviving it at Madison Square Garden,* below, but the scheme never materialized.

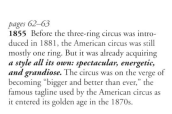

P. T. BARNUM.

P.T. BARNUM'S
OWN AND ONLY
GREATEST SHOW
>ON EARTH.<

Enlarged and Improved Beyond all Former Years for the Season of 1879

GRAND ARRAY OF NEW FEATURES
RARE NOVELTIES
ENLARGED

MENAGERIE
THE ONLY BLACK CAMELS
Ever exhibited in Europe or America
The ONLY WHITE CAMEL
ON THIS CONTINENT.
THE LARGEST HERD OF ELEPHANTS
Ever exhibited together in any show that ever traveled.
50 CAGES OF ANIMALS
TWO HORNED RHINOCEROS
One of the most Ponderous and Gigantic specimen of this interesting Biblical animal ever brought from the African Continent.

MADAME
DOCKRILL
FOUR HORSE BAREBACK
THE ONLY LADY RIDER IN THE WORLD.

P. T. BARNUM'S
GREATEST SHOW ON EARTH.

THE GREAT SEA LION
300 MONKEYS
FINER & RARER
ANIMALS
THAN WERE EVER SEEN BEFORE.
MY AMERICAN MUSEUM
COMPRISING
50,000 CURIOSITIES!
Geological, Geographical, Philosophical and Mechanical, of Rare Interest, and furnishing Food for Reflection, Study and Amusement. LIFE-LIKE AUTOMATA
WONDERS OF MECHANISM
CIREAN TABLEAUX. The great Musical Xartadore, the Wonderful
ORCHESTMELOCHOR
COMBINING ALL THE EFFECTS OF
SIX BRASS BANDS

THE SENSATION OF THE TIME, MY TROUPE OF
20 IMPORTED STALLIONS
From the Imperial Stables of GERMANY, RUSSIA, ITALY and TARTARY. Imported by me at an expense of $100,000.00, in Gold, (when coin was at a high premium.) Exhibited and Trained by **MR. CARL ANTONY**, the Chesterfield and Apollo of the Arena.

TRAINED ELEPHANTS
The most highly educated specimens of their kind ; performing ASTONISHING FEATS
MY COSMOPOLITAN
CIRCUS
Of 200 Peerless Performers!
CONTAINING AMONG OTHER EXCEPTIONAL FEATURES NO LESS THAN
SIX LADY RIDERS ON BAREBACK STEEDS
AMONG THIS GROUP OF STARS ARE:
MADAME DOCKRILL
The Empress of the Arena ; in he GREAT FOUR HORSE ACT.
Miss KATIE STOKES
THE YOUNG AND BEAUTIFUL PRINCIPAL BARE-BACK EQUESTRIENNE.
M'lle LINDA JEAL
The Queen of the Blazing Zone ; in her exciting sensation of leaping with a Bare-back Steed THROUGH CIRCLES OF FIRE.

MISS EMMA LAKE
The Beautiful Princess of the Menage.
SIGNORA MARCELLUS!
In her wonderful Bare-back Act; forming a combination of beauty, grace and skill, which is without parallel.
SIGNOR SEBASTIAN
The best and most daring Male Bare-back Rider in Europe or America.
MR. JAMES COOKE!
And A HOST OF OTHERS, who have no peers in the profession.

THE GIANT OF GIANTS!
COL. GOSHEN
8 FEET HIGH.
LITTLE QUEEN MAB
The Smallest and Prettiest Dwarf ever exhibited.
CAPT. COSTENTENUS
THE TATTOOED GREEK; tattooed from head to foot with innumerable Figures of Birds, Beasts, Fishes and Heathen Gods.

THE ENTIRE ESTABLISHMENT TRANSPORTED ON MY OWN
100 RAILROAD CARS
Divided into FOUR MONSTROUS TRAINS.
A GRAND FREE SHOW, Worh Coming 100 Miles to See
IS GIVEN EVERY MORNING AT 9 O'CLOCK.
A GORGEOUS STREET PAGEANT
In which will appear the HERD OF ELEPHANTS; 10 OF THE 20 ROYAL STALLIONS; THE GIGANTIC
ORCHESTMELOCHOR, which can be heard for nearly five miles.
CAR OF NEPTUNE
With A CORTEGE A MILE LONG, of Dens, Cages, Chariots, Tableaux Cars; combining to make a blaze of Golden Iridescence. WITHER'S NEW YORK BAND. An
AUTOMATIC CIRCUS on WHEELS
In the open street. DO NOT FAIL TO SEE HIS GLITTERING PANORAMA.
☞ REMEMBER MY DAY AND DATE
And do not confound this with any other show. THERE IS ONLY ONE BARNUM AND HE HAS BUT ONE SHOW, which exhibits all advertised, and never disappoints.

ONE TICKET THE CHARGE FOR WHICH IS 50 CENTS, ADMITS TO ALL
CHILDREN UNDER NINE YEARS, 25 CENTS
The Departments. RESERVED SEATS, 25 CENTS EXTRA.
See My Illuminated, Illustrated News, Immense Bill Boards, Mammoth Pictorials, Programmes and Newspaper Advertisements.

The Courier Cones by Show Printing House, Buffalo, N. Y. The Largest in the World; Fire-proof.

LITH OF SARONY

INTERIOR VIEW OF HOWES & CUSH

The interior of the great Tent used by the travelling Troupe of Equestrians attached to Messrs Howes & Cushing's celebrated American Circus presents on all sides a scene of magnificent
extend entirely around the arena, rising one above the other, in amphitheatrical order so as to give to all a full and unobstructed view of every thing performed in the ring. The whole
The sides of the canvass are tastefully adorned with superb silk damask drapery, the seats are covered with rich crimson brocade with all the finest texture, the National Flags of England
columns, from which are also displayed, in dazzling splendor, jets of light formed in a bright galaxy of STARS while a fine refreshing circulation of pure air is admitted
the inclemency of the weather. The facilities of egress from this colossal tent are so abundant and complete that an audience of five thousand people may retire without

GREAT UNITED STATES CIRCUS.

of the most extensive commodious and elegant performing saloons that has ever been seen. The seats, which have been constructed for the accommodation of five thousand spectators, illuminated at night by means of numerous and gorgeous chandeliers lighted with gas manufactured for the establishment in a portable apparatus. interwoven, float in elegant festoons above the audience splendidly decorated banners and armorials, interspersed with the American shield hang around in great variety upon the numerous the top prevailing every part of the enclosure. The top of the pavilion is manufactured from water-proof cloth, by means of which the audience are entirely protected from dible short space of time.

WONDERS
OF THE
WORLD

AWAIT YOU

Dominique Jando

WONDERS
OF THE
WORLD
AWAIT YOU

Dominique Jando

It is sometimes difficult to fathom the importance that live popular entertainment had on everyday life prior to film, radio, television, and the Internet. Until the development of radio broadcasting in the 1920s, the only home entertainment center that could be found in American homes was a parlor organ or a piano—grand or upright, tuned or out of key— and in the most fashionable homes a green, felted card table around which family and friends gathered during cold winter evenings. But if you wanted true entertainment, you went out to the theater or to a nearby vaudeville house or—when it came to town—to the circus. Before the advent of the moving image, the circus was *the* great purveyor of fantasy: "The circus is the only spectacle I know that, while you watch it, gives the quality of a happy dream," said Ernest Hemingway.

opposite
ca. 1890–91 *Grand spectacles and lavish pageantry* were a trademark of the American circus. In 1890 Barnum & Bailey asked Imre Kiralfy, the king of Broadway extravaganzas, to produce *Nero or the Destruction of Rome*, replete with gladiators and chariot races

page 65
1910s *Zelda Boden* looks strikingly similar to silent film star Theda Bara, the original vamp of the silver screen who starred in costume epics such as *Cleopatra* (1917). Yet the modern and exotic Boden preceded the mysterious Bara. Before film's popularity outshone the circus, the circus offered its audiences exoticism in a way that film could never compete with—it was live,

RINGLINGBROS WORLD'S GREATEST SHOWS
SEASON 1914

1902 On Circus Day, when schools shut and businesses closed so everyone could go to the circus, men, women, and children gathered to watch the gigantic, free street parade before the show. *Wild animals from faraway places* paced back and forth in ornate horse-drawn cage-wagons, offering potential circusgoers the first glimpse of the wonders of the world that the circus had brought to town.

Live entertainment at this time, in all its forms, was the equivalent of today's television. It could be distracting, funny, often tacky, sometimes interesting or moving—and even educational, or at least pretend to be so, which was useful in a country where stern puritanism still prevailed. For example, legendary entrepreneur P. T. Barnum, who defined advertising's tricks of the trade decades before his involvement with the circus in the early 1870s, named the theater in his American Museum in New York City the "Moral Lecture Room." While Barnum's museum was a hodgepodge of natural history, curious displays, and sideshow exhibitions, he nevertheless knew that the voyeuristic pleasures they offered needed to be delivered with a semblance of respectability to be truly successful.

A Window Onto the World

The American circus functioned like a blend of Animal Planet, the National Geographic Channel, and the History Channel, but it avoided the unsavory path of tabloid reality that vaudeville eagerly embraced with its presentations of notorious celebrities known for tales of sex, crime, and licentiousness. The businessmen behind

the American circus consciously defined the circus as wholesome family entertainment, in large measure as a result of Barnum's show business acumen and savvy marketing strategies. Barnum, who was a prominent member of the Universalist Church, always played the family card and was keen to stress the propriety of his various exhibits. But Barnum was also a showman as well as an impresario, and he knew very well that true success depended on broadening his audience. His shows had to please both the straightlaced Anglo-Saxon puritan and the fun-loving German immigrant, and had to appeal to men and women alike, adults and children. The circus had to have universal appeal to be profitable, and Barnum knew from his experience with the American Museum that exoticism was a hot ticket. His American Museum had been, by and large, a window onto a foreign and unfamiliar world. There were riches to be made in the presentation of the world's wonders, even if those wonders were fictitious.

The American circus, not unlike the giant fairs of medieval Europe, pushed the doors wide-open onto the outside world, which for a long time had been known only through written testimonies and pictorial renditions. This exotic and thrilling world had taken shape in people's imaginations—even when it was pure invention. But the circus brought its extraordinary reality right to your doorstep. The mysterious "cameleopard" of yore at long last materialized as the amazing giraffe. Africa, Asia, and the Amazonian jungle ceased to be mysterious lands known only to fearless explorers. The circus brought them—or at least colorful and often fanciful interpretations of them—directly to you as live entertainment.

As both a vehicle for performance and as an aspiring educational institution, the circus had roots in its European heritage. When the modern circus was first born in Europe in the late 18th century, it was primarily an equestrian show. This ultimately paved the way for the presentation of other animals as adjuncts to the circus performers, starting with small monkeys, graduating to stags, and then to young elephants. But as a purely commercial enterprise, the American circus had its entrepreneurial roots in the traveling menagerie business. In 1816, at the same time that Baba, the first trained circus elephant, was causing a sensation in Paris, the small traveling menagerie of Nathan Howes was exhibiting Betty, or "Bet," an African elephant, in America. She belonged to Hachaliah Bailey, a farmer who made a fortune with his pachyderm. This inspired many of his neighbors to go into the traveling menagerie business, which proved much more lucrative than farming and soon became a thriving industry. There were no zoos in the United States then (the first of them, the Philadelphia Zoo, wouldn't open until 1874), and traveling menageries were the only places

1914 *Solomon and the Queen of Sheba* was one of many magnificent circus historical pageants, and its purported cast of "thousands" is shown here gathered on the back lot. The false beards were an easy way to give the ensemble a touch of Persian.

1881 The world map depicted on W. W. Cole's circus courier sent a clear message to its readers: The circus will bring them *"the marvels of many nations."* As global trade and travel expanded, the circus mined the world for the latest trends and themes to put in its shows.

OF
GENERAL
LEW
WALLACE'S

KLAW&ERLANGER'S STUPENDOUS PRODUCTION

BEN·HUR

DRAMATIZED
BY
WILLIAM YOUNG
MUSIC BY
EDGAR STILLMAN
KELLEY

THE
STROBRIDGE
LITHO CO
CINCINNATI & NEW YORK

BEN·HUR DRIVES SHEIK ILDERIM'S "STARS OF THE DESERT"
TO VICTORY IN THE ANTIOCH CIRCUS, DEFEATING HIS ARCH·ENEMY MESSALA.

1912 In an America still adherent to Christian dogma, ***biblical stories*** were often dramatized under the big top. The adaptation of General Lewis Wallace's best-selling novel, *Ben-Hur: A Tale of the Christ* (1880), offered a perfect opportunity to see Ben-Hur live. "It is a magnificent sight…the straining, foam-flecked horse, the charioteers with set faces and ribbons flying, the wheels of the chariots cutting deep into the earth." (Ringling Bros. and Barnum & Bailey program, 1929)

opposite
1952 The Ringling Bros. and Barnum & Bailey spectacle *Mardi Gras* celebrated the sights and sounds of the New Orleans festival, and some performers wore Roman-like costumes. It was common for costume designers to take ***artistic license***, conflating eras and historical looks.

below
ca. 1933–36 ***Staged chariot races*** were a staple of the American circus. Breathtaking Roman races, with riders standing on pairs of horses, often concluded the big top performance. In Roman costumes, Al G. Barnes circus performers await their turn on the back lot.

where one could see the animal wonders of the still relatively unexplored American wilderness along with those from more distant and exotic lands. Furthermore, they came to you, whether you lived in a city or in the farmlands.

Several menageries added a circus (then defined as a mostly equestrian show presented in a single ring, which also included acrobats, jugglers, ropedancers, and clowns) to their animal exhibitions, and the combined circus and menagerie, an American creation, was born. Then, in 1835, a group of these animal exhibitors united their interests into one company whose purpose was to "maintain for keeping a large collection of rare and curious animals, and to exhibit them…by means of which the knowledge of natural history may be more generally diffused and promoted and rational curiosity gratified." They had, in effect, cornered the traveling circus and menagerie business. As a result, the circus, which had been until that time in the hands of equestrian performers (where it would remain in Europe), had become in America an industry run by business entrepreneurs rather than by performers.

Every Free Inch a Billboard

Thus, the menagerie and its awe-inspiring collection of exotic animals became part of the lure of the American circus. Where else could you see, live and at close range, a group of graceful giraffes, a hippopotamus or a rhinoceros, the impressive sea elephant, Bengal tigers or Atlas lions, the bizarre okapi, a herd of zebras, the antics of a family of chimpanzees, and the mighty elephant, the undisputed king of the menagerie? Circuses plastered barn walls, wooden fences, and the sides of city buildings with thousands of posters showing roaring lions and tigers, charging rhinos, and furious hippos attacking pirogues of natives hunting on the river Nile.

These powerful and colorful depictions became an integral part of circus magic, a tempting tease of the wonders that awaited you. The circus was the main user of printed advertising at the time. Larger shows plastered thousands of lithographic posters each day; no other industry ever came close to these numbers. A few printing companies specialized in this very lucrative business, but the artists who churned out the true masterpieces of circus advertising worked for the Strobridge Lithograph Company offices in Cincinnati, Ohio, and New York City. The quantity of artwork this company produced during the golden age of the American circus comes in staggering numbers. Some designs were elaborate, others relatively simple, some were elegant, many were gaudy, but all were colorful, charged with energy, exalting the mundane, improving the extraordinary, exaggerating the extravagant. Even before you saw the actual show, the

circus was already delivering its wonders far and wide with its advertising.

Of course, on the circus lot all these animals may have looked somewhat more tame and subdued in their cages and enclosures, gathered as they were in the vast, crowded menagerie tent. Nevertheless they were real creatures of flesh and fur, breathing, moaning, and…stinking! The contact was up close and personal. To city folks, the circus brought them the ultimate escape directly from the wilderness of a distant, exotic world. To country folks, who were more familiar with animals and might have had a chance encounter with a wolf, a bear, or a cougar, the apparent calm and detachment of these exotic beasts belied a latent ferocity they knew might be there. These were truly wild animals. Country folks could sense it, and that made these awesome creatures even more impressive. Nowhere else but the circus could one experience such close contact with wildlife from the most remote parts of the globe.

The Last Unknown People on Earth

Among the other wonders that the circus carried in its cornucopia of attractions was the uniquely American sideshow, the popularizing of which was Barnum's most distinctive contribution to the American circus. He didn't originate sideshow

attractions (they had been traveling with American circuses since the 1850s at least), but they were a feature that he had promoted and cultivated with bold marketing techniques over many years. When the legendary showman accepted the invitation of circus entrepreneurs W. C. Coup and Dan Castello to join them in 1871, he brought to the collaboration what he would be best remembered for: an itinerant version of his American Museum in the circus sideshow, his "great moral exposition of the wonder world," claimed a poster, replete with "moving mechanical wonders life-size" and "animate and inanimate curiosities." Though not as grand and educational as it pretended to be, his sideshow featuring "the Wild Men of Borneo," "the Aztec Children," and Zip, the "What Is It?," evoked dreams of mysterious wonders from lost and faraway worlds. When they came to the circus, audiences were ready and willing to dream.

The advertised exoticism was sometimes legitimate. Crowds gazed in awe at the "Genuine Ubangi Savages," with "mouths and lips as large as those of full-grown crocodiles," who came from an African tribe of plate-lipped women that lived in the depths of the Belgian Congo jungle. Or at "the Giraffe-Neck Women From Burma," who came from the Burmese Padaung tribe where women coiled brass around their necks to give the illusion of elongating them as a sign of beauty and tribal identity. Ringling Bros. and Barnum & Bailey advertised them in 1933 as the "greatest educational feature of all time!" They generated tremendous curiosity and were a huge hit. The circus was a live substitute for today's National Geographic Channel—although National Geographic would certainly never have used the word "Ubangi," which is a river that runs between the Republic of Congo and the Democratic Republic of Congo and is nowhere near the region where the tribe actually came from. Roland Butler, one of Ringling's legendary press agents, had picked the name on a map. It sounded more exciting than Belgian Congo, the tribe's actual homeland. The circus, after all, was meant to sell fantasy.

It is not surprising that the American circus enjoyed its golden age in the Victorian era, shortly after Europe expanded its colonies deep into these unfamiliar territories, triggering a new interest in exploration. The "civilized" world became increasingly curious about other cultures, and the circus—especially the American circus—was ready to satisfy this curiosity. It did this on Circus Day first with its posters, then the menagerie, then the sideshow, and then with the show itself, most notably offering grandiose spectacles and pageants that only the circus could produce on such a phenomenal scale. The circus was like an extravagantly illustrated travel or history book.

Kings, Queens, and Heroes of History

Grand spectacles and lavish pageantry were a trademark of the American circus, even though they had been a staple of the circus since its early days in London. British circus-founder Philip Astley, a former cavalry sergeant-major, was fond of parades and uniforms, but he also borrowed from the theater, adding acrobats, ropedancers, jugglers, and clowns to his equestrian displays, as well as "afterpieces," which were traditionally presented at the end of the show. Afterpieces were mainly farcical plays and pantomimes—elaborate spectacles replete with stage tricks and special effects. Since horses were at the core of the circus performance in its early days, these afterpieces became equestrian pantomimes, known as "hippodramas." They depicted famous battles in history and reconstitutions of spectacular events such as coronations or celebratory parades whose themes were often relevant to current events.

The American circus had become a gigantic traveling affair where theatrical subtleties didn't have a place. The old hippodramas were replaced by pageants—stunning spectacles, or "specs" in circus parlance. They were richly costumed parades involving an endless procession of characters on horse and foot and, of course, including animals from the vast resources of the menagerie. They were elaborate and theatrical versions of street parades, but under the big top. True to form, they often pretended to be educational, such as Ringling Bros.'s *Joan of Arc*, produced in 1913 and advertised as a "magnificent 1200-character spectacle" with "300 dancing girls in entrancing revels." It was undoubtedly "a dazzling scene of life, color, and action" as proclaimed, but the real French saint-warrior might have felt out of place amidst 300 girls cavorting in revels under the big top. Productions such as these were grand, lavish, spectacular, colorful, and on a scale that no theater could ever come near to replicating.

Yet even these spectacles paled in comparison to those staged around the circus' favorite themes, India and Persia, which allowed the participation of exotic animals. These pageants included countless elephants caparisoned with gilded headpieces and ornate blankets in tableaux worthy of legendary Persian storyteller Scheherazade's nightly tales. *Persia or the Pageants of the Thousand and One Nights* was boasted by Barnum & Bailey in 1916 to be "the most gorgeous Oriental display ever seen in any land since the world began!" Equally as grand were the "new big Indo-Arabic spectacle" *The Wizard Prince of Arabia* (1914), an "Oriental wordless play" featuring "1250 characters," and *Aladdin and His Wonderful Lamp* (1917). The public at large was vaguely familiar with Aladdin and Ali Baba, but had never read Sir Richard Burton's

1918 Lavish spectacles such as *In Days of Old* (1918), featuring **King Arthur and the Knights of the Round Table,** brought popular legends to life. These kinds of spectacles had been a major part of the circus for years and were visual inspiration for film epics such as D. W. Griffith's *Intolerance* (1916), *Cleopatra* (1917), starring Theda Bara, and *The Three Musketeers* (1921), starring Douglas Fairbanks.

opposite
ca. 1910 *Tales that allowed elaborate costuming were welcome,* but by the time they reached audiences it was sometimes difficult to pinpoint the costumes' exact style or period. Were these performers dressed as Assyrian warriors? Knights of the Round Table? Costume designers often let their inspiration overrule historical accuracy.

below
1910s Showgirls Miss Rutherford and Miss Divine are poised for their entry into the big top, wearing resplendent royal costumes and oversized fans (indispensable during the summer season). To a mesmerized audience, they seemed like true **Renaissance princesses**.

opposite top and bottom

1891 Famed Broadway director and producer Imre Kiralfy claimed of his production *Columbus*, "In this gigantic undertaking, all my studies, experience and energy have been devoted to placing before the public not a mere series of tableaux, but to supply a faithful, authentic and complete reproduction of the chief historic incidents in the life of that great mariner.... In presenting to the American public the latest and grandest *original historical spectacle of Columbus and the Discovery of America,* I wish to most earnestly assure them that it will be even more magnificent than the great one of last year." (Barnum & Bailey program, 1891)

1903 The *Barnum & Bailey* Book of **Wonders** floridly describes the extraordinary specimens from remote parts of the world that the circus brought to town. The circus' global outlook is exemplified by the hemispheres on its cover.

below

1893 The patriotic pageant *The American Revolution*, presented by the Adam Forepaugh circus, lasted a full hour and described with more spectacle than accuracy the momentous events of the war. Such historical tableaux **helped unite a diverse audience** of Americans, which reflected the swell of immigration to the United States in the 1890s.

pages 76–77

1935 Photographer Edward J. Kelty captured this gigantic and eclectic parade featuring—incongruously—*Asian elephants, Cleopatra, and, in the background, Cinderella.* "So graphically is the story told and so real are the stage effects, the scenery and the tons of properties that the audience seems to breathe the very incense of the past ages and hear the mysteries and the secrets of a dead race whispered from crumbling ruins and buried tombs." (Barnum & Bailey program, 1912)

translation *The Book of the Thousand Nights and a Night* (1885–86); too steamy, perhaps, and much too long for the average reader. No matter, the circus took care of this by abbreviating it and bringing it to life. Then there was Frank "Bring 'Em Back Alive" Buck, the famous animal collector and jungle adventurer, parading in the 1938 spectacular, *Nepal.* His presence confirmed the circus' association with the exotic travels of animal scouts, who combed the world to bring the circus unusual creatures. In reality, the circus often found their animals through the Hagenbeck firm, the world-famous animal dealers of Hamburg, Germany, but their capture was part of the dream the circus provided, and dreams had to be kept alive.

Travel the World Without Leaving Your Seat

The Chinese, Indian, and Persian circus spectacles depicted cultures that were deeply exotic to the American audience at the time. Chinese spectacles, especially, had the additional advantage of including actual Asian performers, although whether Chinese or Japanese, the average spectator didn't know the difference. These troupes and acts were frequent fixtures of the circus show and brought genuine exoticism to the performance (this was during China's pre-Communist era). Asian performers had a specific style that found its roots in the Chinese acrobatic theater, or "the art of one hundred skills," an offspring of the harvest rituals performed by the Chinese peasants of the Han Dynasty (202 BC–200 AD). Chinese and Japanese acrobats brought to the circus their very own specialties (such as plate spinning, perch-pole balancing, trident manipulation, and diabolo juggling), which, performed in Asian costumes, had a very distinct flavor and were markedly different from that of Western performers.

Closer to home, the myth of the American West and its frontiers offered the circus another form of exoticism on which to capitalize. Taking its cue from Buffalo Bill's Wild West, the circus inserted a capsule version of the Wild West show into its own performances, replete with cowboys, Native Americans, stagecoaches, horses, and buffalos. American audiences relished this glimpse into their adventurous recent past, and the shows' military trappings reflected the fascination with colonialism that dominated world politics at the time. The Wild West exhibitions were a uniquely American form of entertainment and extremely popular until World War I. These fictionalized accounts of the conquests of the American West were presented in spectacular, albeit raw, productions with casts that included Native Americans (sometimes with actual legendary historical figures such as Sitting Bull). Although the shows dealt with real and imagined stories of conflicts on the American frontier, they had, in their own way, a significant unifying effect, since heroes often appeared on both sides of the "conflicts."

The history of America's European past was not always that familiar to circus audiences, which consisted of a broad spectrum of the population, including a good percentage of recent immigrants whose formal education could be lacking. The circus took care of that too. Bailey had commissioned Imre Kiralfy, the Broadway director and producer, to stage *Columbus and the Discovery of America* (1891–92). The spectacle *Cleopatra, Queen of Egypt* (1912) brought from the past "the grandeur and opulence of Cleopatra's court," even including an "Antony" character to give the ensemble an additional historical flourish. These pageants, like the menagerie, provided a view of faraway lands and magic kingdoms where maharajahs and their courts paraded on an endless procession of "sacred" elephants. They were also excursions into the past, allowing glimpses of history—however distorted they might have been. Only when Cinemascope and Technicolor appeared in movie theaters did the circus have any real competition. But for all their grandiosity, movies never had what the circus could offer: real-life pageants with the sounds, colors, and smells of living wonders.

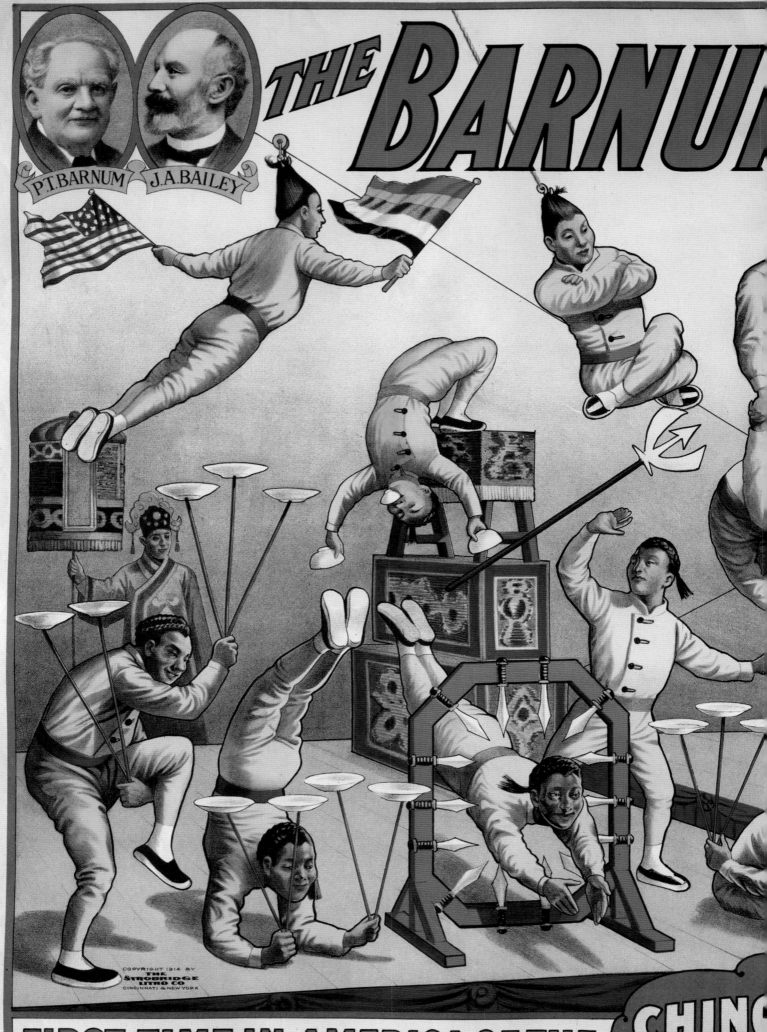

THE BARNUM

P.T.BARNUM   J.A.BAILEY

FIRST TIME IN AMERICA OF THE
IMPERIAL CHINESE CIRCUS STARS

CHIN
TIA
TR

BAILEY GREATEST SHOW ON EARTH

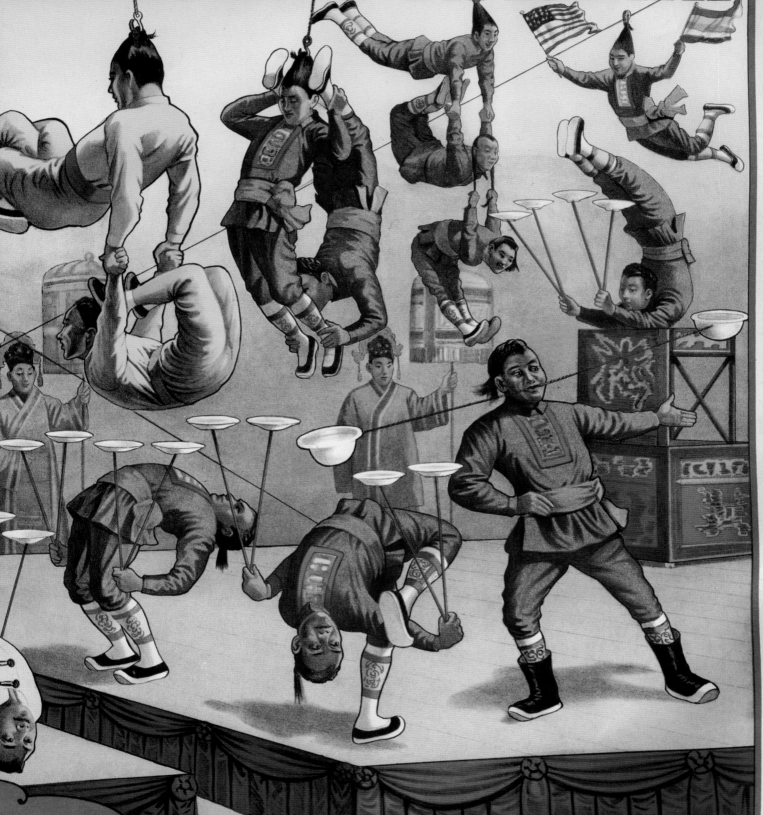

NEW AND STARTLING ACTS PERFORMED ON TWO STAGES AT THE SAME TIME

left, top and center
1914 The Barnum & Bailey spectacle *The Wizard Prince of Arabia* was similar to the Ringling Bros.s' *Solomon and the Queen of Sheba* of the same year. Since 1907, these two circuses, the largest in America, had been owned by the five Ringling brothers. The dozens of dancers wearing Arabian-style costumes were trained by Ottokar Bartik, the ballet master for the Metropolitan Opera in New York who also spent time at La Scala in Milan.

bottom
1914 Zelda Boden poses for a photographer before her entrance into the big top as the *daughter of the King of Baber in the spectacle* **Persia**. Although the Prince of Arabia pursues her against the will of her father, love eventually prevails, and a lavish wedding ceremony, replete with camels, zebras, horses, and elephants, concludes the spectacle.

pages 78–79
1914 *Plate spinning, hair hanging, and hoop diving* are traditional Chinese acrobatic skills and were rarely seen in the Western world in 1914. "These men are the most remarkable specimens of a race of extraordinary gymnasts whose marvelous secrets as wrestlers, balancers, fencers, vaulters, runners and all-around athletes have for centuries excited the wonder of the world." (Barnum & Bailey program, 1912)

COPYRIGHT 1916 BY THE STROBRIDGE LITHO.CO.CINCINNATI & NEW YORK

1916 The spectacle *Persia* allowed the audience to escape into the fairy-tale universe of ***The Arabian Nights***. "The circus," said Henry Miller, "is a tiny closed-off arena of forgetfulness. For a space it enables us to lose ourselves, to dissolve in wonder and bliss, to be transported by mystery." (Henry Miller, *The Smile at the Foot of the Ladder*, 1948)

1924 These Sells-Floto circus showgirls participated in the spectacle ***The Brides and the Beasts***, set in ancient Egypt with costumes that had, for all their mystique, the unmistakable flavor of the Roaring Twenties, thanks to the heavy black makeup. The circus was extremely good at blending the old with the new.

HAGENBECK — WALL
JESS H. ADKINS, MANAGER — HARRY McFARLAN, EQUESTRIAN DIRE

IRCUS ——————
X DE ROSSELLI PRODUCER OF SPECTACLE

PHOTO BY
CENTURY
74 W 47TH ST.
N.Y.C
BROOKLYN N.Y - JUNE 12TH 1931

1914 As America's most popular form of entertainment, the circus inspired early movies. Circus performer **Rosita Mantilla, in an elaborate costume for the production of Solomon and the Queen of Sheba,** strikes a pose that Hollywood vamp Theda Bara famously repeated three years later in *Cleopatra*.

left
1930 By wearing flashy caparisoning, pulling a howdah on wheels, and carrying a showgirl dressed to fit the part, this circus camel becomes *a truly magnificent, regal animal right out of an Arabian tale.*

opposite
1950 For circus owners, there was money to be made in the presentation of the world's wonders, even if those wonders were fictitious, such as this *fictional Persian princess* with the Ringling Bros. and Barnum & Bailey circus.

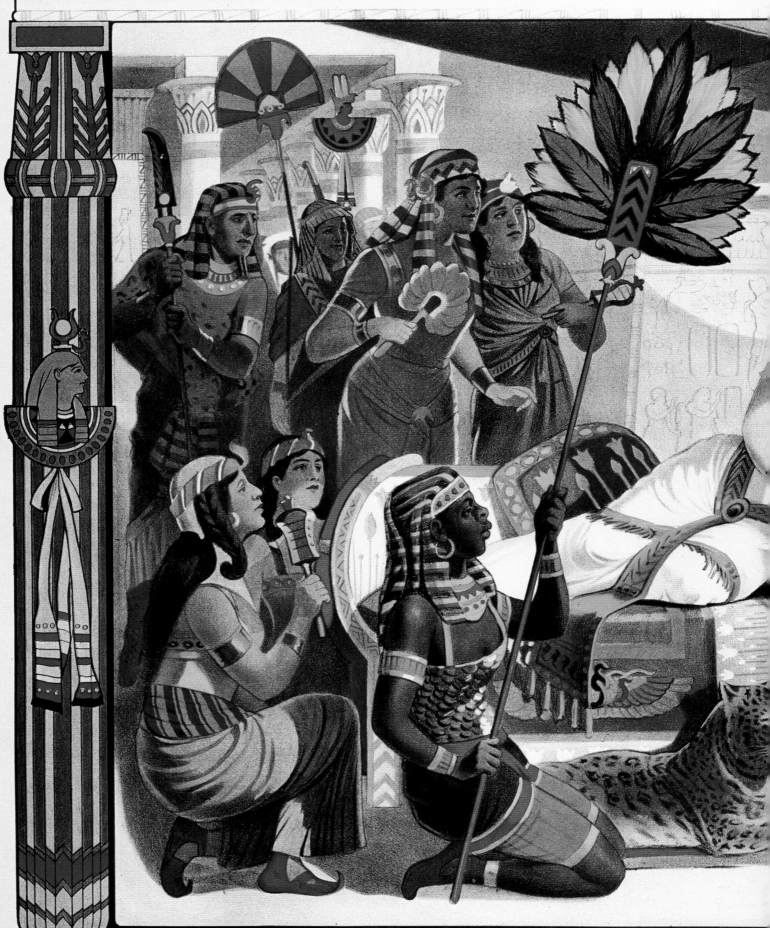

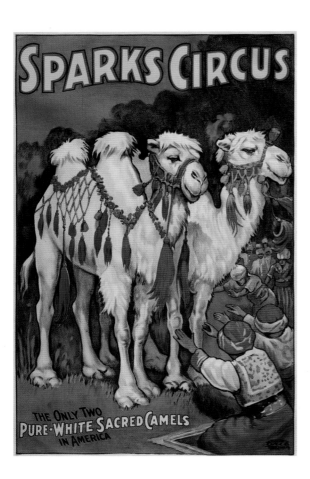

1931 Some Asian Bactrian camels have a very pale coat, which is not unusual, but the circus, always in search of the extraordinary, advertised them as *"pure-white sacred camels"* and offered them up as a rarity to awestruck crowds.

pages 86–87
1912 The spectacle *Cleopatra, Queen of Egypt* brought from the past "the grandeur and opulence of Cleopatra's court," even including an "Antony" character, far right on horseback, to give the ensemble an additional historical flourish. (Barnum & Bailey program, 1912)

1930s Watching the back lot was an attraction in itself: It was like *peeking into a wonderful world all its own or traveling in time.* People seemed not only to come from mysterious parts of the planet but from various periods of history too.

1920s These showgirls represented the four parts of the day—morning, afternoon, evening, and night—*in a nod to the ancient study of astrology*, with headpieces and accessories composing a circus zodiac.

left
1945 The widespread availability of black-and-white television presented a threat to circuses, since it gave potential audiences a reason to stay home. Nevertheless, circuses still represented a world of bright colors with their gigantic lithographs, trains, parade wagons, and the *extravagant fabrics and textures* of their costumes, as seen on this Ringling Bros. and Barnum & Bailey performer.

opposite
1951 This Ringling Bros. and Barnum & Bailey showgirl appeared in ***Circus Serenade, "the stupendous new musical super-spectacle."*** The showgirl's headdress recalls the elaborate headpieces of the Folies Bergère, Moulin Rouge, and Busby Berkeley's cinematic spectacles.

1952 At the circus, performers dressed as ***ancient Egyptian dancers*** were sometimes beautiful blondes, but that didn't matter so long as they communicated another time and place. These outfits were designed for Ringling Bros. and Barnum & Bailey by legendary Broadway costume designer Miles White of *Oklahoma!* and *Carousel* fame.

below
1903 Barnum & Bailey's show ***The Tribute of Balkis*** was advertised as "the most magnificent, sublime and enchanting spectacle ever presented to mortal eyes, embracing over 1000 men, women, children, horses, chariots and tableau cars." Hollywood would later echo this grandiosity in the advertising of its historical epics.

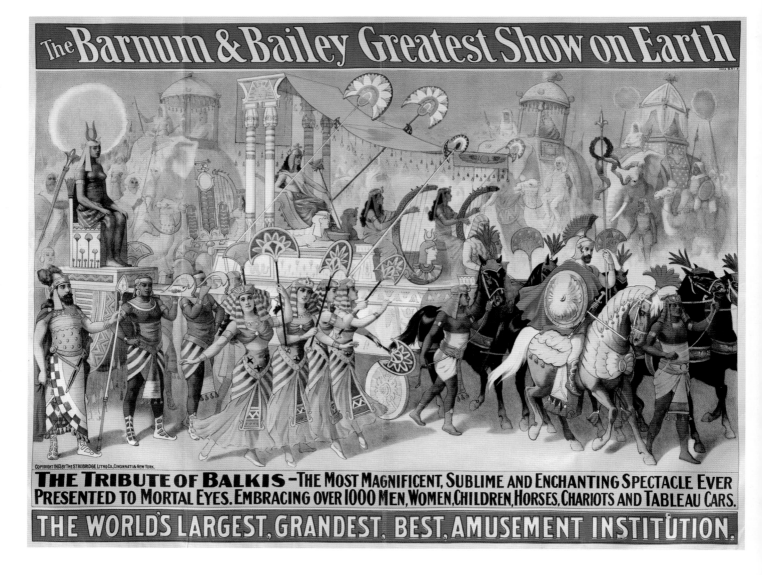

eatest Show on Earth

T ETHNOLOGICAL CONGRESS
OUS PEOPLE FROM ALL PARTS OF THE WORLD
SHOWING THEIR TYPICAL HOME LIFE

EST, AMUSEMENT INSTITUTION.

ca. 1930–31 Harry A. Atwell, a photographer from Chicago, took this backstage photograph of two cast members of the Ringling Bros. and Barnum & Bailey show—*an all-American showgirl and a "Ubangi Savage."*

pages 92–93
1895 As this Barnum & Bailey poster claimed, the circus effectively offered *"a great ethnological congress"* of the peoples of the world available for viewing in three places on the circus lot: the sideshow, the menagerie, and in the pageants under the big top. The circus brought the world beyond America's borders home to the most remote parts of the country.

opposite
1931 "The Ubangi Savages," who performed on a stage in the menagerie, were advertised as having *"mouths and lips as large as those of full-grown crocodiles."* Circus press agent F. Beverly Kelley remembered that they were "gracious and friendly towards the spectators." (F. Beverly Kelley, *It Was Better Than Work*, 1982)

1931 *"The Ubangi Savages"* from Africa quickly got into the circus' commercial spirit on the circus lot by selling postcards of themselves. They were known to happily shortchange their customers by pretending not to see the difference between a quarter and nickel.

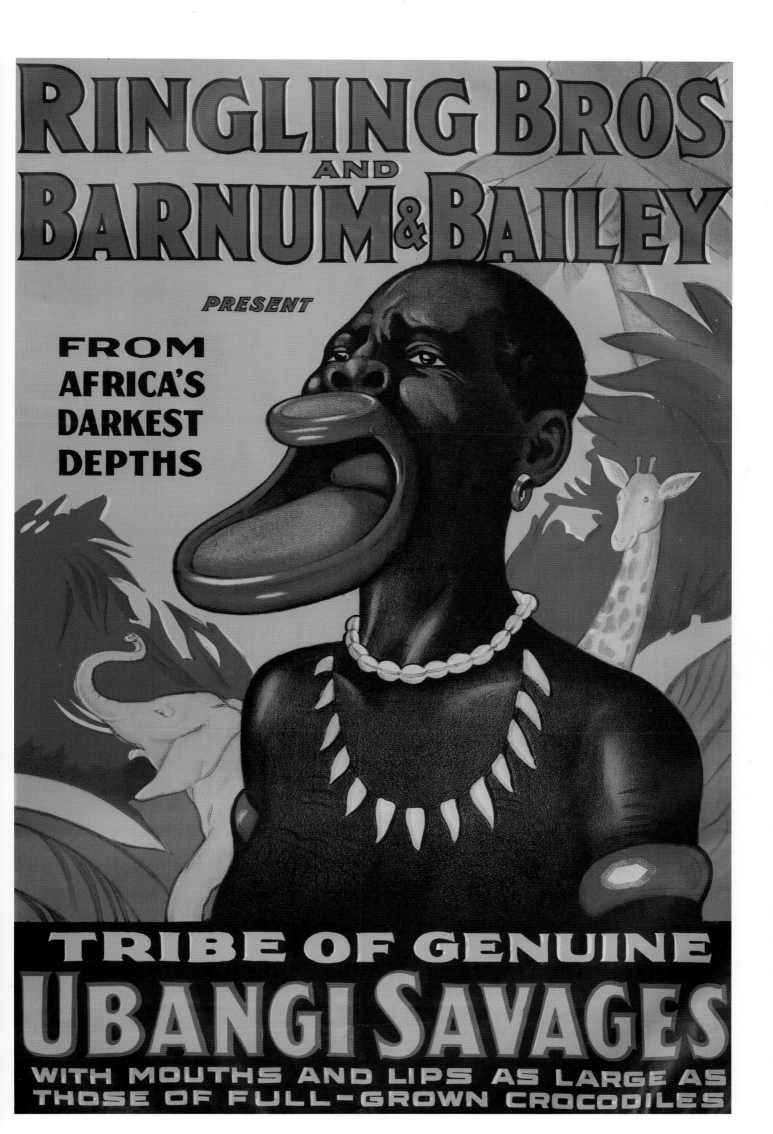

1933 The Ringling Bros. and Barnum & Bailey circus advertised the Royal Padaung ***"Giraffe-Neck Women From Burma"*** as "the greatest educational attraction of all time." Among the "facts" this circus booklet promoted was the claim that tribesmen's matrimonial attraction to the women was proportional to the weight of the brass coils the women wore on their necks and legs, which could sometimes be over 50 pounds. Although facts like these were not always accurate, they introduced circusgoers to a world of foreign customs, giving them a chance to be explorers of hitherto unknown worlds.

1933 The comparison between this poster of "The Giraffe-Neck-Women" in 1933 and a photograph taken that same year is *a fascinating study of circus hyperbole* in its advertising. As astonishing as the photograph may have seemed, the imaginative poster artists could always improve on it. In the circus nothing was too extraordinary—and that attitude is what sold tickets.

below
1933 Harry A. Atwell knew a photo opportunity when he saw one, presenting the imported wonders of the circus at the doorsteps of modern America—*the circus in a nutshell*.

1920s The circus's Asian pageants were gigantic parades mostly defined by spectacular costuming. These *dresses, umbrellas, fans, and wigs said "Asia,"* and one nonwhite performer interspersed in the crowd of performers was enough to validate this Hagenbeck-Wallace circus ensemble.

bottom

1891 *American audiences were fascinated by Asian performers.* Not only was their repertoire often quite different from that of their Western counterparts, but their costumes and, in the case of these Japanese artists, their hairstyles were atypical. Although Asian immigrants were vital to building the Pacific portion of the transcontinental railroad that the circus used, they remained enigmatic to most Americans at the time.

1916 China offered American circusgoers the image of a vast cultural divide, and their customs were thought to be strange and mysterious. The circus was happy to build on this perception, as shown in this Barnum & Bailey poster of the *Jim Wong Troupe* casually sipping tea and eating rice while hanging by their hair.

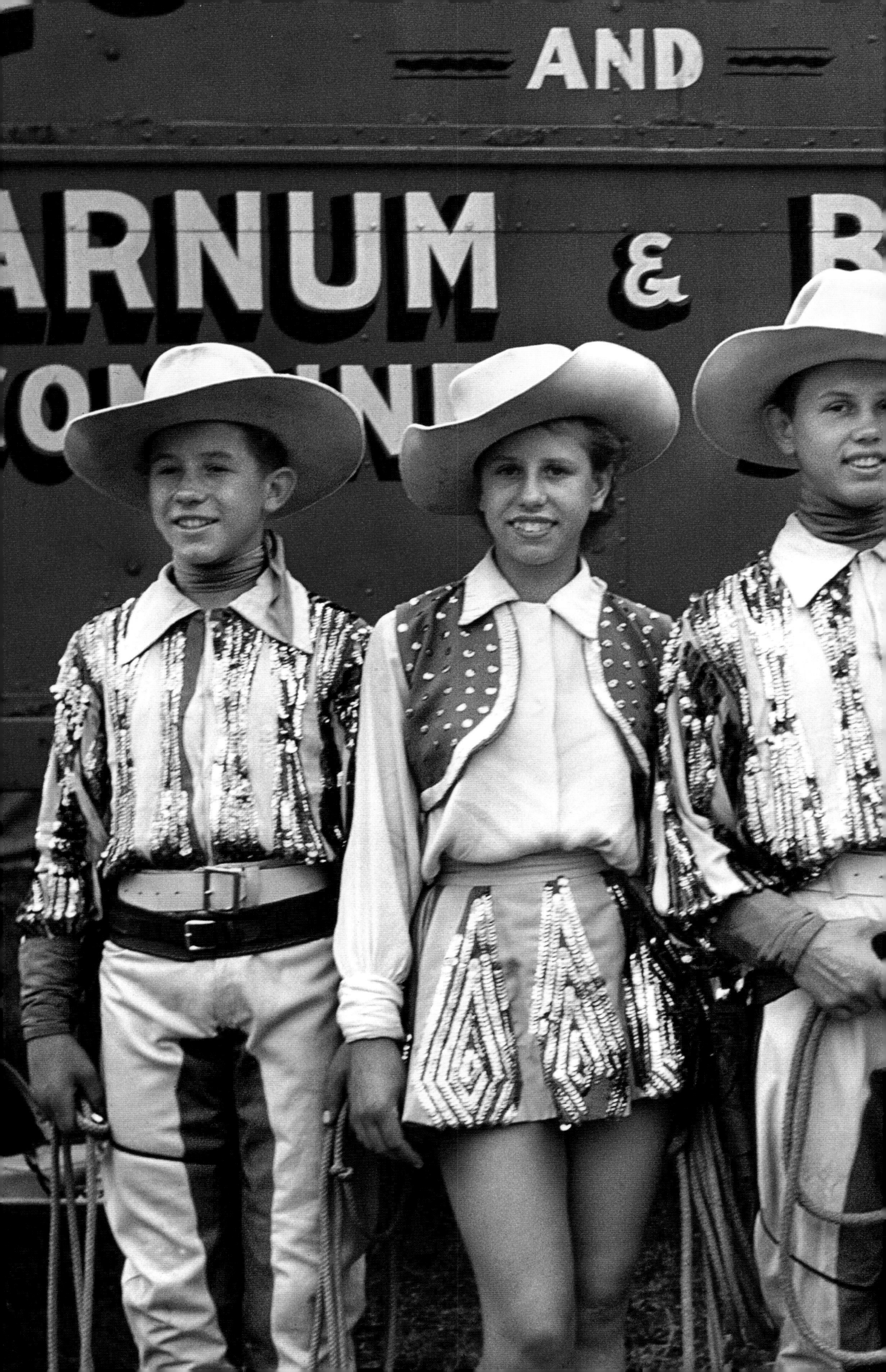
AND
ARNUM &

pages 100–101
1955 *The Cordon Troupe,* who brought the Wild West to Ringling Bros. and Barnum & Bailey in 1955, was actually German, but the adventuresome showgirl who joined them in this picture was American. No true American cowgirl would have donned such a costume, yet this was the circus' exciting version of the Wild West.

ca. 1901 Harry Cole was one of many authentic cowboys turned performers who exhibited their shooting, equestrian, and lariat skills in **reenactments of American frontier conflicts** in the Pawnee Bill's Wild West show. He poses here with his wife and fellow performer.

below
1914 *The Lloyds were a troupe of Native American equestrians* who, claimed the poster, combined "in one marvelous exhibition the recklessness of the red man and the art of modern horsemanship." In 1914 this racist comment guaranteed to its audience an unusually thrilling bareback-riding exhibition.

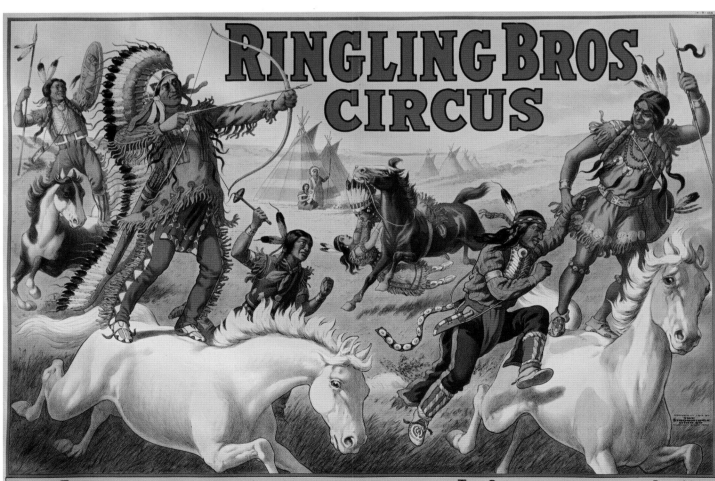

102

right and below

ca. 1913 Chief Iron Tail, a Dakota Sioux, right, Blue Cloud's wife, below right, and another performer in traditional costume, below left, were Native Americans who *played both heroes and foes*, depending on the reenacted scene they were part of in Wild West exhibitions. Although they were Americans, their presence in a U.S. circus was nearly as exotic in the 1900s as that of Chinese, African, or Indian performers.

ca. 1901 *May Lillie* was a remarkable sharp-shooter who claimed to have graduated from Smith College before marrying Pawnee Bill and joining his Wild West troupe. Between performances, she poses in front of the teepees where the Native American performers lived when touring with the show.

1907 *The myth of the American West and its frontiers* offered the circus another historical drama on which to capitalize. Taking its cue from Wild West shows, the circus inserted a capsule version of the Wild West as an aftershow, starring cowboys, Native Americans, stagecoaches, horses, and buffalo.

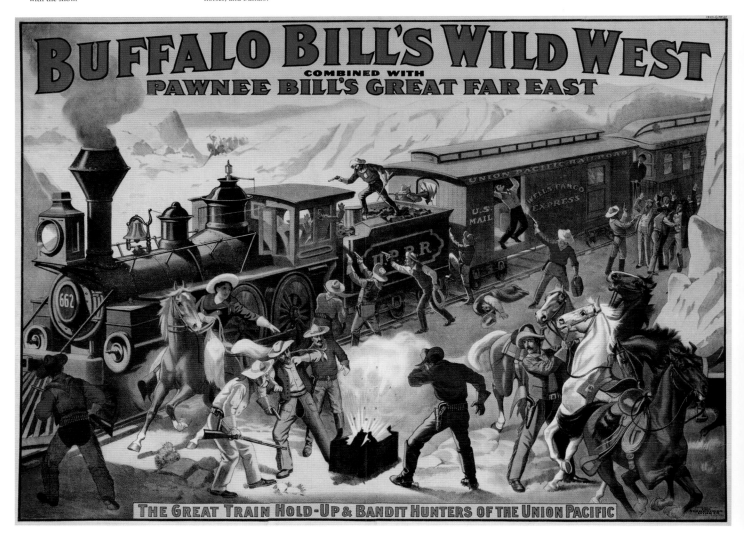

pages 106–107

1907 According to its press agents, **Buffalo Bill's Wild West** *offered a direct line to history*—albeit an idealized version—in its "grand kinetoscopic diorama of the romantic story of the pioneer days of our own country, with interesting reminiscent memories of the fatherlands." (*Buffalo Bill's Wild West* courier, 1907)

1898 *"Buffalo Bill's Wild West and Congress of Rough Riders of the World* with its many men of many kinds inculcate a lesson of true manhood," declared a 1898 Buffalo Bill's Wild West courier. Teddy Roosevelt's famous Rough Riders, who saw action in the Spanish-American War that year, took their name from the popular Wild West exhibitions. But athletic and daring women riders were an important lure to the shows too, like in this poster entitled "Girl Lassoing," even if they would never have been part of Roosevelt's cavalry.

1925 This female performer was featured spinning the lariat in the Miller Bros. 101 Ranch Wild West exhibition. *Women roughriders and sharpshooters* such as the legendary Annie Oakley, the female star of Buffalo Bill's Wild West, were often featured in Wild West exhibitions.

BUFFALO BILL
COMBI
PAWNEE BILL'S

A REALISTIC REPRESENTATION OF TH

V·E·N·U·S·E·S

OF THE AGE

THE

F·E·M·A·L·E

PERFORMER

EMANCIPATED

Dominique Jando

VENUSES
OF THE AGE
THE F·E·M·A·L·E PERFORMER
EMANCIPATED

Dominique Jando

At a time when female sexuality and physical culture were often repressed by the prevailing religious and conservative social mores, the circus did something that no other performing art was able to achieve: It welcomed women for who they were, gave them career opportunities, let them exhibit their bodies and physical strength in public, and managed to do all this without losing one inch of its—and their—respectability. The circus gave women freedom rarely found elsewhere and unwittingly provided a model for female emancipation. Furthermore, as a by-product of the circus' intensely physical culture, sexuality of both genders was brought into the open in an otherwise sexually repressive climate.

opposite
1943 Fans greet *aerialist Ethel Jennier* of the Russell Bros. circus. Anywhere but in the circus or in musical productions her two-piece would have been considered inappropriate. In 1951, five years after its scantier cousin the bikini was introduced, it was banned from the Miss World contest. In Hollywood the Motion Picture Association of America forbid the navel's display on-screen until 1966.

page 109
1945 Beloved performer Corky Cristiani epitomizes *the classic circus woman*—beautiful, healthy, sexy, free, and wonderfully uninhibited. She was part of the Italian Cristiani family of extraordinary bareback riders and acrobats.

Then, as now, sex sold. Burlesque and vaudeville knew that, and even the legitimate theater exploited it. Actresses were seen has having loose morals, and theater impresarios could either fight this perception or build upon it, depending on their interests. Though the Victorian defenders of virtue and moral righteousness have left books, pamphlets, and newspapers articles decrying the "immorality" of female stage performers, there are comparatively few existing texts lambasting female circus performers. The clever marketing of circus pressmen proved to be pitch-perfect to the time in which they lived. They flaunted the circus as family entertainment on one hand and slyly promoted risqué aesthetics on the other without losing their audience or respectability.

At the outset of the Industrial Revolution in the 19th century, before the fast urban development that ensued, society was defined by a mostly rural lifestyle. At the epicenter was the farm or working household, the focal point and often the limit of a woman's universe for her entire life. It was a well-ordered, unsurprising, and unalterable world in which all family members had a preordained role. Although the tasks ascribed to a woman could vary according to her social status and her place in the family, she was a vital part of the homestead economy. She was expected to take care of the household and bear and raise children. Indeed, she gained respect for her ability to reproduce life and continue the family line. Yet popular mores of the day dictated that carnal knowledge and sexual intimacy remain private affairs, and in the public domain the display of female sexuality was associated with actresses and prostitutes. Overdressed and tightly corseted as was fashionable, women were generally not encouraged to cultivate bodily strength and were seen as the fragile sex. Many were overprotected against their will and had few options for living independent lives.

World's First Career Women

In this context, the world of the itinerant entertainers who would compose the circus community couldn't have been more different. By necessity, traveling entertainers lived according to a completely different set of tenets and principles, and in many respects women held a much more egalitarian position. To begin with, the life of traveling entertainers didn't revolve around a house. It centered on the only constant in their existence—the performing space, whether a public square, a bona-fide stage, or, later, a circus ring. Life on the road was hard, and in order to survive everybody in the extended family had to chip in. Money came through

performing, and the better and more varied the performance, the better the income. Consequently, women, like men and children for that matter, contributed to the well-being of the community by performing. However, the life of a female circus performer was not like that of an actress, where being pretty and seductive alone might attract a rich protector and, therefore, a better life. In the circus, one needed talent. Becoming a good acrobat, bareback rider, or ropedancer was far from easy, and no matter your gender, training was hard, long, and painful. Since all members of the circus performing community had gone through this, everyone could appreciate and respect the amount of work behind a successful act, no matter who performed it.

There is no fakery in the circus arts. A somersault can only be a somersault, not the pretense of one. This simple fact defines the attitude of circus folks toward life. Even in the 19th century, circus performers had to wear scanty clothing to be able to do what they did. They didn't have to give the appearance of propriety to be respected. While female performers didn't expect their morality and modesty to be questioned because of their career choice, they were, however, perfectly conscious that their costumes might arouse their male audience. In truth, they didn't have many qualms about that either. They were aware of their bodies and comfortable with them. Their physiques were wonderful tools that had been fine-tuned over the years, and they had no reason to be ashamed of them. Their male colleagues shared this attitude. Female performers wearing circus attire didn't faint, something that was not uncommon in the restrictive clothing of the time. Also like men, women could be strong and have stamina. Like everyone else, circus families abided by a hierarchical structure based on the social mores of the time, but in their culture the divide between the sexes was much less stringent than in the sedentary world they entertained.

Female circus performers date back to its earliest days. In 1772 an early circus performance at Philip Astley's Riding School in London featured two equestriennes. They were the wives of Philip Astley and J. Griffith, the show's principal equestrians. Pamphlets advertising the performance added, "Mrs. Astley will likewise perform with two horses in the same manner as she did before their Majesties of England and France, being the only one of her sex that ever had that honour." At a time when women performers were considered by some to be as disreputable as prostitutes, Patty Astley had been invited to perform for the two most powerful rulers of Europe, George III of England and Louis XV of France, a remarkable

opposite
1917 ***Baring a knee*** (or even an ankle) in 1917 was considered improper unless on a beach, but Barnum & Bailey still used it to advertise its "Lady Artists." The circus differed from vaudeville and burlesque in how it presented women. Although the costumes were similarly revealing, circus pressmen laced their posters with monikers of respect, promoting risqué aesthetics without losing respectability.

below
1924 For young women of good principles—like ***showgirl Stella Rowland***—who were interested in gymnastics and sports, the circus offered a rare and legitimate opportunity to enter the glittering world of show business.

1950s These costumes by Tony Award-winner Miles White resembled those of the famous Parisian theaters ***the Moulin Rouge and the Folies Bergère***. In these theaters, the costumes were considered steamy, but in the circus they were accepted by millions of fans.

feat for a woman at the time. Likewise, when circus pioneer John Bill Ricketts established his circus company in the United States in 1793, one of his principal performers was Mrs. Spinacuta, a female equestrian, who doubled as a dancer and actress in pantomimes.

The Female Performer's Erotic Lure

Equestriennes at the time didn't ride sidesaddle in fashionable outfits that covered their entire body, as would be seen later in the ring when classic equestrian "dressage" became part of circus equestriennes' repertoire. In fact, they were bareback riders, standing on the back of a galloping horse and wearing short dresses that clearly displayed the shape of their legs—a rare vision to say the least and a titillating one for the male audience. This factor certainly contributed to men's interest in the circus, a show allegedly devoted to horsemanship, not to licentiousness, and, therefore, proper for gentlemen. These erotic visions were, in fact, the unspoken lure of the circus, one that was never openly acknowledged but certainly enjoyed. Eroticism is a key ingredient of the circus arts. A beautiful body moving gracefully, showing strength or fragility, has an erotic power—and even more so if this body is not completely

revealed and nudity is teasingly suggested. Circus costumes—whether for male or female performers—are scant for practical reasons, but they are nevertheless revealing. Audiences were not oblivious to this.

The circus female performer was a new kind of working woman, and to many men circus women belonged to another world. While actresses were generally stereotyped as latent harlots—with their makeup and suggestive décolletés—bought and traded by managers and rich protectors, circus women, in addition to their evident sex appeal, were able to perform impressive feats of physicality and daring. They were mystifying, intimidating, and unapproachable, doing things that most male spectators wouldn't have even tried. The German novelist Thomas Mann beautifully expressed this sentiment in his short novel *Confessions of Felix Krull, Confidence Man* (1909): "To imagine her as a wife and mother was simply stupid: a wife and mother or even anyone who could be possibly thought of as one, does not hang head-down from a trapeze…. She was an inapproachable Amazon of the realms of space beneath the canvas, high above the crowd, whose lust for her was transformed into awe."

Women's social condition changed with the far-reaching consequences of the Industrial Revolution, such as the rapid urbanization of the United States in the second half of the 19th century. Many young women from the country left the constraints of the farm to find work, freedom, and a better, more fulfilling life in the city. Their condition was not necessarily improved insofar as men's prevailing attitude toward them was concerned, but women found that they had more options for controlling their destiny. In time, feminism and the suffragist movement would follow. Many found work in the new offices of industrial corporations as typists, telephone operators, or secretaries, brand-new jobs at the time. Others became teachers, salesclerks, milliners, or seamstresses. Their newly acquired freedom let them organize their time as they wished, and they discovered a world that had been up till then proscribed to them: the world of entertainment.

Until the Civil War (1861–65), the American circus audience was predominantly male. It was not considered proper for a woman to attend such a potentially harmful phenomenon as public entertainment. Toward the end of the 19th century, popular theater flourished, and burlesque, vaudeville, and the circus entered their golden age. Young women, and then entire families, began to patronize theaters, vaudeville houses, and circuses alongside men, so long as these shows were considered respectable. (Burlesque, however, was still considered a man's domain.) Show producers quickly figured

The Amazing
MAGGIE
UDDER
IN HER
TITILLATING
INCOMPARABLE
ACHIEVEMENT

out that promoting their shows as upright entertainment was necessary to attract this new, numerous, and diverse audience.

Empowered by their newfound independence, women also exercised their bodies. Urbanization gave men and women more time for leisure, and women engaged in physical education and sports as men did. In 1896 the ancient Greek games were revived at Olympia. That same year, urban America was swept by a bicycle craze, enjoyed equally by both men and women. All this also had a profound influence on women's fashion. You couldn't ride a bicycle or engage in physical activities wearing a tightly buttoned jacket over a blouse and a corset and several layers of petticoats and underskirts all under an oversized dress. This became the age of the "New Woman in Bloomers," as a 1896 courier for Barnum & Bailey proudly announced, where women rode horses "astride in bifurcated skirts." Women abandoned constraining fashions and began wearing lighter, more practical clothes. In the circus ring, circus women had already paved the way.

Nearly Nude, but Always Noble

This new fascination with sports made the exhibitions of female acrobats much more acceptable to the public at large. As performers, they were different from overly made-up women who played lascivious characters in steamy theater productions or dancing girls in burlesque shows who shimmied in revealing outfits to arouse the libido of their male audience. But circus women were no less arousing, with their short skirts cut right under the knee or even more revealing tights and bloomers. They wore pieces of clothing that in public belonged under a dress but in the circus were necessary for their acts. The context was the difference, and circus pressmen understood this and worked to make the female performers inoffensive to everyone.

To young women of good principles who had an interest in gymnastics and sports, the circus provided a rare and legitimate opportunity to enter the glittering and exciting world of show business. They could not only remain respectable but also respected. That having been said, circus producers were acutely aware of the drawing power of female performers on their male audience. Prolific, oversized lithographs plastered every town, showing aerialists, bareback riders, acrobats, and showgirls, who in their dress and athleticism were one step ahead of the general public even as the times and its fashions were changing. But producers were also careful to keep the presence of these female performers acceptable to all audiences lest their shows lose

their clean reputation and, consequently, paying customers. The universal appeal of the show and the diversity of the audience were the keys to the circus' financial success.

Circus press agents wrote extensively about their female performers' respectability, stressing that they were either married or engaged, or that they allegedly belonged to ancient families of European performers (which they often did) with different customs and had been trained by their parents as they trained their own children. Also, since circus women regularly trained and were unusually healthy and fit, they were promoted as examples for urban youth for other women. Above all, as press agents were careful to explain, the public shouldn't perceive female circus performers as sedentary women gone astray. They concocted stories about their love of family and domesticity (which was generally true) and their longing for a well-deserved retirement into a normal, sedentary life (which was mostly untrue). In the 1890s some circuses went so far as to pretend that circus women, embarrassed to show themselves in such revealing outfits, had decided to perform in long fashionable dresses despite the added difficulty. In 1896 the Adam Forepaugh & Sells Brothers circus used a poster depicting the Arrigosi Sisters, billed as "the Flying Wonders, in their astonishing high trapeze, long skirts evolutions, leaps and dives." And there they were, in city outfits—long skirts, high-collared blouses—flying in the air. This fad didn't last, however, as it seriously hindered their ability to perform. Perhaps too much propriety was not so good for business, after all.

Notwithstanding their experiments with "proper" outfits, circuses managed to get away with nudity too. In the mid-19th century, tights were already considered a form of nudity, but, taking a hint from vaudeville, circuses took this one step further with their "living statues." These were supposedly artistic and educational representations of famous sculptures by motionless women standing on a pedestal, whose bodies were entirely covered with white, gold, or bronze greasepaint. The assumption was that the tableaux created by these women, who didn't move an eyelash and pretended to be made of marble or bronze, were artistic, not erotic. On the vaudeville stage, however, similar displays raised more than a few eyebrows: They were often seen as a bit of burlesque bad taste during an otherwise respectable show.

The True Stars of the Circus

To progressive urban women, the circus female performer often appeared as a role model. She was successful, independent, strong and fit, not afraid to show

who she really was, living proof that in many ways a woman could outshine a man. At suffragist rallies, Josie DeMott Robinson, a talented circus equestrienne and a fervent suffragette, attended rallies on her rearing horse, a great image for press photographers and a dramatic symbol of women's liberation. Many female circus performers were stars in their own right, and they acquired that status not because they were pretty, sexy, and appealing (though they could generally claim these attributes) but because they were great performers. They had reached their position by dint of hard work and sheer talent. In their milieu, that called for respect, whether you were male or female. May Wirth, an extraordinary Australian equestrienne and perhaps the greatest female bareback rider of all time, was respected and admired by her peers of both sexes. Her high status in the circus community was unarguable, and her paycheck was in proportion to her talent. The beautiful wire walker Bird Millman also fully deserved her place at the firmament of circusdom; as did Mable Stark, the fearless tiger trainer; Ella Bradna, the great equestrienne; Winnie Colleano and Pinito Del Oro, queens of the trapeze; and the flying triple somersaulter, Antoinette Concello. Each had more talent in her field than most of their male colleagues. And then there was the greatest of them all, the so-called dainty Lillian Leitzel, the

queen of the Roman rings, the greatest star the American circus ever had—and treated as such. Leitzel's expanded suite on the circus train was a true apartment on wheels replete with an upright piano, and her private dressing tent on the show lot was "an elaborate dwelling spread with Oriental rugs, graced with fresh flowers on elegant tables, dignified with an uniformed maid and a majordomo," as remembered by the illustrious equestrian director Fred Bradna. Before her, not even the greatest male performers, not even Alfredo Codona, the king of the flying trapeze, were ever given such royal treatment.

In the circus, Leitzel achieved a position of power that Hollywood stars wouldn't attain in their world until decades later. But on February 13, 1931, the attachment of her aerial apparatus tragically broke during her act in Copenhagen. Leitzel fell and died two days later. Like everyone else in the circus, Leitzel knew that reaching the pinnacle of her profession was not something she could do while shirking from danger or even death. But this had been the choice of a free woman. Lillian Leitzel had been the circus' brightest star and, as such, a powerful, liberated woman.

1953 To a free-spirited young woman, life on the road had charm, notwithstanding the rigorous two-show-a-day schedule. **The nomadic rough-and-tumble lifestyle** might have been off-putting to outsiders, but women learned to prepare for their performances whatever the condition.

top
1934 Many progressive, urban young women joined the circus as showgirls. They were often attracted to the circus by the star female performers, who were successful, independent, strong, and fit, and **not shy about their sex appeal**.

CHAPTER 3

1941 This photograph taken in a circus train playfully contradicts the traditional image of *the clown's unreciprocated longing for the beautiful showgirl*. Publicity shots of flirtatious encounters between clowns and showgirls were often used to add a touch of harmless romance.

pages 118–119
1890s Although at this time the *human cannonball act* was hardly perceived by the public as befitting women performers, women had originated the act 20 years earlier. Here the Frank A. Robbins circus is careful to accentuate the performer's femininity on the poster by including "a wonderful act of grace and beauty."

pages 120–121
1916 Prolific, oversized lithographs showing **aerialists, acrobats, and showgirls** plastered every town. In their dress and athleticism, they were one step ahead of the general public. But producers were also careful to portray these women as acceptable to all audiences, lest they lose paying customers.

opposite
1950 Being a circus showgirl didn't just mean wearing makeup and extravagant costumes. It required ***training and an adventurous spirit***. "When a girl is liable to break her neck any day, she thinks of life—her life here and in the future—in a serious way." (Mickey King, quoted by Bart A. Lynch, "They Split Seconds to Live," *The Detroit Free Press*, February 21, 1932)

1944 Young equestrienne and aerialist Ernestine Clarke prepares to enter the ring dressed as the devil. This is an apt costume: Up through the early 1800s, the unusual skills of itinerant performers were often branded by local religious authorities as the ***work of the devil and witchcraft***.

1948 "Often the ***roads were almost impassable from rain***; the ruts were so deep that the heavily loaded baggage wagons could scarcely go through…. Things did move, somehow…. The spirit animating everybody and everything was that the show had to go on. And it always did." (Josephine DeMott Robinson, *The Circus Lady*, 1936)

opposite
1949 *Aerialist Antoinette Concello*, right, poses with acrobat Fatima Marschary. At the time, Concello was the only woman to turn a triple somersault on the flying trapeze, a feat that was rare even among male flyers. Her male attire here echoes the fashion initiated by free-spirited Hollywood stars Marlene Dietrich and Katharine Hepburn.

1900 In the late 1890s, America had been **swept by a bicycle craze**, enjoyed by both men and women. It had a profound influence on women's fashion, allowing a more masculine style. This became the age of the "New Woman in Bloomers," as a 1896 Barnum & Bailey courier of the period proudly announced.

pages 124–125
1942 *Elizabeth Wallenda* was part of a famous high-wire superstar act with Ringling Bros. and Barnum & Bailey. Stardom for women in the circus came not because they were pretty or sexy—although that had its own appeal—but because they were great performers and had reached their position by dint of hard work and sheer talent.

1900s *May Lillie* was the wife of Gordon "Pawnee Bill" Lillie, of Pawnee Bill's Wild West. She was college-educated at a time when this was rare for women and was a remarkable sharpshooter. In the Wild West show, she chose to emulate the most famous sharpshooter of all time, the legendary Annie Oakley.

1920s *Animal trainer Vera Clark* poses in a victorious pose atop a submissive, froglike creature, the male contortionist DeMarlo. It is an interesting reversal of the traditional gender roles in 1920s America, as well as in the circus, where contortionists were generally female performers.

opposite
ca. 1932–34 *Equestrienne Dorothy Herbert* practices her famous "layback," a dangerous and difficult trick. The 1939 Ringling Bros. and Barnum & Bailey program described the free-spirited Herbert as "the most recklessly fearless and expert rider of reinless, rearing and jumping horses ever known in the circus world."

1894 When the first circus was founded in 1770, *equestriennes were its first female performers*. Their presence brought a dose of sex appeal that circuses like Adam Forepaugh continued to exploit more than 100 years later.

below
1951 The young, pretty, and energetic *British Wallaby Troupe of the Mills Bros. circus* was acrobats with a taste for adventure who worked in American circuses after WWII. Since circus women trained regularly and were unusually healthy and fit, they were often promoted as role models for other women.

pages 130–131

1879 P. T. Barnum billed **Linda Jeal** as the "Queen of the Flaming Zone." Jeal's act changed the traditional image of the sweet, pretty equestrienne into that of a reckless daredevil. "I loved it from the day when, a girl, of 15, I first climbed on a horse's back." (Linda Jeal, quoted by Russell Fore, "Queen of the Flaming Circles," *The Detroit News*, January 29, 1933)

1937 *Legendary press agent Roland Butler* depicted Dorothy Herbert on this program's cover in a costume ahead of its time. Five years before the California one-piece bathing suit hit the scene, this outfit was seldom seen outside the circus, vaudeville, or, increasingly, in movies.

1947 An equestrienne prepares to lead *12 horses at full gallop* around the hippodrome track in an act that dates to the mid-1800s. It required strength and bravery and routinely surprised audiences who didn't expect to see a woman perform such a daring and spectacular act.

1922 This woman was billed as *"the songbird of the circus"* by Sparks circus for her elaborate act with horses and doves. Creative performances are what kept performers employed, and women were encouraged to cultivate a creative independence that was not common in society at large.

1889 In the 1880s, a skirt cut above the knee was by its nature erotically charged. But in the circus it was acceptable attire because of the need to perform freely. Here *equestrienne Lottie Aymar is billed as "Europe's geatest rider"*, with the requisite continental flair to justify her unusual fashion statement.

LOTTIE AYMAR EUROPE'S GREATEST **RIDER** HER FIRST APPEARANCE IN AMERICA ENGAGED AT A **SALARY OF $500 A WEEK.**

pages 136–137
1874 The image of a circus woman standing tall in the face of dangerous lions, tigers, and leopards, and holding one of them in submission with her foot, was ***an unusual motif of female empowerment***. As the suffragette movement gained ground in America at the turn of the century, women performers were counted in the ranks of its activists.

right and below
1926 *Australian-born May Wirth* was one of the greatest equestriennes of all time. Her acts contradicted the common stereotype that some acrobatic feats were beyond a woman's reach. Her handstand on horseback, below, layout somersault from horse to horse, above, and front somersault on a galloping horse were extreme rarities among both male and female equestrians of the 1920s, and still are today. Ringling Bros. and Barnum & Bailey's equestrian director Fred Bradna said that in spite of her being a "tomboy", "she was a fascinating showman [*sic*], delighting the audience with her daintiness and graciousness and, in the backyard, was one of the best loved of all the stars." (Fred Bradna, *The Big Top*, 1952)

1920s A crowd of men look on as *famed animal trainer Mabel Stark tussles with a tiger*. In the 1920s when a journalist asked her what it took to become a trainer, Stark rolled up her trousers to reveal legs covered with scars. Although this was not unusual for tiger trainers, they were testimony to a reality that many at the time thought too tough for women.

1920s Dressed in lighthearted fancy clothes, *Madame Scheel* sits leisurely on a phlegmatic lion—an awesome vision to her spectators. Female trainers were not common but, when they did appear, were very popular.

opposite
1890s This stock lithograph of an anonymous *"lion queen"* served the Clark circus for many years, even when no one was on hand to enter the lion's den. Circus owners knew that the winning combination of feminine beauty and ferocious beasts was sure to sell the circus.

SELLS
THE GREAT
FLOTO
SHOWS
CONSOLIDATED
COPYRIGHT, 1906 BY
THE U.S. LITHOGRAPH Co.
RUSSELL-MORGAN PRINT
CINCINNATI & NEW YORK
9288
TY-BELL SISTERS
SENSATIONAL AERIALISTS

opposite and left
1906 and 1900s In a quest for respectability, some circus owners pretended women performers such as the *Ty-Bell Sisters*, opposite, and the *Grunatho Sisters*, left, were embarrassed to wear revealing outfits. They claimed the women wanted to perform in the long dresses that were fashionable at the time. But the performers didn't care for this propriety—or for the constraint of their movements—and the fad didn't last long.

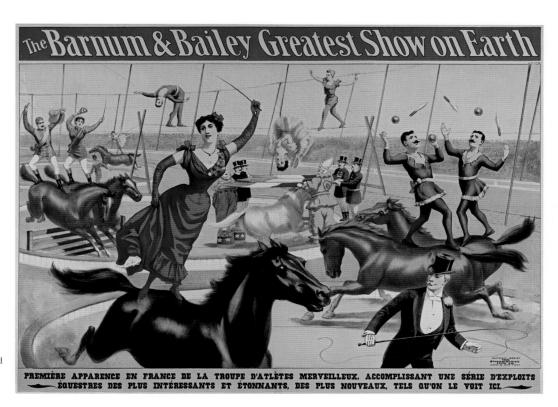

1898 When Barnum & Bailey toured France, they presented *female bareback riders in full city dress*. French audiences thought this an odd form of circus costuming, however, and did not take it as proof of the women's propriety, as American circus owners' had intended.

1930 Circuses were eager to incorporate contemporary fashions into their costumes, especially if they served them in more than one way. In this poster, the trendy swimsuits worn by the performers demonstrated that circus were **hip to the latest fashions**.

below
1920s *The Ernesto Sisters* had come to America from Europe 20 years earlier. Their jump-rope routine on a tightwire was a feat few men accomplished and ensured them a long, profitable career that wouldn't have been possible in the outside world at the time.

pages 142–143
1885 *Mademoiselle Zoe, "Queen of the Air,"* is shown here in a titillating costume performing on the Spanish web and Roman rings. Yet the Barnum & Bailey publicity department was careful to also include a respectable portrait of Zoe, top center, dressed as a true lady in high collar and hat.

opposite
1952 Four showgirls are ready to perform in a Ringling Bros. and Barnum & Bailey aerial ballet with 60 other aerialists in an *all-girl extravaganza*. The circus gave women physical freedom rarely found elsewhere and unwittingly provided a model for female emancipation.

above and right

1920s *Herbert "Berta" Beeson* was advertised by Ringling Bros. and Barnum & Bailey as a female wire walker, "the Mad-Cap Whirlwind of the Mid-Air." But the program also warned, "you expect a lot—and Boy, oh, Boy, you get it." Beeson was the circus's answer to the performer "Barbette," the American cross-dressing wire walker and aerialist who was the toast of 1920s Europe and a protégé of French poet Jean Cocteau. Beeson was riding the wave of the extraordinary celebrity of Barbette but also the popularity of female performers such as wire walker Bird Millman.

opposite

1922 The beautiful *Bird Millman* was one of the greatest female wire walkers in America. Her grace and elegance, as well as her speed on the wire, were her greatest assets. Like other circus performers, she performed publicity stunts such as this one over the dizzying heights of Chicago's skyline.

1935 Tiny Kline was a versatile circus artist who performed this spectacular *"Iron Jaw Slide for Life" over Times Square* in New York City as a publicity stunt. Twenty-five years later, the diminutive yet very talented performer became the first woman to play Tinker Bell at Disneyland.

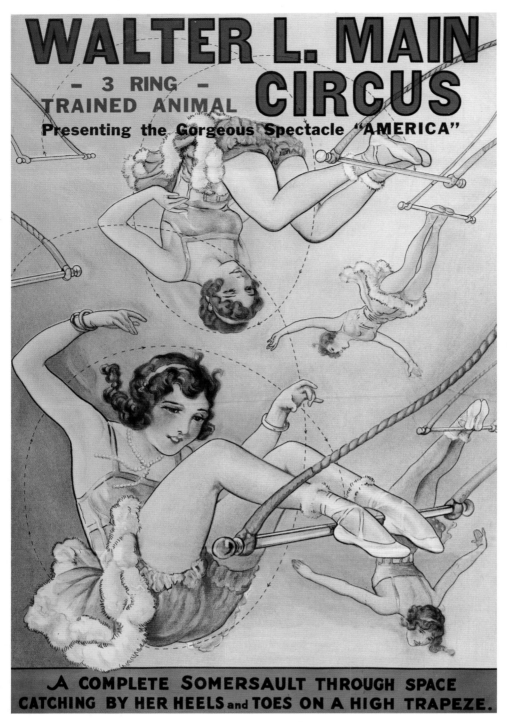

WALTER L. MAIN
- 3 RING -
TRAINED ANIMAL CIRCUS
Presenting the Gorgeous Spectacle "AMERICA"

A COMPLETE SOMERSAULT THROUGH SPACE
CATCHING BY HER HEELS and TOES ON A HIGH TRAPEZE.

1924 A beautiful body moving gracefully through space, showing strength and fragility, has an erotic power—and even more so if nudity is teasingly suggested. As a by-product of *the circus' intensely physical culture*, sexuality of both genders was brought into the open.

opposite
1956 Ringling Bros. and Barnum & Bailey's program called *Pinito Del Oro,* "Spain's stunning steel-nerved trapeze performing star." She was all that and more, a gifted aerialist whose combination of death-defying feats and striking beauty mesmerized her audiences.

below left
1910s One hundred years ago, a woman with bare shoulders doing a split in a short skirt would have signaled deplorable licentiousness had she been in burlesque or vaudeville. In the circus this was viewed as the demonstration of *hard-won flexibility* acquired through rigorous practice.

below right
1923 *Wire walker Naida Miller* with Sparks circus adopted the look and style of the 1920s reigning queen of wire-walking, Bird Millman. The very successful Millman was a role model for Miller's generation of working women.

SELLS FLOTO
CIRCUS

ERMA
WARD

*Erma
Ward*

WORLD'S CHAMPION
LADY AERIAL GYMNAST

above and right
1920s and 1930 In the Roaring Twenties,
Erma Ward, above, could do 100 plange turns
just like the celebrated aerialist ***Lillian Leitzel,***
right, and even lift a man by her teeth. In the
circus, strong and skilled women acrobats were
not the exception but the norm. Many female
performers were stars in their own right. In
1930, Lillian Leitzel, the quintessential circus
star and queen of the Roman rings achieved a
position of power in the circus world that Hollywood stars wouldn't attain in their industry until
decades later.

150

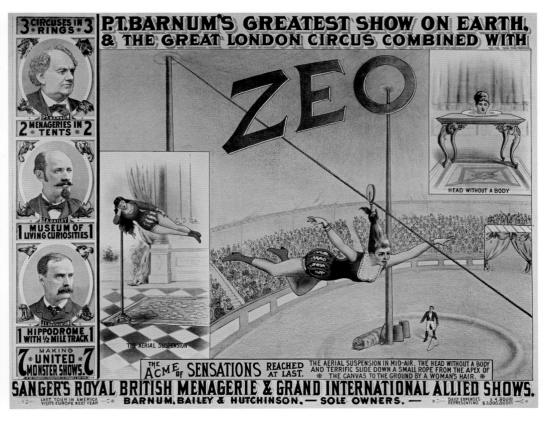

above

1930s *Iron Jaw exhibitions by female performers* were a staple of the American circus. Although requiring little training, it gave women an image of power and strength.

1883 The sideshow magician Zeo performed a *"Slide of Death"* under the big top, hanging by her hair. This was an exciting feat on more than one level: It was not only daring, but the blatant display of Zeo's loose locks was charged with eroticism at a time when seeing a woman's flowing hair in public was rare.

left, top and bottom
1916 Circuses were always eager to accept women in unusual roles. In the Ringling Bros. circus sideshow, **the Bennett Sisters staged boxing and wrestling exhibitions**, a rare and unexpected sight in 1916. The sisters remained circus performers until the late 1920s, steadily building a career for themselves and graduating from staged sideshow fights to acrobatics, trapeze, horse riding, and the Roman rings.

opposite
1912 Barnum & Bailey stressed **Katie Sandwina's "beauty and strength,"** the latter illustrated by her ability to restrain horses with her neck and to play with men as if they were lightweights. Strongwomen were common in the circus, but elsewhere aggressive physical exercise was considered a threat to womanhood.

1910 Strongwoman Katie Sandwina is seen here in a vaudeville act **breaking heavy chains** in front of a chorus line of baffled and rather uneasy Roman legionaries. It was an inversion of gender stereotypes, at the turn of the 20th century, which circus performers brought to the vaudeville stage.

opposite

1910s *Strongwoman Katie Sandwina* had 13 siblings. The Leamy Ladies and a young Lillian Leitzel, far right, were not part of them but were game to demonstrate the unusual strength that gave birth to the fame of their gifted friend and fellow performer.

1900s *Miss Charmaine was a sideshow strongwoman.* Like many circus women, her act went against the social mores of the time. Well-known aerialist Mickey King said in 1932, "Yes, I am very strong. But I have never had to use it, only in my act…nobody has ever tried to molest me. I think I could give one an awful punch in the eye." (Mickey King, quoted by Bart A. Lynch, "They Split Seconds to Live," *The Detroit Free Press*, February 21, 1932)

1890s Madame Yucca was billed in the 1890s as *"the Champion American Female Hercules."* A route book from 1898 claimed that suspending a horse in the air as depicted in this poster was "one of the greatest marvels of the entire performance" and "the most remarkable feat of strength of the century." (Adam Forepaugh circus route book, 1898)

pages 156–157
1880s *Miss Carlotta* performed the Iron Jaw act and spectacular displays of strength depicted here. As was often the case in circus posters of women, the men played a passive, submissive role. In the circus, women got their revenge on the outside world's social convention of damsels in distress.

STRANGE BEASTS FROM FOREIGN LANDS

Dominique Jando

STRANGE BEASTS FROM FOREIGN LANDS

Dominique Jando

Here come the elephants—the grey giants from faraway lands—huge, smart, strong, amazingly agile, stomping through the big top, 15, 20, 30 of them all at once. It is an awesome sight to see them walk on their hind legs just as we do and, in the next moment, do handstands, build pyramids, stand on one foot, or play football, using their nimble trunk to hold the ball. The spectacular elephant act that punctuates the circus performance is matched only by that of the wild beasts, when roaring tigers face a lone cat-trainer inside the center ring's steel arena. Watching the animals in action is a thrilling sensation made all the more potent because we not only see them but hear, smell, and feel their presence too. In the big cage, however, there is no human parody—only a raw, dangerous, and terrifying wild world. We watch with bated breath as wild beasts battle with the trainer inside the cage, a theatrical show of man's victory over nature. In their sheer number and dramatic antics, animals were one of the greatest thrills the circus had to offer.

opposite
1938 A wide variety of animals could be seen at the circus. Additional novelty was often provided by the trainer, like the so-called *Hindu fakir named Blacaman* who came from Sicily in the 1930s and pretended to hypnotize crocodiles and other wild animals to the wonderment of audiences.

page 159
1882 *The Children's Circus and Menagerie Picture Book* perfectly summarized how audiences saw the circus big cat trainer: a man in a cage fending off ferocious, raw-meat-eating wild animals.

above
1930s "Can there be any doubt of the fact that nine-tenths of the children of the U. S. would never see a giraffe, a rhinoceros or any other ***rare and valuable wild animal*** if it was not for the periodical visits of the Barnum & Bailey circus?" (Barnum & Bailey program, 1914)

below
1880s ***Early animal trainers*** worked with small animals that were easy to transport from one location to another and not too difficult to train. Birds, dogs, and small monkeys were most commonly used, as well as some farm animals, and an occasional snake for an added touch of danger.

Up through the early 20th century, animals were a vital part of everyday life. Most people lived off the land and were intimately familiar with the natural world. The circus, from its earliest days in the late 18th century, was enthusiastically received by its audiences because its performances revolved around that most important of all animals in both the city and country: the horse. But with the advent of the Industrial Revolution, working animals were gradually replaced by machines. This, coupled with the loss of nature from human exploitation, meant that wildlife was pushed farther away from the places we chose to inhabit. In this new world, animals became a less familiar part of life. Gone was their vital usefulness. What was left, however, was the fascination they, particularly exotic and wild animals, generated in the public's imagination and their ability to entertain us, sometimes parodying human attitudes, behaviors, and foibles.

Tried-and-True Audience Favorites

Right from its inception in the late 18th century, the circus incorporated animals into its performances. When Philip Astley, the British equestrian who invented the circus in 1770, brought other entertainers to perform in his show, he chose acts that were tried-and-true audience favorites. Among the ropedancers, jugglers, and "posturers" (as acrobats were then called) were the ever-popular trained animals. Most trainers at the time, whether in theaters, public squares, or, eventually, the circus ring, worked with small animals. They were easy to transport from one place to another and not too difficult to train. Birds, dogs, and small monkeys were most commonly used, as well as farm animals such as donkeys, geese, and pigs, clowns' partners of choice up till the early 20th century. Pigs had long been typecast as the comic characters of the farming world, and to those clowns with a penchant for political satire (a common characteristic of clowning at the time), they served as a metaphor for politicians, figures of power, or profiteers.

Equestrians used to working with horses soon tried their hands at other sizeable mammals like wild beasts. Early circus equestrians were not only performers, they were also riding masters and, as Astley put it in one of his early advertisements, available "for breaking horses for the Army, Road, Field, Draft, Shooting, Stroking, &c." Training wild animals not only made for a great show, it enhanced a riding master's reputation. As early as 1779, Astley also showed a zebra in his circus in London. Not long after, in Paris, the Franconis, the French circus pioneers, scored a huge hit when they exhibited a trained stag, Coco, at their Cirque Olympique in the 1810s. An even bigger sensation was Baba, a young Asian elephant they acquired in 1816. It was the

CHRISTY BROS. 5 RING WILD ANIMAL SHOW

RIVERSIDE PRINT CO. CHICAGO 3370

1920s Nineteenth-century colonialism led to *extensive wild animal trading,* which triggered the traveling menagerie business in the U. S. With the subsequent development of urban menageries and zoos, traveling menagerie owners moved on to the circus business, bringing animals with them.

first trained elephant ever presented in a circus. These novelties brought great business, and the variety of animals presented in the circus broadened over time.

Wild-Animal Trade Runs Rampant

An important factor in the audience's growing fascination with wild and exotic animals in the 19th century was the fast expansion of European colonial empires and the extensive exploration that ensued, notably in the unknown wilderness of Africa. Colonialism didn't limit itself to geographical exploration alone. Local peoples were often exploited or traded as slaves, and unfamiliar indigenous animals were captured and traded as exotic curiosities. In the wake of these colonial pursuits, European countries developed a thriving wild-animal trade, and this triggered the development of zoological exhibitions and menageries, both stationary and itinerant. The blossoming of the menagerie business was nowhere more evident than in the young, entrepreneurial United States. It started in 1809, when Hachaliah Bailey, a local cattle dealer in New York state, began exhibiting an elephant he called Bet. He made a fortune, and his success prompted several of his neighbors to go into the traveling menagerie business where they, too, found great wealth.

With the growing menagerie business came more animal trainers, especially "tamers," as they were called then, of wild and dangerous animals such as lions, tigers, leopards, bears, and wolves. At first, their exhibitions were limited to the confines of the traveling menagerie. But when their acts evolved from basic confrontation between man and beast to more elaborate performances, they moved to the theater and circus stage before eventually landing in the circus ring. One of the first wild-animal trainers to become an international celebrity was Isaac A. Van Amburgh. Born in Fishkill, New York, he began working in menageries in 1829. A true pioneer in animal training, he trained his animals to move together at his command, to hold prearranged positions, and to lie together with him. He also pretended to fight them, which made the audience believe (with the help of some savvy press agents) that he had extraordinary powers to "will" his charges into submission. Van Amburgh also appeared in melodramas in New York's popular theaters. In 1833 in *The Lion Lord; or The Forest Monarch,* he tangled with a Bengal tiger, a petrifying vision for an audience not used to seeing such terrifying creatures, let alone a tiger, in a fighting mood. This type of presentation made him a household name and, eventually, an international star.

In their pursuit of profit, animal exhibitors eventually took over the traveling circus business, unifying two kinds of entertainment that in form and content had been

destined to bond. In the days before the railroad, however, the number of animals that early itinerant enterprises could show was restricted by the difficulty of transporting them. Before the American circus adopted railroad transportation on an unprecedented level in the 1870s, circuses and menageries traveled by horse-drawn wagons. Show horses and some exotic mammals like camels, zebras, and even an elephant or two could walk along the routes, but this required a number of capable handlers. Wild beasts, which had to be kept in a cage, needed wagons and heavy horses to pull them. This added to the expense, and if the show was more expensive to produce, a larger audience and a larger tent were needed to ensure success. When P. T. Barnum hit the road in 1871 with his Grand Traveling Museum, Menagerie, Caravan and Circus, his show was huge, as its title implied, in more ways than one. Success was immediate. But how far could such a gigantic enterprise expand while remaining logistically manageable and, above all, profitable? The quest to find a solution to this logistical problem eventually determined the evolution of the American circus. Always the visionary, Barnum had the answer: In 1872 he and his partners moved the entire show by rail. It was not easy at first, but his imaginative associate, William C. Coup, established systems that would remain in use until the end of the railroad circus era in the 1950s. With this new mode of transportation, everything changed for American circuses. They were now capable of the colossal undertaking that would make the circus and menagerie business immensely profitable. The American circus now entered its golden age.

A Zoo on Wheels

During this time, the menagerie tent was second in size to the big top, and in major circuses it was larger than the big top of many smaller shows. The tent was traditionally erected right behind the entrance marquee and served as a foyer to the big top. The audience walked through this thrilling animal maze to get to the circus tent, a perambulation that was sure to build tension and expectation. The menagerie could house up to 20 or 30 ornate cage-wagons lined up along its sidewalls, full of all sorts of animals—from Atlas lions, Bengal tigers, and African leopards to perhaps a rhinoceros, a hippopotamus, a polar bear, a family of sea lions, and even a sea elephant. In the center of the menagerie tent, large herds of exotic animals like zebras, dromedaries, and camels could be lined up, and several giraffes, and perhaps ostriches and emus, dallied in mesh enclosures. In the far end of the tent, close to the big top entrance, was the long line of elephants. There were also a few animal oddities—a five-legged calf, a three-horned goat, and a "mysterious" species thrown in on occasion. In 1937

THE REALISTIC JUNGLE MENAGERIE

...IAL VIEW OF THE INTERIOR OF THE MAMMOTH MENAG...
...AVILION SHOWING SOME OF THE STRANGE HUMAN FREAKS,
...G CURIOSITIES AND RARE AND VALUABLE ANIMALS. ALL
...HICH ON EXHIBIT WITHOUT EXTRA CHARGE.

pages 164–165
1897 The circus became immensely profitable with the development of the railroad because it could move quickly from city to city and transport bigger tents, more animals, and more performers. This meant higher profits and extravagant displays such as this *"realistic jungle menagerie,"* replete with potted palms.

opposite
1882 P. T. Barnum brought *the mighty Jumbo* to America in 1882, the greatest animal attraction the circus ever had. Even though his career only lasted fours years, the huge African elephant was such a success that his name has become synonymous for "colossal."

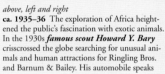

above, left and right
ca. 1935–36 The exploration of Africa heightened the public's fascination with exotic animals. In the 1930s *famous scout Howard Y. Bary* crisscrossed the globe searching for unusual animals and human attractions for Ringling Bros. and Barnum & Bailey. His automobile speaks of the trader's wealth, even if it was not ideal for traversing the wilderness. The memory of *Jumbo, P. T. Barnum's elephant superstar* of the 1880s, never faded. This large tusker pictured was certainly impressive but never made it to America. Bary was still searching for the ultimate elephant as late as 1955.

Ringling Bros. and Barnum & Bailey advertised a "herd of the smallest full grown pigmy elephants on the face of the globe," which were, in fact, baby African elephants. Cute nonetheless, they were a sure winner with the audience. This was fair game in the good old Barnum tradition of giving spectators what they wanted, even if you had to fake it. Whether you lived in a city or a village, and whether or not the animals were really as advertised, the giant menagerie tent was a sight to behold.

Not all animals in the menagerie appeared in the big top performance. Most of the caged animals were there for exhibition only. The performing big cats and bears were kept apart in cage-wagons near the performers' entrance. There, a long, removable caged tunnel, known as "the chute," connected them to the large steel arena in the center ring (or, sometimes, in all three rings). To those onlookers lured to the circus by posters of roaring lions and tigers, the nonperforming big cats in the menagerie could be a little disappointing. Lying in their cages, the fierce wild beasts looked more like languorous pussycats, listlessly gazing at the audience or even sleeping.

Battling Fangs and Killer Claws

When the performing big cats appeared in the steel arena, however, with circus spotlights beaming on them, they sprang into action. Snarling, roaring, jumping, they "fought" a trainer dressed in a pseudomilitary uniform or a jungle-explorer outfit replete with boots, jodhpurs, and pit helmet. This transformation was fascinating to watch. How could a single individual survive such an explosion of fury and raw ferocity? And how did this intrepid "officer" or "explorer" keep in check a group of 20 or 30 wild, aggressive beasts, sometimes of various antagonistic species, put together in the same cage? In truth, the wild animal acts were pure theatrics. These courageous performers were not "tamers" who forced their charges into submission as the circus wanted us to believe. They were skilled animal trainers, and sometimes, as in the case of the legendary Clyde Beatty, they were great actors who could beautifully stage their act. Yes, danger was inherent in working closely with wild animals, but what the audience saw in the ring was the *performance* of danger. They had read about the ferocity of these animals in the popular literature of the day; now they could witness the fierceness of the wild beasts with their very own eyes.

With the advent of nature documentaries, the audience's perception of wildlife began to change. In the classic Disney animated films of the 1930s and '40s, animals think, speak, and behave like people. In a similar manner, Disney's highly influential early wildlife documentaries of the 1940s and '50s portrayed animals as anthropomorphic inhabitants of an idealized natural world in what could be called the "Bambi" syndrome. During the golden age of the American circus before film entered the scene, wilderness was still seen as being wild, and great animal trainers like Clyde Beatty and Terrell Jacobs delivered a taste of this wilderness to their audiences. Even Mabel Stark, the legendary female tiger trainer of the 1920s, was shown in press photographs "fighting" big cats, not "seducing" them, a performance style more befitting a female performer of this era. In reality, animal trainers have to have a special bond with their animals to perform as they do. They live with their animals, take care of them, and work with them in an all-consuming, round-the-clock job. On the other hand, audiences thrilled to the appearance of hostility between the trainers and their charges. In the 20th century, this image would tarnish animal trainers' reputations considerably in the eyes of animal rights activists.

In the 1940s the French big-cat trainer Alfred Court and his assistants were featured with Ringling Bros. and Barnum & Bailey, and their laid-back style, which stressed complicity between the trainer and his felines, highlighting the animals' beauty instead of danger, was hailed as a novel method of animal training. Yet Court's training methods and those of Beatty, Jacobs, or Stark were the same: patience, rewards, and a good understanding of animal psychology. The only difference was the style of performance. The famous German trainer Gunther Gebel-Williams, who hailed from the same European tradition as Court, would have the same effect in the 1970s, but by this time his approach coincided with audiences' changing attitudes toward animal welfare.

Zebras, camels, dromedaries, llamas, guanacos, water buffalos, Watusi cattle, even hippos, and other exotic menagerie animals of gentler dispositions often appeared in the ring, sometimes in bona fide circus acts or led by costumed handlers in the sumptuous exotic pageants that punctuated the circus performance. Less manageable animals such as rhinos and buffalos could also be seen on display in the big top, standing in a richly decorated horse-drawn (or camel-drawn, or elephant-drawn) cage-wagon, or on a large, flat wagon. This included Gargantua, the terrifying gorilla originally known as Buddy, who was the superstar of the Ringling Bros. and Barnum & Bailey menagerie from 1938 to 1949 and the greatest animal celebrity since the days of Jumbo, Barnum's legendary elephant.

Jumbo: International Pop Star

The illustrious Jumbo was such a successful attraction that his name has become part of the English language, a synonym for everything huge, gigantic, colossal.

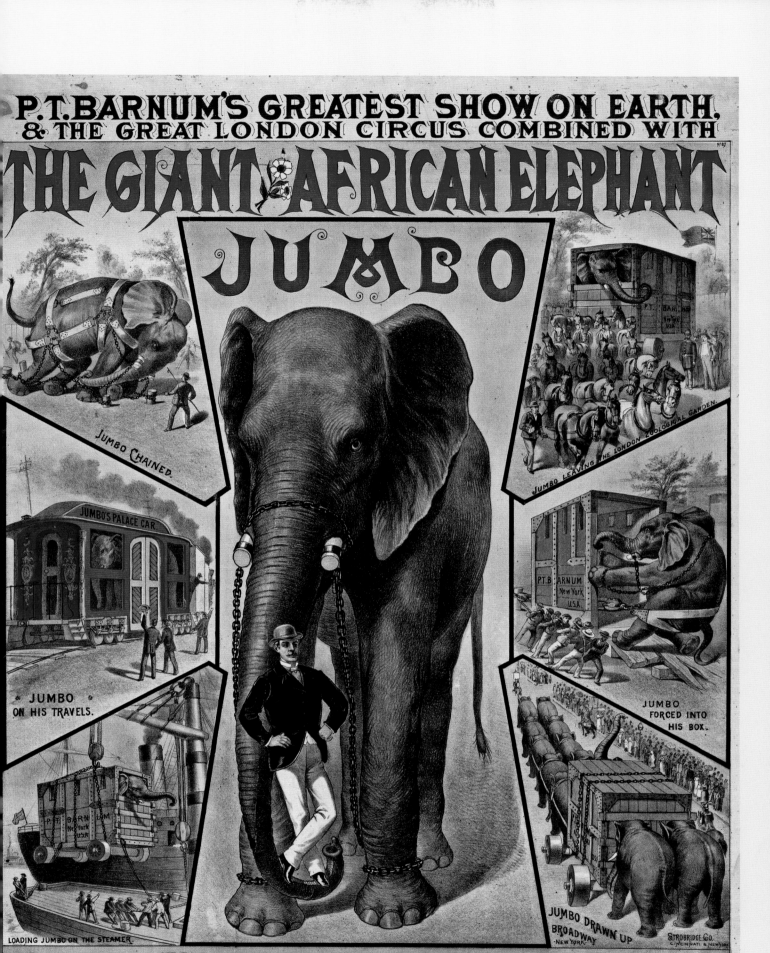

pages 170–171
1933 ***The menagerie tent*** was second in size only to the big top. Large ones could house several dozen cage-wagons and a large collection of animals. Movies like *Tarzan the Ape Man* (1932) gave audiences a peek at the animal kingdom, but the circus gave them the chance to experience it in person.

opposite
1910 After the extraordinary success in Europe of a "gentleman" chimpanzee named Consul, many U. S. trainers exploited this trend. ***Charles 1st***, a chimp with the Barnum & Bailey circus, parodied a perfect gentleman and bore a name befitting a king.

1947 ***Life on a circus back lot*** was as exotic as the menagerie. To children who grew up with the circus, performing chimpanzees such as the Varga chimps of Ringling Bros. and Barnum & Bailey were part of their extended family.

ca. 1943 ***Chimpanzees were an audience favorite,*** especially when they mimicked human behavior. In this photograph by Weegee, young women hold souvenir chimp dolls in New York City's Madison Square Garden, which they likely purchased at one of the ubiquitous concessions stands.

Jumbo was a male African elephant born in Sudan, then a French colony, and was first exhibited in Paris in 1861 when he was four years old. He was acquired four years later by the London Zoo, where he became very popular giving rides to young zoo visitors. His name, which was actually *Jumbe* in Swahili, means "chief," and at over 11 feet tall at the shoulder, Jumbo was an imposing creature. With great fanfare, Barnum purchased him in 1882, and with his ballyhoo machine in full gear, Jumbo ultimately became the greatest attraction the circus has ever known. Jumbo's impact on the American psyche is all the more striking when one considers that his American career lasted only a little more than four years. The huge beast was accidentally killed on a running track by an unscheduled train during the 1885 season.

If Jumbo's fame was partly the result of Barnum's promotional know-how, it was also due to the audience's fascination with elephants. For more than a century, elephants were the true animal stars of the American circus. Circuses proudly claimed to be "bigger and better than ever" each year, and elephants played an important role in advertising this claim. Elephants were smart, strong, big, and seemingly gentle. They were also expensive to find, expensive to buy, and expensive to keep. For American circuses, owning elephants was the ultimate status symbol of financial power and success, and circus owners proudly advertised the number of elephants the show carried. The larger the herd, the more successful and, thus, reputable the circus.

Unlike elephants many exotic animals in the menagerie were for exhibition only. Although colorful circus posters depicted spectacular captures in the wild, they were generally purchased from the world's largest animal dealer, the Hagenbeck firm, founded by Gottfried Hagenbeck in the 1850s and based in Stellingen, near Hamburg, in Germany. In Stellingen Carl Hagenbeck, who succeeded his father, also created in 1907 a groundbreaking zoo. It would become the model for all zoos built in the first half of the 20th century and is in existence to this day. Hagenbeck provided the major European circuses with most of their wild and exotic animals, as well as the lucrative American circus market. The sheer number of wild animals that the great railroad circuses carried was an attraction in itself. Urban zoos, which developed at the end of the 19th century, couldn't offer the same immediate impression of variety and quantity, not to mention mobility. The circus menagerie offered an exotic world, with all its sounds and scents, that circusgoers could see in a single short walk through a tent that was the anteroom of the big top itself. At the end of Circus Day, you could safely say you'd truly seen the world.

RINGLING BROTHERS AND BARNUM & BAILEY COMBINED MENAGERIE

BROOKLYN N.Y. MAY 19TH 193

W.C.COUP'S NEW UNIT

THREE TIMES LARGER THAN EVER. EXHI

A LIVING HORSE IN A BLAZE OF FIRE JUMPING THROUGH HOO
BURNING GATES OF BLAZ

FARINI'S GREAT PARIS

EXHIBITED ON THE GREAT TRACK NEARLY ½ MILE. EN

MONSTER SHOWS.
IN 3 RINGS AT SAME TIME. – COMBINED WITH

Nº 8.

G FIRE, FIRING A CANNON STRAPPED TO HIS BACK WHILE LEAPING OVER
TIVELY TO BE SEEN AT EVERY PERFORMANCE OF THESE COMBINED SHOWS

PODROME. EXCURSION TRAINS ON ALL RAIL
NG THE 2 GREAT RINGS. ROADS TO THESE GREAT SHOWS.

pages 172–173

ca. 1880–82 From its earliest days in the late 18th century, the circus centered around **the era's most important animal: the horse.** Circus equestrians were not only performers, they were riding masters and available for hire, as circus founder Philip Astley put it in a 1779 ad, "for breaking horses for the Army, Road, Field, Draft, Shooting, Stroking, &c."

1955 "A circus without elephants would be like *Hamlet* without [Hamlet]. It is a safe guess that his pachydermic majesty **draws about 75 percent of the audience.**" (Robert Edmund Sherwood, *Here We Are Again: Recollections of an Old Circus Clown*, 1926)

1918 Each year, circuses would claim to be bigger and better than ever, and elephants played an important role in these declarations. They were **the ultimate symbol of a circus' power and success** and were advertised doing extraordinary feats such as playing football with their nimble trunks.

opposite

1947 For more than a century, **elephants were the true animal stars of the American circus.** They were smart, strong, big, and gentle to strangers, as this excited circus fan in the back lot of the Ringling Bros. and Barnum & Bailey circus has learned.

The Barnum & Bailey Greatest Show on Earth

MOST WONDERFUL ADDITION TO THE CHILDREN'S CIRCUS. AN EXACT ILLUSTRATION OF THE MARVELOUS PERFORMANCES OF THE TROUPE OF TRAINED CATS AND PIGS, WHOSE CLEVER AND REMARKABLE ACTS AMAZE AND ASTOUND ALL BEHOLDERS. ACTUALLY EXECUTING A SUCCESSION OF HITHERTO IMAGINED IMPOSSIBLE FEATS.

THE WORLD'S GRANDEST, LARGEST BEST, AMUSEMENT INSTITUTION.

1890s Trained pigs have been part of the circus animal cast practically since its inception, but *trained domestic cats* were rarely seen in the ring. When featured, they were a favorite of children, who likely returned to their homes and tried, in vain, to train their pets.

1900s Playful and smart, *Jack Russell terriers make excellent canine performers,* and this one with the Barnum & Bailey circus was no exception. In spite of his small size, his unbridled energy made him the focus of attention in the vast expense of the big top and a sure crowd pleaser.

1919 Alf Loyal passed his family's equestrian skills on to his dogs, who were proficient at *jumping off the batoude over several men,* just like human tumblers. By the looks of this poster, his dogs were also able to "juggle" rings. What attracted the audience was the animals' ability to mimic their human counterparts.

ca. 1903–10 *Charles Carlos is partnered with his dog* in his balancing act. This kind of novelty never failed to please audiences. Perhaps it distracted them from the fact that Carlos may have had unexceptional acrobatic skills.

opposite
1900 Dogs playing soccer is a joyous mayhem belonging more to the world of clowns than to sophisticated wild animal training. This clown's punkish hairstyle dates to the 19th century, when the ***famous mohawked English clown Grimaldi*** reigned on the London stage.

pages 180–181
1932 ***Circus illustrators were known for embellishing reality***. Famous equestrian director Fred Bradna remembers less idyllic bears than pictured here, recalling that they had "the same schedule at every appearance. Nothing could be skipped or the bears would be confused…and for days thereafter refuse to perform." (Fred Bradna, *The Big Top*, 1952)

left and above
1951 ***The Arwood dogs*** performed balancing feats with their trainers at the Polack Bros. circus. These vivacious and playful Jack Russell terriers resembled ordinary house pets. For dog owners in the audience, their acrobatic feats likely awakened training vocations, albeit short-lived, in many a home.

STRANGE BEASTS FROM FOREIGN LANDS

RINGLING
BROS
COMBINE

PALLENBERG
BRUINS THAT DANCE, SKATE, WALK TIG

pages 182–183

1949 Trained bears performed long before the circus existed. For centuries, they have fascinated audiences with their ability to mimic human behavior, a talent trainers emphasized by dressing them in clothes. Some, like *the Clausen bears and their trainers,* even wore matching outfits.

1931 These performers were with *Gangler's Novelty circus,* a small circus in New York City. Dressed as clowns, they present their trained bears. Performing bears were often thought of as the clowns of the animal kingdom despite the real danger they represented.

opposite

1918 "In its natural condition, the Bear is comparatively harmless…and is *playful in its frantic comicalities.* But, if driven to close quarters, or desperation from hunger…then it is becoming to 'stand from under,' for there are few Davids who are able to defend either themselves or their flocks and herds from its ravages." (Barnum & Bailey's menagerie guide, ca. 1875)

1900 During its European tour, Barnum & Bailey advertised a wide variety of performing animals, from elephants, sea lions, and bears to domesticated pigs, dogs, goats, and even a clown dressed as a rooster. With the right presentation, *any animal could be a star* under the big top.

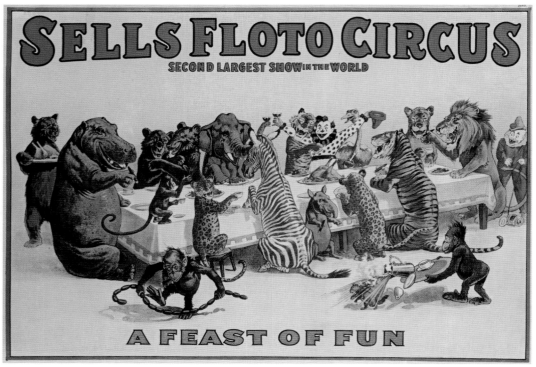

1920s Great apes never cease to fascinate, and the Al G. Barnes circus capitalized on this in its poster of chimpanzees, baboons, and orangutans who are taking care of *"monkey business de luxe,"* as any of their circus fans would at home.

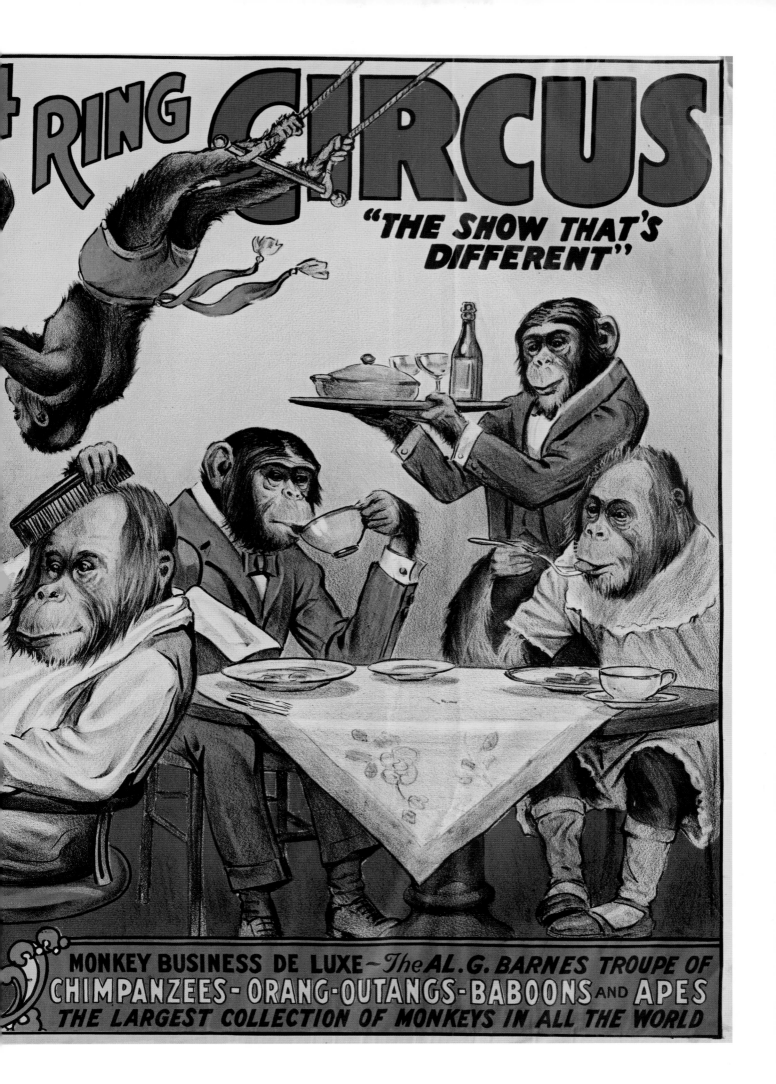

opposite
1947 Natal Favetier created havoc in the Ringling Bros. and Barnum & Bailey big top *playing an escaped ape from the menagerie.* At the end of his act, Favetier removed his mask and revealed himself, and for a brief moment the tables were turned. It was not an animal aping human behavior but a human playing the ape.

1938 *Gargantua was the superstar* of Ringling Bros. and Barnum & Bailey from 1938 to 1949. His original name was Buddy, but Ringling's vice president, Henry "Buddy" Ringling North, felt uncomfortable sharing his nickname, so he gave the animal a more fearsome moniker. Gargantua became the greatest animal celebrity since the days of Jumbo, Barnum's legendary elephant in the 1880s.

1947 *Chimpanzees delighted audiences* because of their close resemblance to humans. Trainers had the apes parody human behaviors such as having a smoke, like in this back lot photomontage.

pages 192–193
1893 In the 1890s Barnum & Bailey advertised this orangutan as *"the veritable 'missing link,'"* showing it rocking by a cozy fire, doing calisthenics, and finding a love interest to this young woman's chagrin.

eatest Show on Earth

AT THE BREAKFAST TABLE.

IN TRAINING FOR THE CHAMPIONSHIP.

AN AFTERNOON SIESTA.

THE STROBRIDGE LITH Co. CINTI & NEW YORK

LT SPECIMEN IN CAPTIVITY, IN THE WORLD. A MOST WONDERFUL ANIMAL, MORE CLOSELY RESEMBLING MAN THAN ANY ST; USING KNIVES, FORKS, SPOONS, CUPS AND OTHER ARTICLES, IN PRECISELY AS A HUMAN BEING. THE VERITABLE "MISSING LINK."

1936 Publicity photos provided by circuses had to be spectacular. This one of *trainer Clyde Beatty and his lion Menelik* is actually a montage of two pictures taken on different days. The photographer put Beatty and his lion together in closer proximity than they had been, and the press had their shot.

opposite
1923 A lion jumping through fire under a trainer's control was *a popular image used to represent the wild-animal act.* The snarling, roaring, jumping animal was often depicted with a trainer in uniform or a jungle-explorer outfit replete with boots, jodhpurs, and pit helmet.

1930s Small cats like *leopards and cougars are more difficult to train* than lions and tigers and, therefore, were not often seen in cage acts. This colorful, energetic Cole & Rogers circus poster trumps its circus rivals by promising this rare animal act.

left and above
1922 A former nurse, *Mabel Stark was the star tiger trainer* with Ringling Bros. and Barnum & Bailey in the 1920s. One of the highlights of her spectacular act was a staged fight with a full-grown tiger. The fight was not always easy to control, as her scar-covered body bore witness.

below
1915 Barnum & Bailey depicted *Mademoiselle Adgie* with roaring and ferocious lions. In fact, lions are often languorous creatures that trainers have to coax into roaring. "The lion is lazy, a sort of poser among animals." (Robert Edmund Sherwood, *Here We Are Again: Recollections of an Old Circus Clown*, 1926)

1936 This spectacular depiction of a lion's twisting body turning on the illustrious trainer Clyde Beatty *plays up the apparent hostility between trainer and animal.* Such confrontational depictions would in time tarnish the reputations of animal trainers in the eyes of animal rights activists.

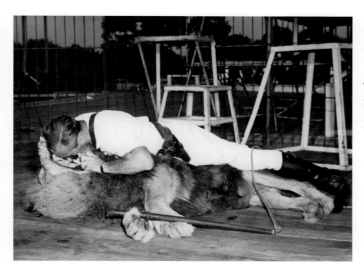

1950s This photograph of *cat trainer Dick Clemens* putting his head in a lion's mouth is the classic image of risking one's life in the big cage. In reality, no cat trainer has ever been mauled doing this stunt.

pages 198–199
1938 Blacaman's pretense that *he hypnotized his charges into submission* was a claim dating back to the early 18th-century trainers of traveling menageries. But it never failed to impress audiences.

CIRCUS ACTS

CONTROLLED MAYHEM
TO DAZZLE AND DELIGHT

Dominique Jando

CIRCUS **ACTS** CONTROLLED **MAYHEM** TO DAZZLE AND DELIGHT

Dominique Jando

It's circus day in Small Town, U.S.A. The usual grind of everyday life has come to an abrupt halt, and the long awaited day is now in full bloom. It had started early this morning with the arrival and unloading of the circus trains and the endless parade of horses and exotic animals to the circus lot. There, hundreds of antlike workers moved wagons, and raised gigantic poles and acre after acre of white canvas in a flurry of unbridled activity. Industrious children carried buckets of water for the animals in exchange for a coveted free pass, while grown-ups watched in awe, reminiscing about their own childhoods. Later, after a leisurely visit to the sideshow, everyone will wander over for the "come in"—the most exciting moment of all. The circus is ready to unleash its dazzling world of fantasy, all the incredible images pictured on the giant posters that had appeared a few weeks earlier on every available space for miles around. Thousands of men and women and children pass through the mammoth menagerie, taking a whiff of the circus' unmistakable aroma—a bouquet of grass, sawdust, hay, animal manure, peanuts, popcorn, and cotton candy—and enter the cathedral of this magic kingdom, the big top.

opposite
ca. 1943–46 *Heidi LaLage, seen here in New York City's Madison Square Garden,* succeeded Lillian Leitzel as the queen of the Roman rings. The magical atmosphere of the circus is visible in this dramatic photograph by Lisette Model: The ethereal aerialist defies danger with grace in the spotlight's glare.

page 201
1949 Lottie Brunn came from Germany to Ringling Bros. and Barnum & Bailey in 1948. She was billed as *"the World's Fastest Female Juggler"* and was as fast—and as talented—as her illustrious brother, Francis. Both were taught juggling by their father, who had learned the craft in an Allied prison camp.

1920s *Multiple acts are typically performed in quick succession,* creating an exhilarating pandemonium under the big top. On the ground beneath the three wire walkers, a rolled-up flying-trapeze net waits to be rigged for the next act.

below
1904 *The Siegrists were a famous German family of aerialists.* Charles Siegrist, not pictured, once said, "I will never quit the long road until I have to.... What is there to life anywhere else?" (Charles Siegrist, quoted by Bart A. Lynch, "They Split Seconds to Live," *Detroit Free Press,* February 21, 1932)

opposite
1930s The feats depicted on this Walter L. Main circus poster were actually performed on a low wire, but "high wire" sounded more spectacular. *To the audience, even a low-wire act was extraordinary,* especially when performers wore urban outfits, just like them.

On the back lot, acrobats, aerialists, jugglers, equestrians, animal handlers, showgirls, clowns, and the ring crew are getting ready for the grand entry, smoking a last cigarette, warming up, chatting. They, too, are excited. Performing in the ring is what they live for. Theirs is not a job, really—it is a way of life, a religion, a culture, and it is often the only life they have ever known. They live in a world of their own, with its tenets and principles, the only border of which is that of the circus itself. They speak German, Italian, or French—the main languages of the trade—but also Spanish, Russian, Chinese, Hungarian, and English, of course. The circus is Babel on the move, and that only adds to its mystique. Many of these artists come from Europe, others from Mexico, Australia, or Asia, and many belong to old dynasties of acrobats and equestrians. Few are American (or American by birth). The United States is still a new world and one of entrepreneurship. Becoming an entertainer is not a calling that entails instant financial gratification, and America's puritanism at this time does not encourage such avocation either.

It's Showtime!

Inside the big top, the equestrian director, in black riding jacket, white jodhpurs, top hat, and shiny black boots, gives a last look at the intricate web of rigging ropes and cables, at the colorful props set around the rings and the hippodrome track, at the steel panels of the big-animal cage erected in the center ring. He then signals to the bandleader and the announcer (who would later become known as the ringmaster) that everything is ready for the show to start. The announcer then shouts in a stentorian voice, "Laaaadies and gentlemen…"—which creates a gigantic outburst of applause, laughter, and uncontrolled enthusiasm—it's showtime!

The circus begins its magic carpet ride with a magnificent parade of hundreds of performers, riders, and dancers in sumptuous costumes. Some stand on elaborate gilded floats, others shepherd herds of exotic animals and an endless line of caparisoned elephants. In today's show the Asian pachyderms are the highlights of a mesmerizing Arabic tableau entitled *Cleopatra*—but who cares about the historical and geographical inconsistencies? The mammals' appearance is what everyone was waiting for. Before the last elephant has left the tent, the rings have already been filled with the organized mayhem that is the uniquely American three-ring circus. In the side rings, dogs, ponies, and "stubborn mules" (not so well-trained, that is) frame the center-ring attraction: a ferocious group of roaring lions and tigers put to their paces with ostensible courage and audacity by an animal trainer like the legendary Clyde Beatty. Beatty,

whip in hand and a gun ready in his holster, grabs a chair to protect himself from the sudden attack of a "mean-spirited," black-maned lion.

After the theatrical "taming" of the beasts, the wild-animal act, in this case the first act of the program, is over. The arena is now quickly dismantled. The audience's attention is distracted by an army of clowns who have invaded the hippodrome, while in each side ring elephant and pony duets perform in unison. In the meantime, all around the house "candy butchers" noisily promote cotton candy, pink lemonade, and peanuts: the thrills of the big cage always lead to a sales boost. It is pure confusion: sales clowns are all over the place, dozens of them, moving from one spot to another to perform a quick visual gag and keep the audience entertained during the transition.

Fast Feats and Fearless Heights

The next tableau of today's program is the aerial ballet, featuring 30 or more beautiful showgirls. The glamorous circus showgirls dance, ride elephants, perform an aerial act, and be just stunningly pretty—hanging all over the hippodrome track, while three solo trapeze artists perform simultaneously above the rings. They are sparsely clad, and their daredevilry make them all the more seductive. Sex (albeit dis-

NATIONAL SHOW CO. INC, OPERATORS
WALTER L. MAIN
3 RING
TRAINED WILD ANIMAL
SHOWS
HIGH WIRE
ARTISTS
INTRODUCING THE MOST DIFFICULT
AND
DANGEROUS FEATS EVER DEVISED
BY HUMAN INGENUITY.
2591

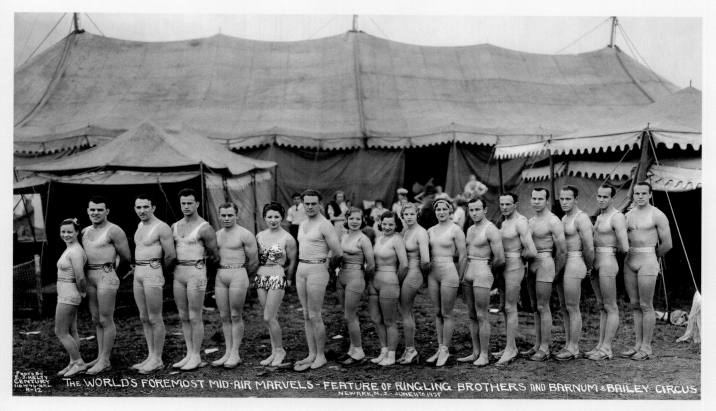

THE WORLD'S FOREMOST MID-AIR MARVELS - FEATURE OF RINGLING BROTHERS AND BARNUM & BAILEY CIRCUS
NEWARK, N.J. JUNE 11th 1935

1935 The impressive lineup of flying trapeze stars featured with Ringling Bros. and Barnum & Bailey included the brightest of them all, *triple somersaulters Arthur and Antoinette Concello,* fifth and sixth from left. Although they are all wearing white leotards, Antoinette, the star, sports sequins on hers.

opposite
1891 Although the Cornellas were billed as America's best acrobats, *their name reveals their European circus heritage.* European circus performers could make a good living in the U.S., where work was plentiful, and many artists chose to stay, like the Cristianis, Lillian Leitzel, Lou Jacob, and the Zacchinis.

below
1860s *French aerialist Jules Léotard* never worked in America, but his name is well known. Not only did he invent the flying trapeze in 1859, he originated the skintight costume that bears his name, which made him the first sex symbol in the history of show business.

cretely veiled under the cover of costume requirements) is part of the age-old lure of the circus. For practical purposes, circus costumes are minimal and snug—like the revealing leotard, originated by Jules Léotard, the French gymnast who in 1859 invented the flying trapeze. A huge international star in his time, Léotard was also show business' first sex symbol.

An exciting troupe of jockeys, or bareback riders, and two graceful "ballerinas on horseback" form the next display. Theirs are the oldest specialties of the circus. The ring, with its standard diameter of about 42 feet, was designed for their "feats of horsemanship," as they used to say in the old days. They are the true descendants of the 18th-century circus pioneers and master equestrians: Philip Astley, Charles Hughes, John Bill Ricketts, and Antonio Franconi. Although the audience often thinks that aerial disciplines are the most dangerous, bareback riders actually perform the most perilous acts. They need tremendous balancing and acrobatic skills (which must be learned at an early age) and have to work on a platform as unstable as it is uncontrollable. A sudden halt of their heavy mounts and the centrifugal force generated by their circular movement can propel these acrobats out of the ring. A horse rearing up, an unexpected quick move, can also cause unpreventable accidents, especially since horses are prone to impulsive frights.

Chaos Like Clockwork

Next to follow in the typical circus show are displays of specialty acts: acrobats, jugglers, hand-balancers, tumblers, tightwire dancers, and imaginative novelty acts. The list of these specialties can be endless; circus performers are always looking for new ways to thrill the audience. In this particular display, a troupe of acrobats builds precarious balancing pyramids in the center ring. On one side of it, a trio of jugglers swiftly passes a flurry of rings and clubs to one another in intricate patterns, and on the other, a duet of tumblers performs a joyous knockabout routine. In a larger circus, a couple more acts could be added on stages placed between the rings. The audience's interest sweeps from one ring to another, sometimes directed by the announcer's voice, who asks to pay special attention to a supposedly unique feat, "never to be seen anywhere else!" Spectators are fed a succession of unrelated, extraordinary images that form a true kaleidoscope of visual sensations. The emotional pandemonium of the American circus is, in many ways, an exhilarating experience. There is no time to think, the acts come fast and furious, and the moment an amazing exploit takes your breath away, another one immediately tops it.

Performing in a three-ring circus, however, was not always easy for European

performers. Used to the smaller audience of a one-ring circus (and often in a comfort-able and elegant circus building) who could focus on the subtleties of their craft, the performers often felt slightly debased when first performing with an American three-ring circus. To add to their occasional distress, they had to stop their performance whenever the center-ring act was over and the equestrian director blew his whistle. Many never adapted and returned to their native lands once their contracts ended; others modified their work accordingly. The less ambitious performers replaced the true difficulties of their act, which were not always appreciated under the vast big top by a distracted audience, with a couple of spectacular "tricks" whose effects were guar-anteed, even though their difficulty (or danger, in some instances) was not always real. Others, unwilling to surrender their hard-earned artistic status, simply made their work more spectacular, whether or not this meant increasing its difficulty. These per-formers became the true stars of the circus. In any event, in order to survive the three-ring competition, circus acts performed in American circuses had to be spectacular, and European talent scouts who worked for the major American circuses ensured that this dictated their choices.

Mighty Midair Marvels

One of the greatest stars ever of the American circus was Lillian Leitzel, another Austrian. She was a dainty aerialist, not especially pretty, with an average talent on the Roman rings. But she had a great personality, irresistible charm, and immense charisma. She could "sell" her act, catching everyone's attention, even up to the most remote seat in the last row of the bleachers. And she had a perfect ending that was her signature "trick": Up in the air, hanging from a hand loop, she performed an endless series of shoulder dislocations (known also as "plange" turns), which are rapid gyrations of the body around the arm. It was (and still is) a display of sheer strength and stamina, but artistically, the trick had very little merit. It could even have been boring after a while were it not for her carefully chosen musical accompaniment (Nicolay Rimsky-Korsakov's *The Flight of the Bumblebee*) and the fact that the audience was encouraged by the announcer to count her never-ending rotations. "On the 40th roll," reminisced legendary equestrian director Fred Bradna, "she loosed a hairpin, and her hair swept profusely about her shoulders during the final gyrations." And each time, the audience went wild. Leitzel once did 243 turns like this, although she usually did 60 to 100 in a normal performance. Spectacular she was, and under the big top she had no competi-tion: She performed alone above the center ring.

After a short solo exhibition in the center ring or the hippodrome track (like Eddie Rice having a car driven over his body, or the legendary elephant trainer Frank "Cheerful" Gardner being carried around with his head in the mouth of one of his pachyderms, or a huge trained hippo parading at a leisurely pace), the rings are again filled with a hodgepodge of acrobatic and dexterous acts—a group of Japanese perch-pole balancers in the center ring, flanked by a somersaulting wire walker emulating the graceful Australian Con Colleano on one side and a "tempo" juggler on the other. Tempo jugglers work fast, making their act more exciting. If they add to their speed a few acrobatic jumps and truly spectacular tricks, the audience will pay attention, and the jugglers could reach stardom. The German dynamo juggler Francis Brunn became a legendary proponent of this electrifying style. The Russian juggler (of Italian descent) Massimiliano Truzzi may not have been as fast, but he was certainly nothing short of spectacular and another star in his own right. The ability to keep several objects in the air at the same time has always been a fascinating skill. The difficulty of doing so is easily appreciable, since anyone can always give it a try at home after the show.

The show is typically punctuated by a spectacular performance of elephants. The "ponderous pachyderms," as declared one program, now occupy all three rings. In a display such as this, there could be 15, 20, even 30 elephants. Huge, impressive, and amazingly agile, they use their dexterous trunks as hands, walk on their hind legs, stand on their heads, build colossal pyramids mounted by showgirls, and move swiftly all under the control of trainers—another metaphor for human achievement.

The grey giants exit in the traditional "long mount"—all the elephants line up, standing on their hind legs, their forelegs resting on the elephant before them—draw-ing a thunderous ovation. A hard act to follow, but the show goes on, endlessly deliv-ering its world of wonders, startling, awesome, fear-provoking, funny, dazzling, spec-tacular, surprising, chaotic perhaps, yet working like a perfectly tuned Swiss watch. Nothing is left to chance here. It is not, as is often said inaccurately, "a circus." Dozens of white or chestnut stallions proudly prance in the ring (presented "at liberty," with the trainer in the center of the ring) or around the hippodrome track, mounted in "high school," or haute école, a display of classic equestrian dressage. Smartly trained exotic animals, amazing acrobats, and unruly clowns take their turns, garnering their share of applause, and disappear—all of it in a breathless succession of enchanting images. The bewilderment never ceases.

It is now time for one of the heavily advertised star turns, the solo performance of a high-wire act. Most great high-wire acts in the American circus came from Ger-

208

NOVEL AERIAL ACTS BY THE · WORLD'S · GREATEST · ARTISTS ·

opposite
1956 Japanese performer Takeo Usui would transform his near misses on the high wire into another trick: He would catch the wire and spin around it as if on a horizontal bar, stopping for a short instant in a handstand position, after which he would resume his wire dancing. He kept the audience amazed. Usui was a true artist of the high wire.

1890s The *inventive ingenuity* of circus performers is boundless, and although this stock poster was the product of an artist's imagination, any of the apparatuses and tricks depicted could have been seen at the circus.

1944 Si Kitchie balances on his head before a full house at the Dailey Bros. circus. Trapeze artist Mickey King once said about performing for a crowd, "I like people in the audience to like me. I want them to applaud and cheer me. I know that when I please those who come to see me, I can be with them a long time, and that is a great thing for a performer to know." (Bart A. Lynch, "They Split Seconds to Live," *Detroit Free Press*, February 21, 1932)

many. Ropedancing was a much revered art in 18th-century German states, and it became a national specialty, like tumbling and acrobatics were a specialty of the Italian states. The Wallendas, of course, were the undisputed stars of the highwire. When they arrived in the United States, their success was immediate. Theirs was a spectacular act, not only for the danger it presented but also for the variety of their repertoire, the originality and audacity of their stunts, and their sheer artistic talent. Much later, to revive interest in his act, Karl Wallenda would add a stunt he had performed in Germany when he was with other troupes: a precarious, three-tiered human pyramid of seven persons slowly crossing a three-quarter-inch cable at a vertiginous height. It was an old classic, a superb high-drama final stunt for any truly great highwire act. But one day in 1962 the pyramid of the Wallendas collapsed during a performance, and the tragedy was caught on film. The Wallendas' accident was widely publicized, reminding everyone of the circus artist's vulnerability and of the true danger often lurking behind his or her astonishing exhibitions. The Wallendas became part of circus lore, and in the process the seven-man pyramid became theirs.

Man's Dream to Fly

This is what the circus is all about: a codified ritual of survival, a reminder that we can always overcome our fears and limitations. Yes, we can tame the wilderness, walk on a wire, fly in the air—the proof of which is presented to us at this point in the performance. Enter a triple display of the king of all aerial arts—the flying trapeze, or "flying return," act. This is a crowd favorite and perhaps the most spectacular and elegant of all circus acts; a true ethereal ballet where amazingly graceful and fit men

and women literally fly from a swinging trapeze bar to the hands of a "catcher," do intricate acrobatic figures in midair on the way, and then fly back to their point of departure. The superstar of the flying trapeze was Alfredo Codona, an exceptionally elegant and charismatic Mexican flyer, and the third man (and fourth person) ever to complete the then unattainable triple somersault to the catcher.

Codona married Lillian Leitzel, and they became the royal couple of circusdom, the Douglas Fairbanks and Mary Pickford of the Sawdust Circle. Sadly, Leitzel fell to her death in Denmark in 1931 when her rigging broke during her act, and Codona never truly recovered. Victim himself a few years later of a bad fall in the safety net, he was forced to quit flying. In 1937, during a divorce hearing in his lawyer's office, he killed his second wife and former trapeze partner, Vera Bruce, and then shot himself. The heartbreaking story of Leitzel and Codona has become the stuff of legend, a tragic part of circus lore. Arthur Concello, whose private life was less eventful, succeeded Codona as the great triple-somersaulter, and he was quickly followed by his wife, Antoinette Concello, the first woman ever to complete the legendary trick since its originator, Lena Jordan, did so in 1890. Antoinette Concello had a brilliant career as a flying trapeze artist before becoming a illustrous choreographer for the aerial ballets of Ringling Bros. and Barnum & Bailey.

The daring men and women on the flying trapeze bring the show to a close. In a last outbreak of uncontrolled enthusiasm, the traditional races invade the vast hippodrome, a final wink to the Roman circus of yore, with the most spectacular being the Roman race, whose riders stand on the backs of a pair of horses galloping side by side. Then comes, as the program screams, "By popular demand—a living person shot through space with terrific force from the mouth of a monster cannon," aka, the human cannonball. The show finally ends on a bang, literally. Patrons are often invited to remain for the after show. Today, it is a short Wild West exhibition, delivering a last bouquet of thrills and adventure. And then it's all over. Tomorrow, the magic city of canvas will be gone.

Starry-eyed spectators slowly leave the big top, exhausted and ecstatic. While on their way out, they begin to reminisce about the joyous, delightful, and dazzling images they are taking home with them. They will remember these magical moments until next year when the circus comes back to town. John Steinbeck beautifully summed up their exhilarated feeling: "The circus is change of pace—beauty against our daily ugliness, excitement against our boredom…. Every man, woman, and child comes from the circus refreshed and renewed and ready to survive."

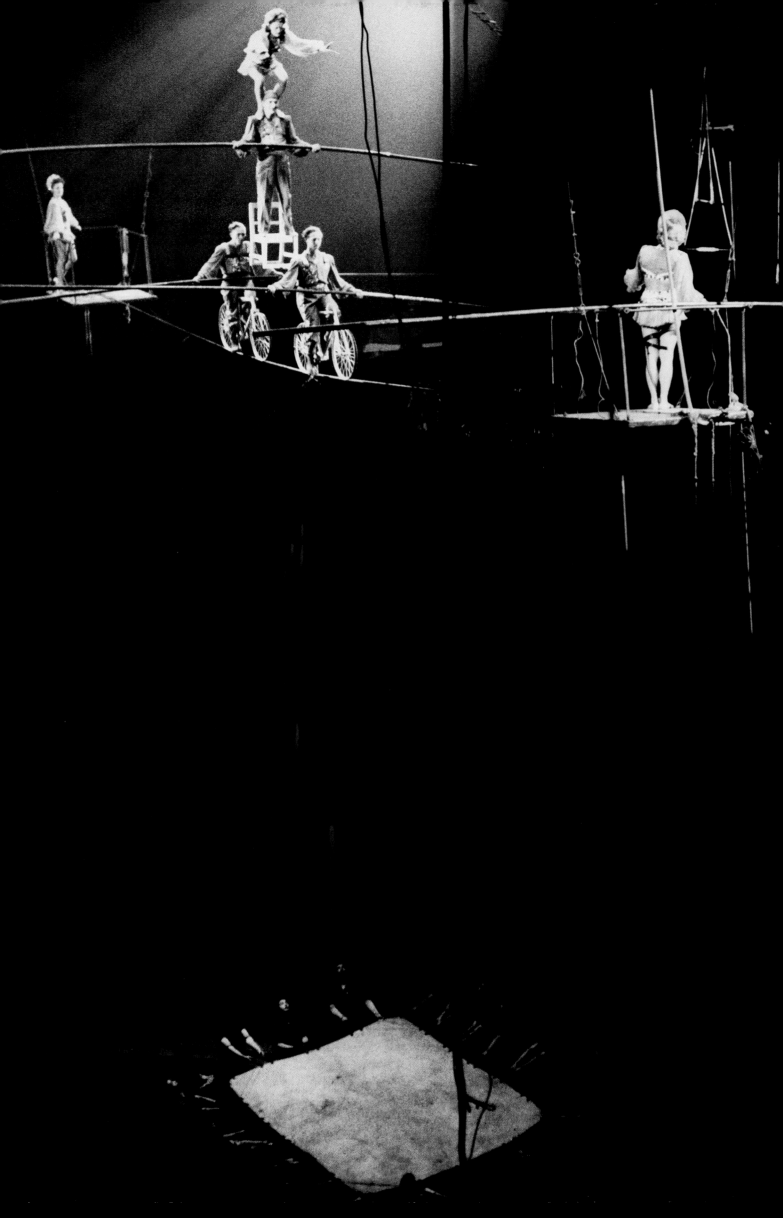

1937 The Cole Bros. circus performed in a single ring at New York's mighty Hippodrome on Sixth Avenue. The cast was as impressive as always, *a hodgepodge of diverse nationalities* that formed a true Babel on the move. Among them are two legendary hobo clowns, Emmett Kelly, seated front right, and Otto Griebling, standing behind the man with the American flag at extreme left.

NEW YORK HIPPODROME–1937

pages 214–215
1899 The inclined ramp seen on the right side of this poster was used for the *Charivari*, in which tumblers, including a few clowns, vaulted over horses and elephants. This act was a staple of any good circus performance when Barnum & Bailey presented it during its European tour.

CIRCUS ACTS: CONTROLLED MAYHEM TO DAZZLE AND DELIGHT

213

The Barnum & Bailey

GRAND TURNOÍ PAR 20 CHAMPIO

L'INSTITUT DE DIVERTISSEMENT LE PLU

1900. B N° 63.

AUTEURS LES PLUS RENOMMÉS.

PRINTED IN AMERICA.

AND ET LE PLUS MAGNIFIQUE DU MONDE.

above left
1950s *Dieter Tasso* used his feet to throw cups and saucers to a precarious pile on his head, while balancing on a slack wire. When age caught up with him, he transformed his act into a hilarious parody of itself with even greater success.

above right
1942 Passing clubs is not an easy juggling feat. Doing it while standing on one leg and spinning a ring on the other only adds to the difficulty. *The Naittos, an amazing troupe of Japanese acrobats,* did this on a tightwire. In a three-ring environment, performers had to invent ever more spectacular tricks to catch the audience's attention.

1925 Dozens of Ringling Bros. and Barnum & Bailey performers exhibited their talents simultaneously on three rings and four stages, while candy vendors, aka candy butchers, sold their goods *to some 12,000 to 14,000 spectators.* It was a dizzying, gigantic display of incredible achievements.

BROTHERS GREAT SHOWS CONSOLIDATED

99. S. Nº 70

COPYRIGHT 1899 BY
THE
STROBRIDGE
LITHO CO
CIN'TI & NEW YORK

S MALE AND FEMALE ACROBATS.
CROBATIC SKILL AND DARING EVER SEEN.

pages 218–219
1899 *The Carl DaMann family* perform a Risley act, from the name of its originator Richard Risley Carlisle, in which an acrobat "juggles" his partner on his feet. The members of the DaMann family were also talented floor acrobats, which increased their chances of engagement.

right
1930s *Antoinette Concello* was the first woman ever to perform the legendary triple somersault on the flying trapeze since its originator, Lena Jordan, did so in 1890. "Toni" Concello had a brilliant career before becoming a great choreographer for the aerial ballets of Ringling Bros. and Barnum & Bailey.

1940s The audience, young and old, experienced *all sorts of emotions* during the circus. As their attention was diverted from one ring to the other, down and back up again, they were continuously fed cotton candy, popcorn, and pink lemonade by the ubiquitous candy butchers.

opposite
ca. 1931–32 This stock poster shows the *great diversity of thrilling aerial acts* that a major circus (which Snyder Bros. was not) could present, from flying trapeze to Roman rings, from balancing trapeze to the Sky Walk.

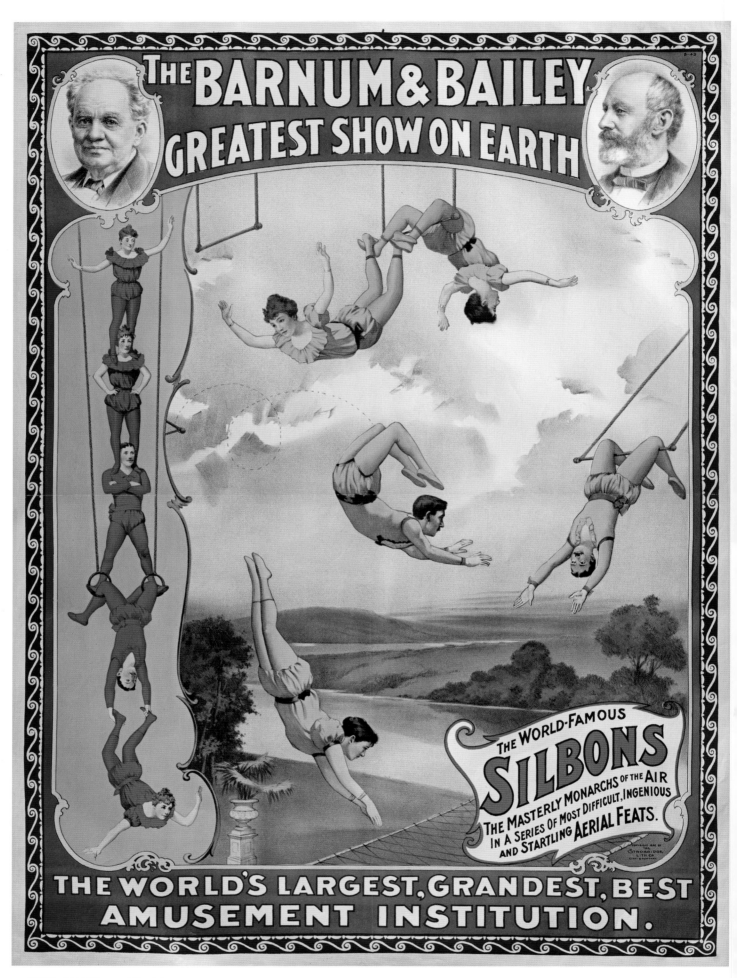

1896 The British Silbons would later join the German Siegrist family through a series of marriages to create an even more impressive flying trapeze act. In some ways, circus unions were *like royal marriages:* They were a way to expand one's influence and reach.

1956 *La Norma's energetic trapeze swings,*
her perfect style, her beauty, and, of course, her
talent as an aerialist propelled her from a side
ring to the center ring of Ringling Bros. and
Barnum & Bailey—the pinnacle of the American
circus world—in the space of two seasons.

right
1910 *Ernest Clarke of the Clarkonians* was
one of the greatest flyers in history and one of
the first aerialists to complete a triple somersault.
The Clarkonians's remarkable acts were, according to a Barnum & Bailey program, "performed
with utmost celerity and exquisite grace of movement, while they compel the hearts of the spectators to stand still by their recklessness and apparent disregard for life."

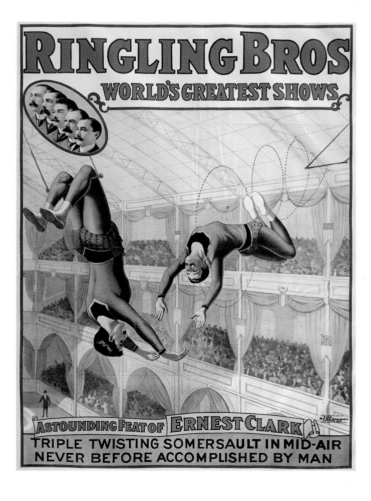

*To my good friend
Dr. Mann.
most sincerely
Alfredo Codona
1935.*

above
1935 The **legendary Alfredo Codona** was, according to star aerialist Lillian Leitzel, "the personification of grace in the air and just as graceful on the ground as he is when working." He was also her husband, but all who saw him shared her opinion. (Lillian Leitzel, as told to Paul Brown, *The Circus Scrap Book*, Vol. 1, No. 1, January 1929)

left
1942 **Aerialist Juanita "Neets" Deisler,** a flyer with the Flying Randolls of Ringling Bros. and Barnum & Bailey, carefully bandages her wrists before climbing up to her trapeze platform under the big top. This is a traditional practice for every flyer, as it helps them avoid slippery and painful catches.

right
1950 *The Geraldo Troupe* were a remarkable couple of aerialists who performed a spectacular double-trapeze act. They performed rarely seen and extremely dangerous ankle-to-ankle catches, and the gymnastics chalk covering their lower legs helped to prevent them from a potentially deadly slip.

above
ca. 1928 Lillian Leitzel was one of the greatest stars of the American circus. She had a great personality, irresistible charm, and immense charisma. She could really "sell" her act, catching everyone's attention, even the most remote audience member in the last row of the bleachers.

right
1930s Flying trapeze star Antoinette Concello is uncharacteristically the catcher here, hanging from a pair of Roman rings and holding Gracie Genders. Theirs is not a job, really—it is a way of life, a religion, a culture, and it is often the only life they have ever known.

HAROLD BARNES FEATURED WITH COLE BROTHERS-CLYDE BEATTY CIRCUS

1930s Considered one of the greatest wire-walkers of all time and a major international circus star, the *Australian Con Colleano* was born Cornelius Sullivan and took the name of his mother, who came from a Mexican circus family. His was the first to do a front somersault on the wire, but, above all, he was a remarkably graceful and charismatic performer.

above
1935 *Young Harold Barnes, a talented tight-wire acrobat,* poses for a publicity shot with Cole Bros. circus showgirls in tennis outfits used during the show. Barnes's front split, which was already a rarity among female wire dancers, has rarely been duplicated by male wire walkers.

opposite
1928 "Here *brave and brawny athletes tumble and tussle* in desperate efforts to excel; here skilled acrobats writhe and contort…here are executed the most original acts and daring feats ever seen or heard of." (Barnum & Bailey program, 1896)

pages 228–229
1956 *British performer Harold Alzana* was a remarkably daring high-wire acrobat who worked most of his act solo, although he ended it with this bicycle stunt. It was indeed spectacular but was actually not very difficult and was less perilous than the rest of his breathtaking act. In the circus, appearances are sometimes deceiving.

opposite
1953 In this Cornell Capa photograph, the small net stretched under **Harold Alzana at Madison Square Garden** was there because New York State law required it. Were Alzana to fall, the net would have probably been useless, but Alzana had other ways to break a fall. Generally those ways worked, but for some in circus history they didn't. High-wire performers accept the high stakes of their trade.

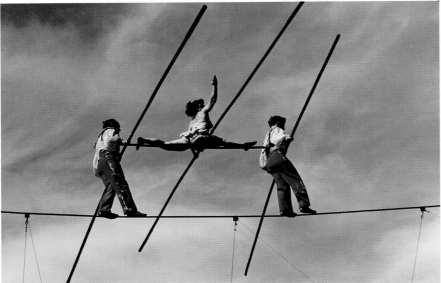

1957 "I never saw the Wallendas perform without *a tingling spine and a tight, dry throat.* Here was steel nerve which had taken three generations to perfect. Death-tempting stars are often taut, superstitious and sentimental. Not so the Wallendas. They are calm, intelligent, gracious people. To them, their turn was a professional performance to be done twice a day with scientific precision and without fuss. No matter what the conditions, whether lightning, storm or illness, they never declined to work." (Fred Bradna, *The Big Top*, 1952)

right
1904 *Mrs. Ancillotti of Barnum & Bailey* hailed from an old circus family and was the wife of a celebrated daredevil. A talented acrobat herself and an amazingly strong woman, she could pull a stunt or two of her own, too, as she demonstrates backstage.

below
1910s On the back lot *the Belford Troupe practice a difficult three-man-high column,* where the top mounter increases the difficulty of the exercise by balancing head-to-head with the middle man.

1910s *The Marvells* performed a balancing act with elements from a Risley act using their feet. They pose for the photographer in an unusual position that was not part of their act.

1899 The diverse acts that acrobats come up with are endless. Performers are always looking for new ways to thrill the audience, from juggling objects of different sizes and shapes to contorting in all possible positions to, at far left, performing the once *famous act Jackley Drops,* which was unique to the circus.

The Strobridge Lith. Co, Cin'ti, O.

TEN PHUNNY PHOOLS IN A FEW OF THEIR COMICAL DIDOS.

HOW TO MAKE HOME BREW

above
ca. 1881–87 In early circuses, clowns were generally skilled performers who brought outrageousness (and costumes) to genuine acrobatic, juggling, and equestrian feats. Then they began to speak, sing, and even play musical instruments. Slapstick clowning became prominent later to suit the size of American circuses. These *"Phunny Phools"* may have worn outrageous costumes, but they were actually talented acrobats.

left
1921 The perfect method to make **home brew during Prohibition,** according to clown Eddie Raymond of the Hagenbeck-Wallace circus, is likely concealed between the covers of his oversized book. The audience will discover the secret in a few moments when he flashes the gag during his "walk-around" under the big top.

opposite
1900s Turn-of-the-century contortionists often wore leotards with longitudinal stripes to *accentuate the lines of their body* and emphasize their extraordinary flexibility, which was the result of years of training that often started at an early age.

left
1860s In the early days of photography, capturing clowns meant that they had to hold deathly still. ***In real life clowns entertained fast and furious:*** "Real clowning should always be in full gallop, the style ferocious and emphatic. Clowns at work should behave like perfectly mad creatures." (Bill Ballantine, "The Art of Clowning," *The New York Times Magazine*, March 28, 1954)

above
1900s The entire cast of the ***Ringling Bros. and Barnum & Bailey Clown Alley*** poses in the back lot in front of the big top. This army of clowns will invade the hippodrome in a few moments to distract the audience with an atmosphere of pure mayhem and confusion.

1920s "You discover that *each audience presents a different laugh problem.* Factory and mill towns come ready for fun; small town audiences are more reserved than big city. Farmers are extremely careful laughers." (Bill Ballantine, "The Art of Clowning," *The New York Times Magazine*, March 28, 1954)

opposite
1945 Many clowns work with animals, and dogs and farm animals such as pigs, ducks, and geese are among their favorites. Ringling Bros. and Barnum & Bailey *clown Harry Dann poses with his feathered friend.*

above
1951 Midget clowns Paul Horompo and a colleague entertain two young visitors on the Ringling Bros. and Barnum & Bailey's back lot. In *a society still racially divided,* the contrast of black and white must have attracted the photographer.

right
1947 Legendary clown Paul Jung poses with *characters from Disney's animated feature,* **Song of the South** *(1946),* which appeared in a Ringling Bros. and Barnum & Bailey parade.

1890s Clowns often performed acrobatic and physical skills like stilt walking and used trained animals as partners. *Pigs were their partner of choice.* The natural clowns of any barnyard, they served as an easy metaphor to mock human foibles, especially those of the rich and powerful.

The Barnum & Bailey Greatest Show on Earth

P.T. BARNUM

J.A. BAILEY

THE AMERICAN MECHANICAL CLOWNS, DONKEY, PIG, CAT, ROOSTER & OTHER INGENIOUS MANAKINS. IN MOST LAUGHABLE PERFORMANCES. BARNUM'S FROLIC CARNIVAL FOR HIS LITTLE FRIENDS

THE WORLD'S GRANDEST, LARGEST, BEST, AMUSEMENT INSTITUTION.

1950 Another *juggling legend, Massimiliano Truzzi,* seen here with Marian Cristiani of the King Bros. circus, was Russian in spite of his very Italian name. His family had moved from Italy to Russia in 1880 and created one of the Russian Empire's most important circuses. Truzzi had been trained in part by the juggling "god" Enrico Rastelli and mesmerized U.S. audiences.

opposite
ca. 1950 Although this is a still photograph, one can sense the *fantastic speed and energy of the famous juggler Francis Brunn.* "Brunn's act ranged from the spectacular to the sublimely simple—from juggling 11 objects at once to juggling a single ball." (Francis Brunn obituary, *The Villager,* June 9–15, 2004)

1949 Like all great jugglers, Francis Brunn still practiced minutes before entering the big top. "There is one movement for every eight minutes. It's supposed to be, let's say, *like a ballet.* It would be impossible for me to start in the middle. I would love if the audience is so fascinated that nobody applauds in the end." (Francis Brunn, quoted by Jennifer Dunning, "Meeting Keeps 600 Jugglers in Motion," *The New York Times,* July 23, 1983)

pages 242–243
1936 The German Otari Troupe found a way to differ from other flying trapeze troupes. They worked with two trapeze rigs crossing each other, maintaining the old tradition of flying from trapeze to trapeze instead of trapeze to catcher. They later presented their act with black lights.

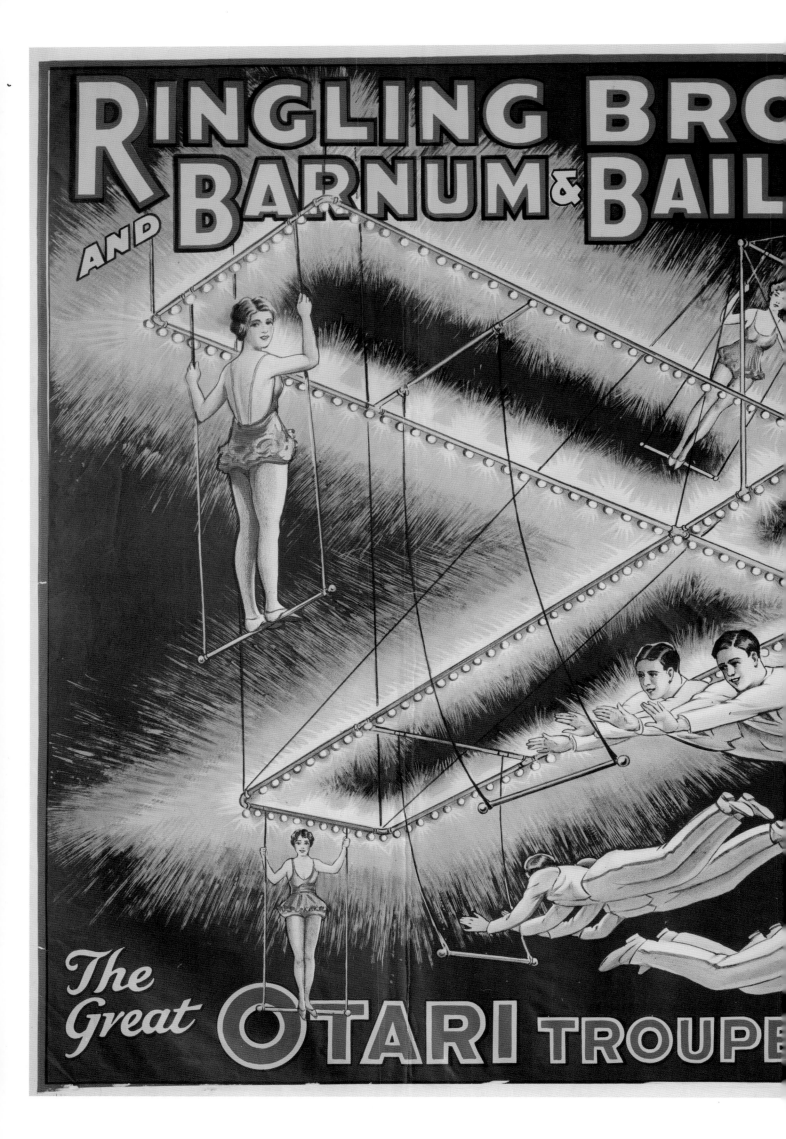

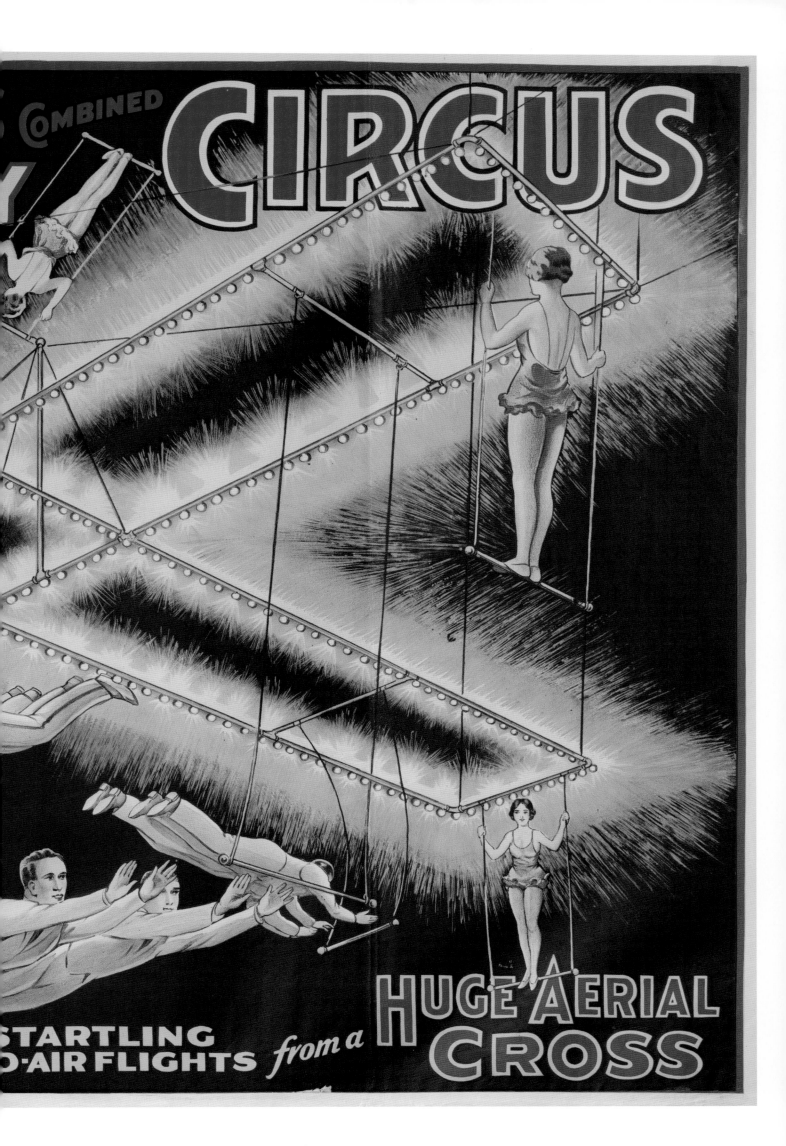

EATING
FIRE
THROWING
KNIVES

FREAKS &
WONDERS
OF THE SIDESHOW

Linda Granfield

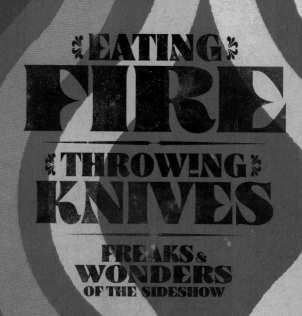

EATING FIRE *THROWING* KNIVES

FREAKS & WONDERS OF THE SIDESHOW

Linda Granfield

It is the late 1890s on a circus lot, and the air is thick with the pungent smell of animal dung and hay. The scent of popcorn and boiled peanuts waft down the midway, the area between the ticket wagons and the big top entrance where visitors can take in the sideshow tent. The talker, the man standing on a platform outside the sideshow, calls out to circus-goers: "Ladies and gentlemen, don't miss this rare opportunity to see the world-famous Albino Family! And, wait, in just minutes, a fearless fire-eater will extinguish a burning torch by swallowing its dancing flames! Yes, he will *eat* fire, right before your eyes!" Who could resist these glimpses of a world unknown, unheard of, and unimagined?

opposite
1920s The sideshow was a world of extremes, and press departments emphasized this. Here, *Major Mite* (Clarence Howerton), "the Tom Thumb of the Jazz Age," strikes a pose with his colleague *Clyde "Tiny" Hicks*.

page 245
1889 Sideshow acts were shown in a special tent erected on the circus lot. Due to their immense popularity, some acts even became center ring attractions, like this Barnum & Bailey fire-eater *"the Human Salamander."*

below
1900s *Armless wonder Charles Tripp*, who could write with his feet, poses with his legless colleague Eli Bowen. Although they didn't perform together, they were friends. Bowen would allegedly quip to Tripp, "Keep your hands off me," to which Tripp retorted, "Watch your step!"

American circus owners in the second-half of the 19th century found that while their audiences greatly enjoyed watching graceful young women step with breathtaking drama upon tightropes, or seeing young men leap from the ground onto the backs of galloping horses, there was also profit to be made during the extra time curious spectators spent on the lot before and after the show. Their willing suspension of disbelief and their downright curiosity played into the hands, or rather pockets, of circus owners and the sideshow operators who presented the acts. The routine of daily life and the expectation of all things out of the ordinary at the circus led to the incredible success of the sideshow. If one had just parted with hard-earned cash to spend an entire afternoon or evening at the circus, then why not pay a little extra to enjoy all there was to see during that one day away from the daily grind?

There's a Sucker Born Every Minute

The 19th-century world was an ever expanding one to most people. Exploration by the scientifically curious, like Charles Darwin, in the 1830s brought new

animals and people from the far ends of the world to the attention of the general public. Societies for the study of all things new flourished, issuing reports, sponsoring public lectures, producing books, and exhibiting many novel items in the increasingly popular dime museums that were opening up in cities across the country. Nineteenth-century businessmen like P. T. Barnum quickly saw the financial profit to be gained in displaying discovered (and sometimes concocted) oddities to the general population—for a small fee, of course. When Barnum's first career as a country-store owner came to an end, a new career as an entertainment entrepreneur, for which he would ultimately become famous, began. While he never actually uttered the famous phrase attributed to him, "There's a sucker born every minute," Barnum did recognize that there was fun and profit to be had by capitalizing on human curiosity. He understood that people wanted to see for themselves the incredible new curiosities and discoveries they were reading about in newspapers. Barnum became their facilitator, in essence, their educator, setting the stage for the freak show to become an enduring part of popular entertainment. Above all, he legitimized the sideshow by nationalizing his advertising campaigns, taking the show beyond local venues, and making it a profitable business enterprise in its own right. Along the way, the curious public would meet human oddities like Krao Farini, advertised as "the Missing Link" and "living proof of Darwin's theory of the descent of man," and Jo-Jo, "the Dog-Faced Boy," and believe that they were staring into the face of a specimen of humanity's evolution.

In 1841 Barnum purchased John Scudder's failing American Museum, filled with curiosities from all over the world. Located at one of the busiest intersections in New York City, only blocks from where ships unloaded their immigrant passengers, the museum provided a glimpse into life on a global scale. There were gems and minerals, stuffed birds, freaks, small living mammals, and a writhing anaconda that the advertising claimed could eat "a good-sized dog." Barnum's belief in enticing advertising turned the business around and it flourished until 1865 when it burned down (only to be reopened and destroyed by fire again in 1868). Customers had to be hurried through the floors of exhibits in order to accommodate the long lines of ticket holders waiting outside. Curiosity, coupled with fear of the unknown and legitimized by the notion that these exhibits were "educational," sold thousands of American Museum tickets. In fact this museum enjoyed the most foot traffic of any institution in America at the time, coaxing 38 million people through its doors. It was a place where, if you believed the promotional signs, you could see what new species had

above
1922 This lineup shows the *freaks, novelties, and minstrel band* of the Sells-Floto sideshow. The banners behind them exaggerate the performers' distinctive characteristics to heighten their intrigue, but the banners' bold colors and tableaux also ensure their visibility from across the circus lot.

been discovered and the new finds that scientists and historians were conspicuously debating in the press.

What Is It?!

Since the early 19th century, circus owners sometimes brought along with the show unusual people or strange objects that couldn't be verified by the viewers (a petrified Finnish ogre's toe, anyone?) to flesh out the program. These extras, also seen on fairgrounds, developed into circus sideshow acts. Circus sideshows typically consisted of many acts shown together in a "ten-in-one." These acts were advertised in varying degrees of veracity and artistic license on the painted canvases that made up the sideshow bannerline, and by the talker who stood outside the sideshow tent colorfully describing the novelties to be seen within. Sideshow banner artists like David "Snap" Wyatt, Fred G. Johnson, and Bill Ballantine translated the mysteries and excitement of the sideshow as they imagined them, not necessarily as the acts actually appeared onstage, employing artistic license to attract a crowd. Each sideshow act was painted larger-than-life in bright, bold colors onto massive canvases heavy enough to withstand the strongest winds. Some banners added the word "Alive" in a circular "bullet" to denote a living person or animal to a public that had grown wary of being duped by phony displays of papier-mâché mummies inside glass cases.

A bally of acts, or free samples in sideshow parlance, often took place outside the sideshow tent near the talker on a small portable stage to further convince visitors to pay for the trip inside. Perhaps an exotic snake charmer sat on an elevated chair and played with her serpent from the "great jungles," or Barnello swallowed fire with

1890s *Famous bearded lady Annie Jones* was first exhibited in 1866 as a one-year-old (with her mother) in P. T. Barnum's American Museum. When she died from illness at age 37, she had married twice.

1880s–90s *Knife-throwers*, fakirs, magicians, sword-swallowers, and other novelty acts were shown alongside the freaks in the sideshow. Some knife throwers attached to their knives cloths doused in gasoline that were then set alight, heightening the acts' sense of danger.

incredible dexterity and fearlessness, or a tough-footed performer walked up a sword ladder with bare blades glistening. No matter that the performers didn't always appear exactly as depicted on the banners. The excitement of the bally act and the near constant, mesmerizing spiel of the talker usually worked.

Some people genuinely hoped that they or their children would learn something; circuses were advertised as being educational as well as entertaining. Other people simply enjoyed the sideshow displays and acts for their invention and fun, while others, particularly men, found titillation inside the tent. After all, the daughter of the sheik of Araby, who grew up in the hot, dry deserts so far away (perhaps as far as Brooklyn, New York), would have to wear as little clothing as possible, wouldn't she? Around 1900, women in the circus, in the sideshow or elsewhere on the lot, flashed a lot more skin than was seen on city streets where corsets, high collars, and long skirts kept women restricted and modestly covered. "Cooch dancers," what we might think of as exotic dancers today, did bump-and-grind shows and sometimes for a few extra coins offered a topless viewing, or "blow-off," for men only in a cordoned-off section. The variety of performances to see in the sideshow tent sent two quite different messages to adults and children, appealing to both in different ways.

Wild, Weird, and Wonderful

Sideshows typically included three different kinds of exhibitions: novelty acts touted as superhuman, exotic, or extraordinary; miscellaneous exhibits involving curious taxidermy displays (although these were more common to carnival sideshows than circuses); and freaks, otherwise known as human oddities, including

1890s George Williams was born with misshapen limbs and stood only 18 inches tall as an adult. Always looking for a unique, sellable angle, press agents called him **"the Turtle Boy,"** sometimes even claiming he had a shell.

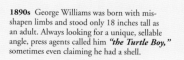

armless wonders, conjoined twins, leopard-spotted people, fat ladies, dwarves, giants, and so-called made freaks, which were typically illusions or those who accentuated a certain aspect of themselves like tattoos. The novelty acts consisted of those performers who had developed a particular talent. This part of the sideshow included sword-swallowers, knife-throwers, fire-eaters, strongmen and -women, magicians, human pincushions who felt no pain, those who walked on nails or broken glass, and others who "charmed" snakes. Their knowledge of procedure and safety, spiced up with exotic costumes and expert timing, created tantalizing performances. Certainly a true element of danger was present in many of the acts, but it was the performers' acting skills and comic flair that convinced the audience that they were in more danger than they actually were. This was early performance art, and thematic music, painted backdrops, and atmospheric lighting could add spine-tingling drama. Many of the acts used props such as fire and snakes or featured elaborate, exotic costumes and makeup to ensure that the viewers would see something extraordinary.

Illusion, too, played a great part in many sideshow acts. The "Talking Head—Alive!" was actually a woman speaking normally while everything but her head was concealed by mirrors. Or one might see a "live" mermaid shown in a fishbowl on the banner outside, but in reality the mermaid was a projection of a live woman *onto* a bowl. The legless woman—"Half Woman—Alive!"—might be half concealed, but she might also be a woman truly born legless, otherwise billed as a freak. General ignorance about these conditions made the act all the more believable: Seeing *was* believing. The deception caused both a delicious anxiety upon entering the tent and also the hoodwinked rush after viewing. And some of the concoctions on view were so unappealing and delightfully creepy that you had to peer at them through your fingers.

The Talk of the Town

Spectators moved through the sideshow expecting the unexpected and getting it. They also brought with them the desire to be shocked by what they saw and to leave with plenty to talk about. Circus owners knew this. The more provocative the sideshow, the greater number of tickets could be sold on the circus' one- or two-day stopover. Even if the show was in town for only one day, as was typical, seemingly disappearing into thin air overnight, the buzz generated in one town could translate into increased sales in the next as word-of-mouth spread, and as newspaper and, later,

radio stories were read and heard. While the sideshows of county fairs and carnivals could also be quite profitable, it was paramount that the traveling circuses, with their huge operating costs, have the biggest and best freak shows to guarantee financial success.

The freaks, both natural born and concocted, generated the most buzz on the midway. Exotic, stuffed animals were one thing, but living, breathing, moving exhibitions of humans were quite another. Once inside the sideshow tent, viewers paraded before a raised platform upon which sat or stood an array of these oddities, discovered, so the signs claimed, in faraway places around the world. Often talkers or lecturers walked the crowd past each performer, speaking of his or her unusual lineage and drawing attention to each one's specific traits. Sometimes the performers spoke about themselves. Viewers could be lulled into believing that the invented biographies of the sideshow freaks were true, that what they were seeing was real science. They could be convinced that history was manifest before them in the tattoos (fake or real), the unfamiliar bodily forms and costumes, and the exotic backdrops that reeked more of linseed oil than of the silt of the Nile or Amazon. It may be difficult for modern viewers to comprehend what was considered a sideshow spectacle during the heyday of the traveling circus in America. An "Illustrated Man" was a man with a lot of tattoos. In 1907 tattoos were most common amongst sailors and prostitutes, and there were few chances to see someone's body completely covered in them. By the 1950s awed circusgoers could see "the Tattooed Lady," Betty Broadbent, whose body was covered with over 400 tattoos. Today, people pay *for* tattoos, not to *see* them.

Height, or the lack thereof, was also another recognized crowd-pleaser. One of Barnum's first successful exhibits was Charles Sherwood Stratton. Renamed General Tom Thumb, Stratton was a midget of 3 feet 4 inches and began working with Barnum when he was only five years old. He dressed as Napoleon, sang, danced, toured the world, and even met President Lincoln. Thousands flocked to see him standing on a normal-sized chair or beside a tall person. Today's sports world has made seeing a professional player of over 7 feet tall a common occurrence. We may be bemused standing next to the basketball player who towers above us, even want our picture taken with him. The difference between then and now is that the audience of long ago paid to see the height, not the talent.

1930s Known as *"the Living Venus de Milo,"* *Frances O'Connor* was the most popular arm-less attraction from the 1920s to the 1940s. Her greatest title of glory, however, was a part in Tod Browning's film *Freaks* (1932), a biting critique of discrimination set in a sideshow, in which she played alongside several of her colleagues.

7.

opposite
1889 The sideshow offered *visual illusions* that mesmerized viewers nearly as much as the real freaks. These acts were very successful in their own right, so much so that by 1889 Barnum & Bailey had dedicated a separate tent to them.

pages 254–255
1953 *The Ringling Bros. and Barnum & Bailey sideshow banners*, left, enticed the crowd to "step right up"—as a talker would say—and for a few nickels see mysterious acts and all kinds of freaks, from a bearded lady to a three-legged man.

Super Freaks

The most dramatic and sometimes alarming exhibits on the platforms were those who suffered from various physical afflictions. Today the public has more occasion to learn about conditions that made for popular attractions, such as anorexia ("the Skeleton Man"), cranial abnormalities ("the Human Gargoyle"), glandular problems ("the Fat Lady"), hormonal conditions ("the Bearded Lady"— was she a he?), and lack of pigmentation ("the Albino Family"). Conjoined twins were also popular attractions throughout the 19th century. Chang and Eng Bunker were born in Thailand (Siam, hence the term "Siamese twins") and were the first conjoined twins to become famous. Joined at the lower chest, the brothers report-edly disliked one another and quarreled often, yet married sisters and between them fathered 22 children. Their exhibition in the circus and on tour brought them wealth and respect.

By the time the Bunker brothers retired from the circus world, Millie and Christine McCoy were born—as slaves. Joined at the buttocks, they were sold and exhibited, and examined at show venues by doctors to verify their attachment. The women were intelligent, multilingual artists. They sang as "the Two-Headed Nightin-gale" and danced on tour around the world. Their autobiography was sold at their appearances, adding income and providing readers with medical descriptions that further fueled their curiosity.

Family members of people born with birth defects, disabilities, and medical problems often sought out sideshow proprietors. Parents, like those of Tom Thumb, realized that such employment offered more than life might have otherwise afforded their children. The costs of the few, if any, available treatments would have been prohibitive. In many respects, life was difficult for those freak-show performers who, as the result of public insensitivity, were often the objects of nervous laughter and ignorant comments from those who paid for the entertainment. There was also the realization, theirs and ours, that for many the alternative would have been worse. Society's ignorance, coupled with little scientific development, meant that they might have been locked in a room or barn at home, hidden from others, shunned by those they did meet. Institutionalization, if available, would have been another option, yet often these institutions were more dehumanizing than accommodating. Taken into the sideshow world, these people had an opportunity to make a legitimate income. They were embraced by a new family of sorts, the circus family, bound by the way the world saw their various disabilities and deformities.

Some of the performers, often helped by managers, made extra money by selling autographed postcards, and later "pitch cards," that usually featured their photograph, or by selling illustrated booklets that told their life story, often in the first person and not always accurate. Some made careers moving successfully between the circus and carnivals. Others appeared in films, like Tod Browning's *Freaks* (1932). Made by the director who a year before had achieved success with *Dracula*, *Freaks* startled audi-ences who expected a typical Hollywood production. Controversy arose because the sideshow freaks that appeared in the film played their parts as sensitive, "normal" humans, while beautiful and handsome actors played the "ugly" characters. In a powerful plot twist, the radiant but murderous trapeze beauty becomes a sideshow beast. The real stars of the film are the freaks: Prince Randian, billed as "the Living Torso," rolls his cigarettes using only his mouth; Johnny Eck, born without legs and only a shortened torso, walks with his strong arms; Pipo and Flipo, the famous "pinheads" suffering from microcephaly, are charming. Once greeted with outrage at the role reversals and banned for its violence and so-called grotesque casting, *Freaks* was deemed worthy of preservation in 1994 by the U.S. National Film Registry Archive.

At the turn of the 20th century, the freak aspect of the sideshow had to share the midway with new inventions like the kinetoscope, which was used to show films in the special black sideshow tent, gradually giving way to other inventive and creative performances and illusions. In addition, medical developments and improved health care reduced the number of physical afflictions over time. By midcentury a growing mass media, in particular television, offered alternative entertainment that resulted in the mainstreaming of phenomena once considered special. Yet the unique-ness of the sideshow personalities and their challenge to our understanding of normalcy and acceptability still inform new generations of performers. Rock concerts, music videos, and some of the more extreme reality and stunt television shows con-tinue to channel the individuality and self-display embodied by these early showmen and -women.

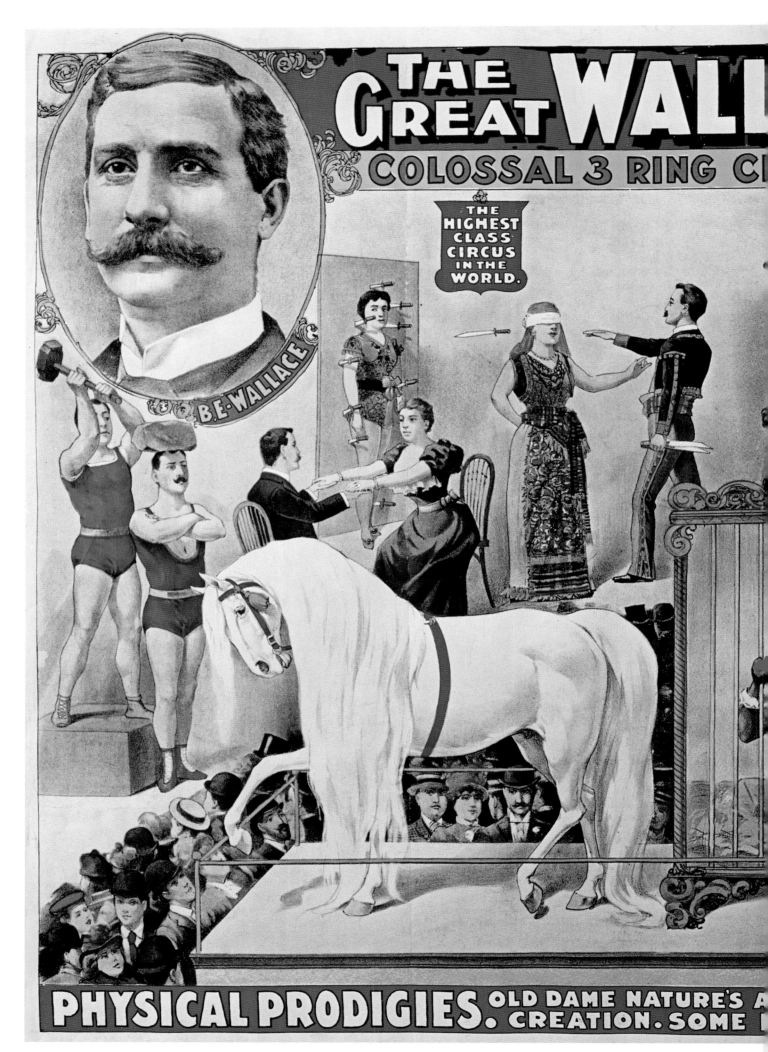

1898 This poster is a *good illustration of the sideshow's variety,* from "missing links" to strongmen and long-maned horses to Punch and Judy puppeteers, snake charmers, knife-throwers, tattooed men, and exotic dancers.

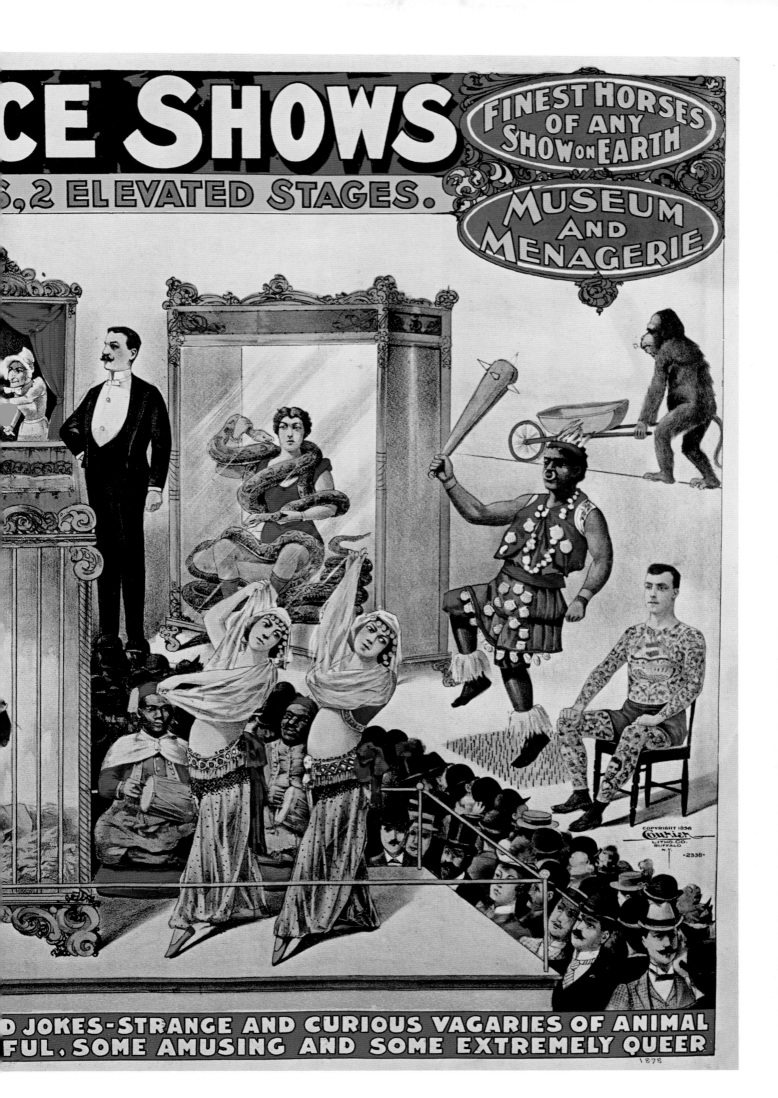

opposite

1930s This elegant *Jazz Age trio of African-American dancers* stand next to a sideshow tent. While jobs in the sideshow were often available to nonwhite performers, it would be decades before the circus hired African-American dancers as showgirls under the big top.

right, top and bottom

ca. 1928–30 Sometimes *African-American dancers* performed on the bally stage at the sideshow's entrance to entice passersby, like in these photos by Walker Evans. In a country still racially divided, African-American entertainers were more likely to be seen in the sideshow than under the big top.

1932 The sideshow was the *last refuge of all-black minstrel bands*, front row in this photograph, which had evolved out of the more popular blackface vaudeville and theater performances by white minstrels. They were hired as musical accompaniment to the sideshow and were an important conduit for spreading African-American music nationally.

CONGRESS OF FREAKS-RINGLING BROTHER

1925 Photographer Edward J. Kelty took this group portrait of the Ringling Bros. and Barnum & Bailey *"Congress of Freaks."* A large number of sideshow celebrities are present, including Zip, in fur suit, bottom left; Eko and Iko, bottom center; Koo Koo, back row, to the right of the giant; and the Doll family of midgets in the back row. Kelty sold his group pictures as season souvenirs to the freaks, performers, staff, and crew.

BARNUM & BAILEY COMBINED CIRCUS.

CARLSON SISTERS
Combined Weight
1146 lbs.

1940s *Dorothy (Dotty) and Florence (Flo) Carlson* were known as "the Half-Ton Twins" and "the Boxing Fat Sisters." To add a little drama to an otherwise motionless display in the sideshow tent, they performed a fake boxing match for their viewers.

pages 264–265
1902 The *Barnum & Bailey freaks* left a lasting impression on audiences during their turn-of-the-century European tour. Although several European circuses tried to emulate the American-style sideshow, it never caught on with their audiences, who preferred freaks confined to the fairgrounds.

ca. 1925 *Fat people* were an astonishing sight in sideshows in the years before the obesity epidemic hit America. From left to right are Tom Ton (Mexican-born Theodore A. Valenzuela), Jolly Irene (Amanda Siebert née Quinn), and "the Half-Ton Twins," Dotty and Flo Carlson.

opposite
1949 Fat people like *Jolly Dolly Geyer* (Celesta Geyer née Herrmann), portrayed in this sideshow banner by Nieman Eisman as "Dolly Dimple," were a sideshow staple. Geyer even made the Guinness Book of World Records when, after a heart attack in 1950, she lost 443 pounds. At a mere 112 pounds, however, her sideshow career was over.

CENTURY
144 W 46 ST
2171-B
CONEY ISLAND

DREAMLAND CIRCUS SIDE SHOW
FEATURING
TOM TON, JOLLY IRENE AND CARLSON SISTERS

The Barnum & Bailey

CURIEUSE EXHIBITION d'HOMMES & FEMMES

P.T. BARNUM'S GREATEST SHOW ON EARTH AND GREAT LONDON CIRCU[S]

TRAVELING THIS SEASON ONLY UNITED ACTUAL EXPENSES DAILY $ 4.500°°

THE CHINESE GOLIATH, CHANG-TU-SING.

THE MOST GIGANTIC & FINELY PROPORTIONED MAN IN EXISTENCE HIS COMPARATIVE SIZE WITH ORDINARY HUMAN BEINGS, ACCURATELY DISPLAYED ON THIS PLATE. AN EDUCATED AND REFINED GENTLEMAN, SPEAKING 26 LANGUAGES FLUENTLY. RECENTLY ARRIVED FROM EUROPE, UNDER CONTRACT WITH P.T. BARNUM, JAS. A. BAILEY & JAS. L. HUTCHINSON, AT A SALARY OF $ 600°° PER WEEK.

AMONG THE MYRIAD ATTRACTIONS

THE STROBRIDGE LITH. CO. CINTI. O.

right
ca. 1860 and 1863 *P. T. Barnum,* far right, was among the famous sitters of renowned 19th century photographer Mathew Brady, whose New York City studio was across the street from Barnum's American Museum. Barnum established his fame and fortune exhibiting human oddities in his museum and on tours. The most famous was midget **Tom Thumb (Charles Sherwood Stratton),** at right impersonating Napoleon, with wife Lavinia Warren, also photographed by Brady.

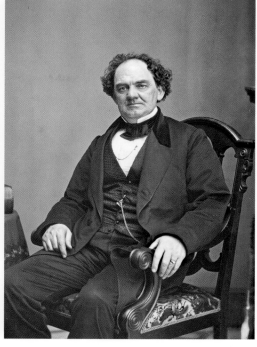

opposite
1880s *Chang Tu Sing, "the Chinese Goliath,"* allegedly stood 7 feet 10 inches. He had a successful international career in China, where he appeared at the court of the emperor, before coming to America. When he joined P. T. Barnum's *Greatest Show on Earth* sideshow, the advertising posters made much of the fact that he towered over his fellow performers.

1881 P. T. Barnum became a celebrity in Europe when he exhibited Tom Thumb in England in 1844. **Thumb performed for Queen Victoria** three times during his three-year European tour, an accolade that Barnum didn't fail to make use of in subsequent years, as in this Barnum & London poster.

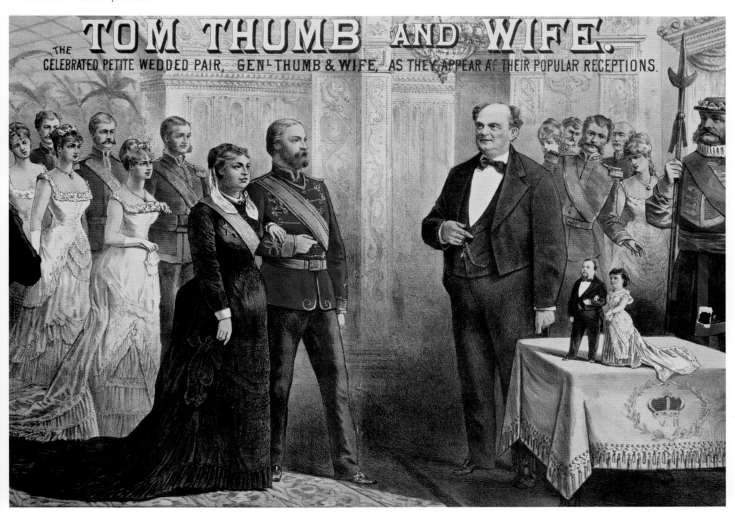

1936 Twenty-eight-inch *Major Mite (Clarence Howerton)* barely reaches the tops of 8-feet-6-inch Jack Earle's boots. Earle appeared in more than 40 movies in the silent film era, like *Jack and the Beanstalk* (1924). Two years after this photograph was taken, Howerton would also set foot in Hollywood, performing in *The Wizard of Oz* (1938).

left and below
ca. 1872 and 1915 *William Henry Johnson, known as Zip,* was one of P. T. Barnum's most successful freaks. Mathew Brady, "the father of photojournalism," took the first known photograph of Zip, left, in the 1870s. There were at least three Zip impersonators over the years, but the most successful was Johnson, who also played the violin, as seen in this rare photo, below, on the bally stage in front of the Barnum & Bailey sideshow.

opposite
1907 *Lionel, "the Lion-Faced Boy"* was born Stefan Bibrowski in Poland. The 1903 Barnum and Bailey program sang the praises of his unexpected virtues: "[He's] unusually bright and intelligent, and may be spoken to in perfect freedom. He is polite and attentive to everything that is said to him."

pages 272–273
1881 Long-haired women were a popular sideshow attraction, but the most famous were the *Seven Sutherland Sisters* who toured with Barnum & Bailey. They had a combined total of almost 40 feet of hair and got rich selling their own brand of hair grower.

1887 *"The Sacred Hairy Family of Burma"* was said to have been the good-luck charms of the king of Burma. After they were exhibited in New York City in March 1887, *The New York Times* declared, "The Siamese twins, the double-headed nightingale, the tattooed man, Tom Thumb, and Chang, all rolled into one, could not compare."

below
1885 Jo-Jo (born Fedor Jeftichejev in Russia), *"the Dog-Faced Boy,"* was a member of the Barnum & Bailey sideshow. Booklets like this and other souvenirs were sold in the tent and were one of the main ways performers, and their managers, made money. Although a major success, Jo-Jo never performed for the tsar, as this cover depicted.

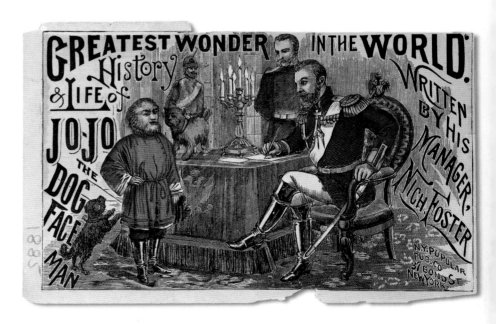

LIONEL
LION FACED BOY.

7.

THE SEVEN WONDERS. THE HIRSU
FLOWING TR

SHELBY, PULLMAN AND HAMILTON'S 8

CON

"VEILED BY HER LOVELY TRESSES FLOWING TO HER FEET
SHE STOOD IN MAIDEN MODESTY"

N°3.

THE STROBRIDGE LITH. CO. CIN. O.

WITH

RAND UNITED MASTODON SHOWS

left
1900s *Circassian beauties* with teased hair were billed as the world's most beautiful white women. They were said to come from the Caucasus mountains in Circassia (part of today's Russia) and adopted non-Western names like Zoe Meleke and Zalumma Agra for an added dose of authenticity.

opposite
1930s George and Willie Muse were featured as *Eko and Iko, "the Ambassadors from Mars."* They were African-American albinos, "discovered" near a crashed spaceship in the Mojave Desert. They began their career as "the Sheep-Headed Cannibals from Ecuador," but the Mars angle proved more popular.

below, left and right
1861 and ca. 1860 On display in the 1860s at P. T. Barnum's very popular American Museum were *"the Aztec Children,"* bottom left, and *Rudolph Lucasie's "Albino Family,"* bottom left and below. Both would later tour with P. T. Barnum's *Greatest Show on Earth* and, later, Barnum & Bailey.

Are They Ambassadors From Mars

opposite
1906 *The Davis family of the Cole Bros. circus sideshow* was advertised as leopard people. Their vitiligo, or skin discoloration, and their unusual hairstyles were enough to qualify them as freaks and ensure a profitable career in the sideshow.

right
1880s Canadian-born Guillermo Farini was a great promoter of daredevil acts and human oddities, which he exhibited in both Europe and America. *"The Leopard Boy"* was one of his discoveries, shown here at London's Royal Aquarium.

1960s This Snap Wyatt sideshow banner depicts *Sadie "the Leopard Woman"* as a white-spotted beauty living among leopards. Inside the sideshow tent, the public would see an African-American woman with vitiligo.

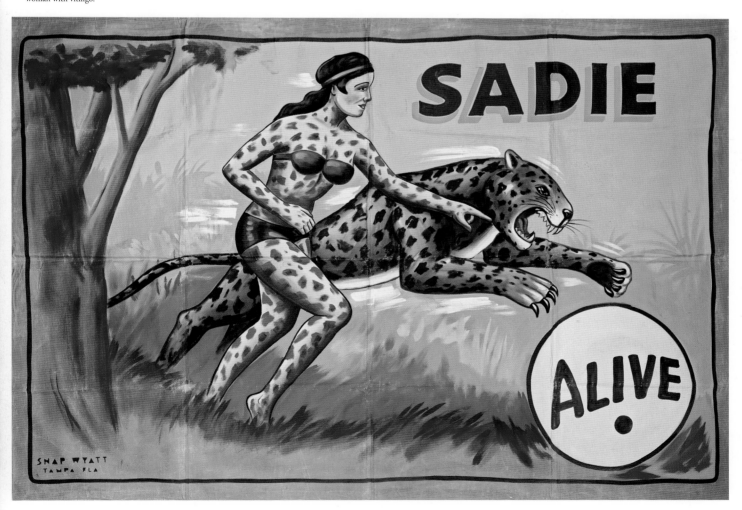

1902 ***Mademoiselle Octavia*** is shown on the bally stage outside the Ringling Bros.' sideshow. She wears more clothing than later snake charmers, yet quite a bit less than the women watching in conventional floor-length dresses under the hot summer sun.

below
1889 Barnum & Bailey claimed that their ***"Young Hindoo Snake Charmer"*** worked with "boa, constrictors, anacondas, pythons...." Whether or not she handled these dangerous snake varieties was irrelevant. She handled snakes, and that was intriguing enough to draw a crowd.

FREAKS & WONDERS

HINDOO SWORD SWALLOWER

1930s Whether in the 1890s, the Jazz Age, or today, snake charmers do not much differ apart from their costumes. They often perform smiling **with a snake coiled around their necks.** But a kiss on the reptile's nose is as much excitement as one could expect to see during this act.

opposite
1970s In the sideshow, created acts like tattooed people, along with working acts like **snake charmers and sword-swallowers,** shared the spotlight with genuine freaks. But quantity was important in the sideshow tent, often more than quality, and banners such as this one by Fred G. Johnson transformed even mundane acts into visions of drama and danger.

ca. 1885 *Snake charmer Lulu Lataska* protects the public from her charges with a mesh enclosure. Her costume and the poster on the underside of the trunk's lid at right suggest she may have infused some animation into her act by dressing as a Circassian beauty.

1950s *Booptee, the antlered pinup girl*
by sideshow banner artist Snap Wyatt, may
have been a woman with a skin ailment, or a
woman adorned with fake antlers. While the
real nature of her act has been lost to obscurity,
she evidently styled herself in bikini and regal
cape to resemble the costumes of her "normal"
circus colleagues under the big top.

1960s A so-called *"Electric Girl"* was a sideshow performer who played with static electricity for the benefit of her viewers. It was a fascinating act for audiences, particularly in the late 19th century before electricity was widespread in the U. S.

below and right
1902 These two rare photographs taken inside a sideshow tent show *sword-swallowers Charles E. Griffin* with the Ringling Bros. circus, left, *and Mademoiselle Clifford* of Barnum & Bailey, above right, preparing for their sword-swallowing acts. Circus sideshows were lined with stages where performers sat or performed as viewers moved from one act to the next.

1890s–1900s To change up their acts, some sword-swallowers, like **Miss Victorina**, used several swords of different shapes and sizes at the same time.

opposite
1950s *Sword-swallower Lady Jean* brought a modern touch to a classic act by using not just swords but a neon tube. In time, the stunt would be perfected so that when the lights were dimmed, the lit neon tube could be seen inside the performer.

1928 X-ray photographs of sword-swallowing acts were sometimes displayed as proof of the stunt. Here the **Mighty Ajax** is shown mid-act. To make this photograph, photographer Edward J. Kelty used the actual X-ray, like one would a celluloid negative, to expose a piece of photographic paper.

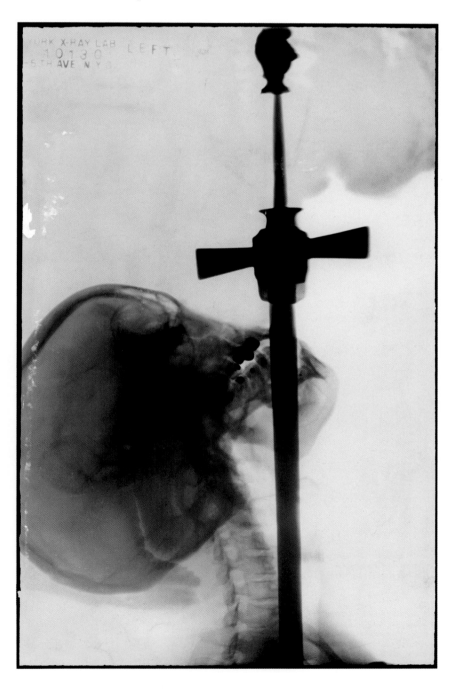

1912 Born in 1857, Edward A. Barnwell began his career as a child actor. He allegedly learned his fiery trade from a tribe of West Coast Native Americans. When he hit the stage after living with them for almost a year and a half, he renamed himself *Signor Barnello, "the Human Volcano."*

pages 288–289
1940s "He is fireproof" declares this Nieman Eisman banner of a fire-eater billed as the *"Son of the Devil."* Instead of breathing fire out, he "swallowed" fire from a blowtorch. The banner's brightly painted environment efficiently illustrates his alleged family ties.

right
1898 *"King of Fire" Delkano*, with Barnum & Bailey, had an elaborate display, including skulls, ornate stands, and a carefully planned devilish costume.

opposite
1888 *Mademoiselle Katamorpa's* fire stunt is embellished with carefully hand-drawn smoldering flames in this detail of a cabinet card. Her fire-eating act combined the excitement of sword-swallowing with the danger of burning flames. It was rare to see woman performers handle fire at this time.

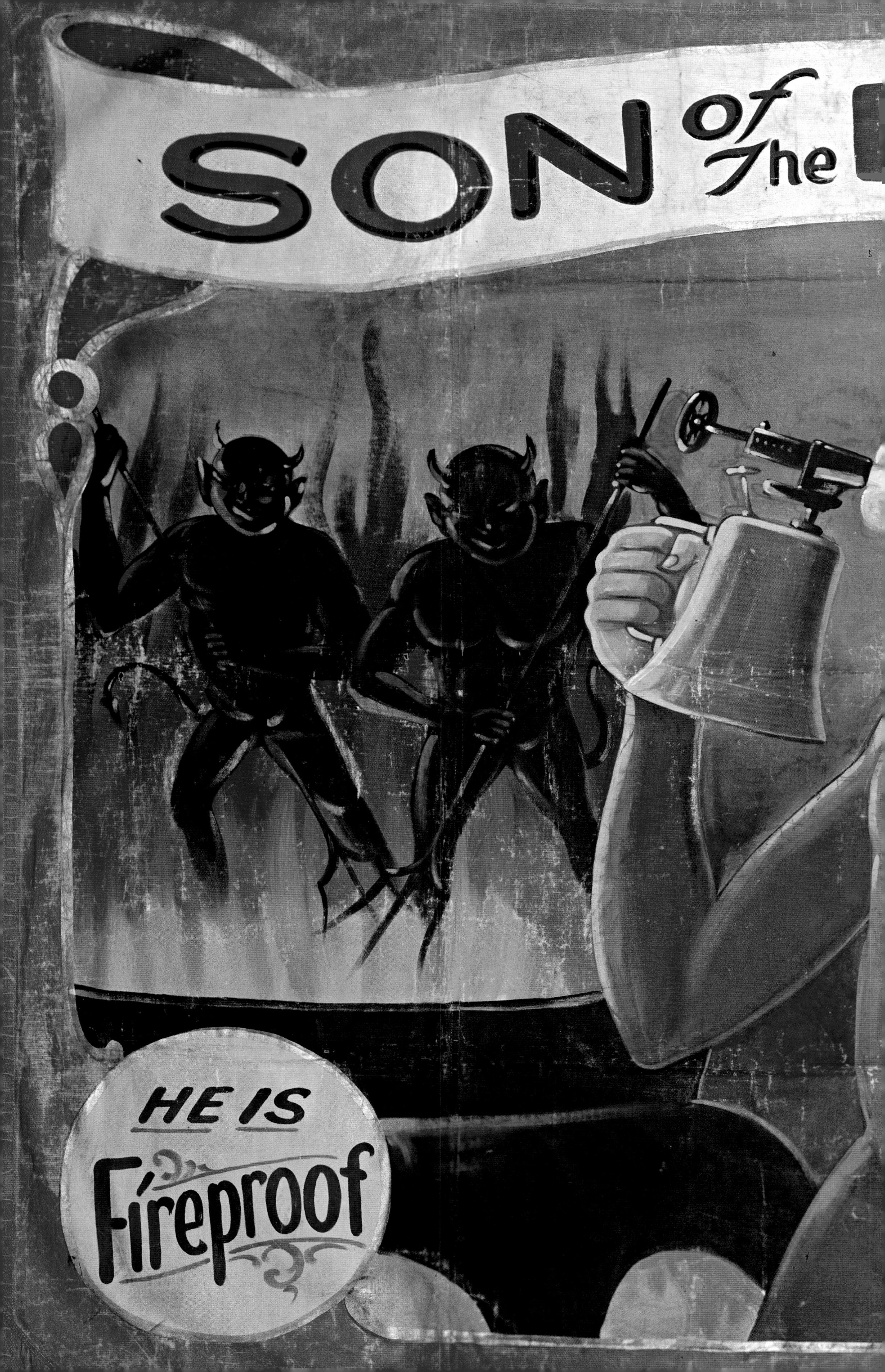

SON of the
HE IS
Fireproof

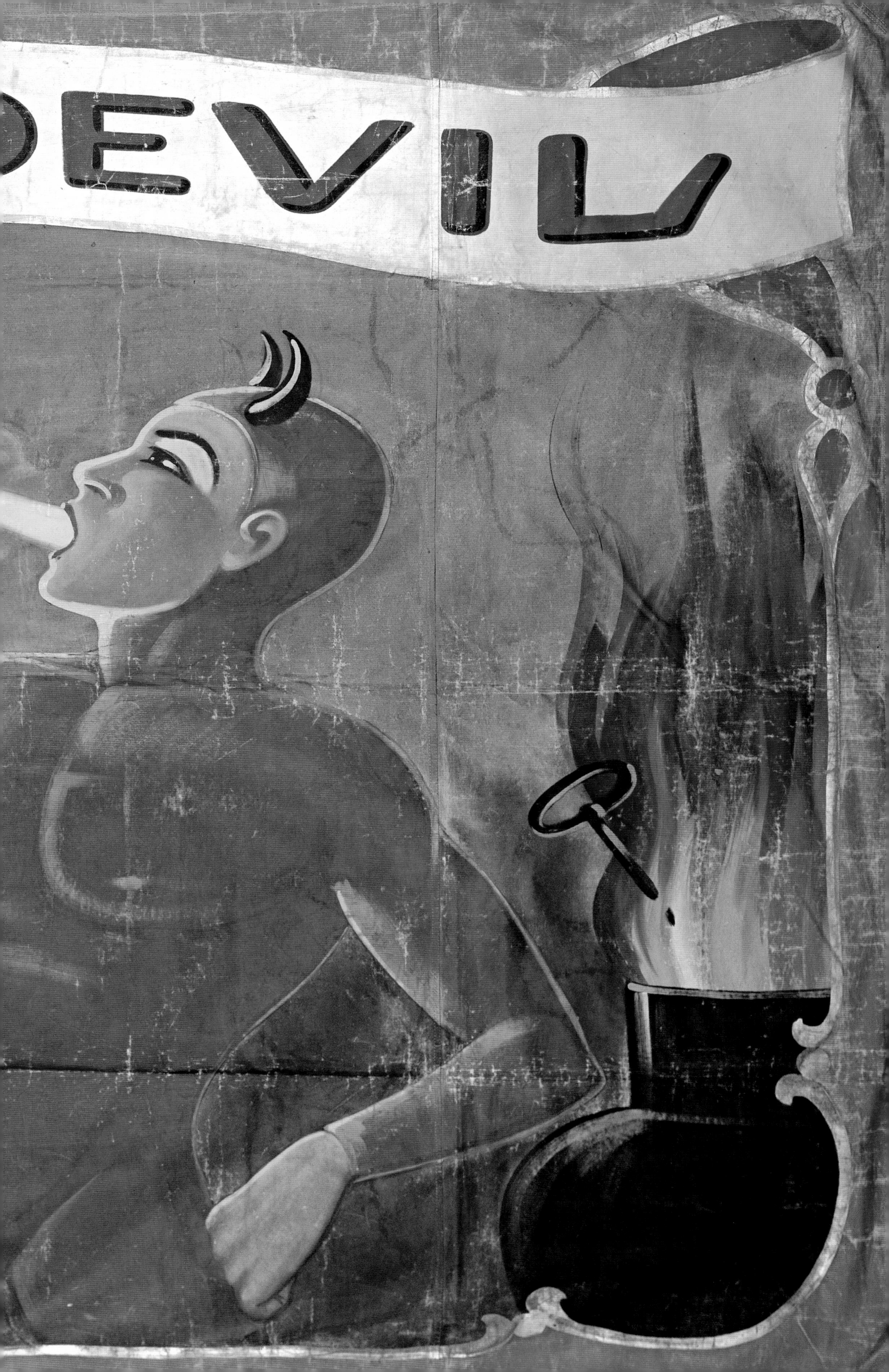
DEVIL

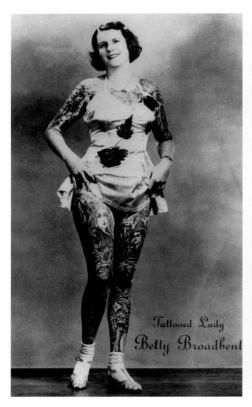

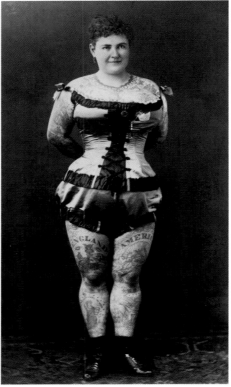

1950s "The freak tent is a large one, and it is necessary to pad it with a few mediocre features. There is, therefore, still a place in the world for ***a smart tattooed girl in a low-cut dress.***" (Alva Johnston, "Sideshow People, Part II," *The New Yorker*, April 21, 1934)

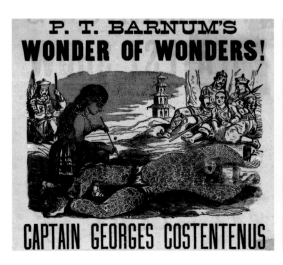

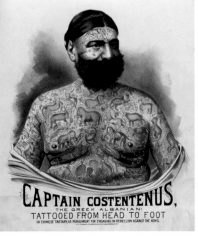

right
1899 _Charles Tripp_ was a famous member of the Barnum & Bailey sideshow for many years. The 1903 program described him as having "educated himself to use his feet with a deftness that few men of even mechanical bent attain with their hands."

below
1960s _Sideshow banner art_ was crafted to be eye-catching, dramatic, even poetic, with bold colors and clean lines. This spoof photograph depicts show painter Bobby Wicks pretending to be the well-known banner artist Snap Wyatt painting his armless subject.

1883 *Millie and Christine* were born into slavery in Welches Creek, North Carolina. Their owner sold them in infancy to a sideshow, and despite being sold again several times and stolen twice, they were eventually reunited with their mother. Gifted singers, they became a worldwide sensation and died wealthy in 1912 at 62.

center
1870s *Conjoined twins Chang and Eng* were among the most famous freaks ever shown. Born in Siam in 1811 (thus the name Siamese twins), they were brought to America in 1829. At first they traveled alone with a showman, then with dime museums and sideshows. They married sisters Adelaide and Sarah Ann Yates and fathered 22 children, but they apparently couldn't stand each other.

right
1920s British-born *conjoined twins Violet and Daisy Hilton* made a fortune in sideshows and vaudeville singing in harmony and playing instruments. They had well-publicized affairs with celebrities, and their tumultuous lives were adapted into a movie, *Chained for Life* (1951), and a Broadway musical, *Side Show* (1997). They also appeared in Tod Browning's *Freaks* (1932).

left and below left
1910s Sicilian-born ***"Three-Legged Wonder"***
Francesco A. Lentini came to America in 1898
at 10, and embarked a few years later on a
sideshow career that lasted 50 years. He died in
1966 leaving a widow and four children. The
pitch card, below left, was a common souvenir
sold at sideshows, along with portraits or first-
person booklets, one of which read, "I am sometimes asked how I buy my shoes; well here's how:
I buy two pairs and give the extra left shoe to a
one-legged friend of mine who had the misfor-
tune to lose his right leg."

below
1890s Texas-born **Myrtle Corbin, "the Four-
Legged Woman,"** was born with an extra pair of
legs hanging between her normal legs. She was a
popular attraction on major American circuses
for many years and commanded a weekly salary
of a hefty $450. She eventually married a Ken-
tucky man and had five children.

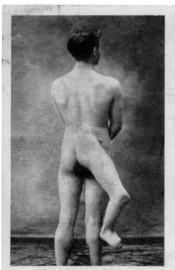

FRANK A. LENTINI

The only man in the world with 3 legs, 4
feet, 16 toes, 2 bodies from the waist down.
Operation impossible, doctors claim it would
cause death or paralyze my entire body. 3rd
limb connected at spine. THANK YOU.

Please show this photo to your friend.

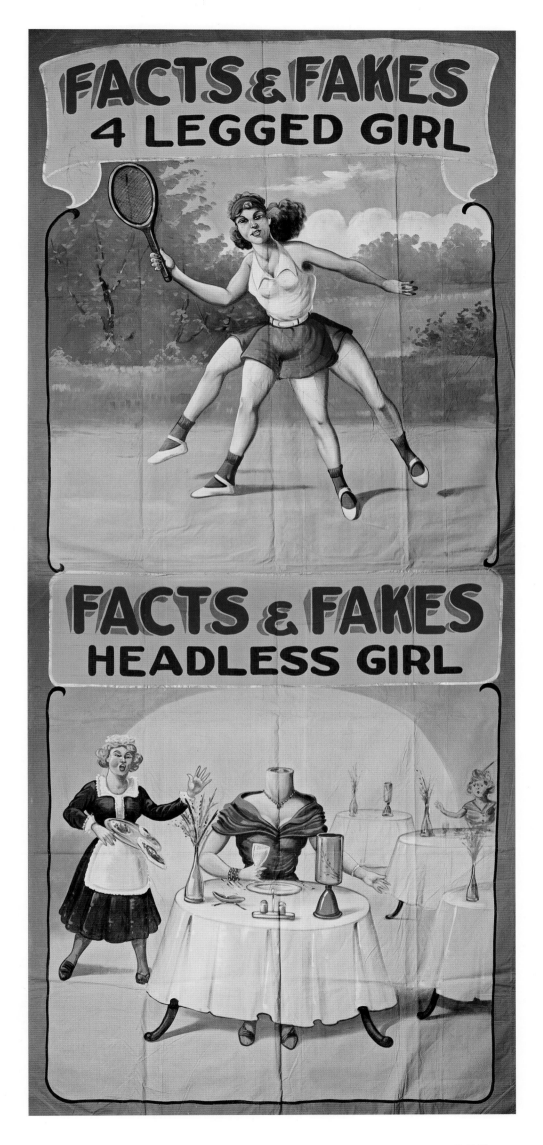

The **Barnum & Bailey** G

CHASTE, CHARMING, WEIRD & WONDERFUL SUPERNATURAL ILLUSIONS, A
HEADLESS BODIES, TALKING HUMAN HEADS, REVOLVING SPRITES, BEAUTIFUL MER-

THE WORLD'S LARGEST, GRANDES

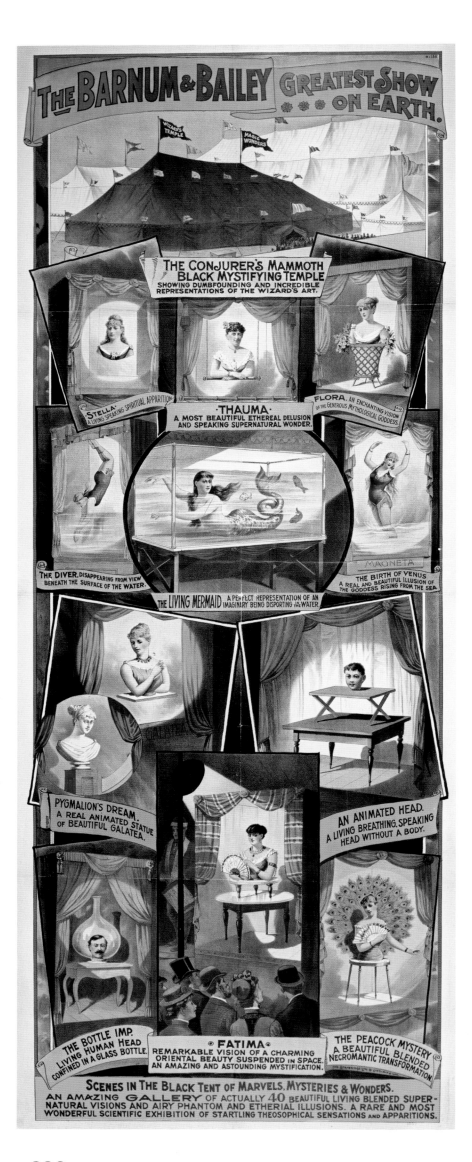

SCENES IN THE BLACK TENT OF MARVELS, MYSTERIES & WONDERS.
AN AMAZING GALLERY OF ACTUALLY 40 BEAUTIFUL BLENDED SUPER-
NATURAL VISIONS AND AIRY PHANTOM AND ETHERIAL ILLUSIONS. A RARE AND MOST
WONDERFUL SCIENTIFIC EXHIBITION OF STARTLING THEOSOPHICAL SENSATIONS AND APPARITIONS.

left
1889 One can see the enormous popularity of sideshow illusions in this *rare Barnum & Bailey poster.* The poster artists have rendered not one but a dozen acts in detail. The illusion tent was black and dimly lit so the illusions, which often depended on mirrors, set pieces, and curtains, remained concealed.

opposite
1890s Genuine freaks were extremely popular but also hard to find, necessitating improvisation. The *tent of illusions* was exactly that and used normal people in startling headless, legless, and other surreal motifs.

pages 300–301
ca. 1880–81 The *"Mysterious Man and Woman Fish"* was a breathing-underwater illusion using concealed air tubes. In the sideshow, illusions were fair game as spectacles. What mattered was that the attractions were strange and unusual enough, whether real or fake, to bewilder spectators.

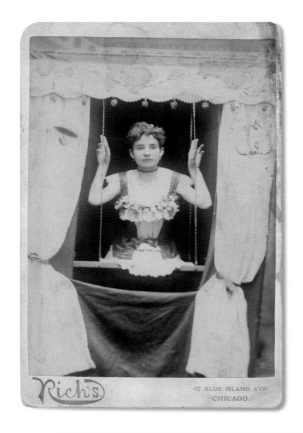

Rich's.
97 BLUE ISLAND AVE.
CHICAGO.

MLLE. GABRIELE.
THE ONLY LIVING HALF LADY IN THE WORLD.

left
1890s Thrice-married Mademoiselle Gabrielle was the *"Living Half Lady."* She said in an interview, "Women really don't need legs. I can enjoy life and do everything I want to do without them. I don't envy any woman the possession of them." (interview cited by Wallace Short, "The Psychology of the 'Limbless Complex,'" *London Life*, 1938)

above
1889 The elaborate setting surrounding this woman is a *telltale sign that this is an illusion*, not a genuine legless woman. Illusions of absent body parts played on the popularity of the freak celebrities.

JUST ADDED IN A BLACK TENT | THE BARNUM & BAILEY GREATEST SHOW ON EARTH | 40 MARVELOUS MYSTERIES
A NOVEL SURPRISING AND STARTLING SUPERNATURAL ILLUSION DEPARTMENT. WEIRD, ENCHANTING AND GHOSTLY APPARITIONS BLENDED AND JOINED AND NOW EXHIBITED FOR THE FIRST TIME. IN A COMMODIOUS SPECIALLY CONSTRUCTED BLACK CANVAS TENT. A RARE DEEPLY INTERESTING AND INSTRUCTIVE EXHIBIT OF WONDERFUL SCIENTIFIC CREATIONS.

40 SUPERNATURAL ILLUSIONS | A QUAINT AND NEW ADDITION. WITHOUT EXTRA CHARGE. | THE BLACK TEMPLE OF MAGIC WONDERS
THE WIZARD'S MARVELOUS AND ASTOUNDING MODERN PRODUCTION. AN EXTENSIVE GALLERY OF 40 BEAUTIFUL LIVING MYSTERIES, SUMMONED AT THE COMMAND OF THE FAMOUS CONJUROR PROF. HOFFMAN. ALL SHOWN UNDER THE RAYS OF 100 INCANDESCENT LIGHTS.

THE NON-DESCRIPT MYSTER
AS THEY APPEAR IN THEIR GREAT ORIGINAL SU

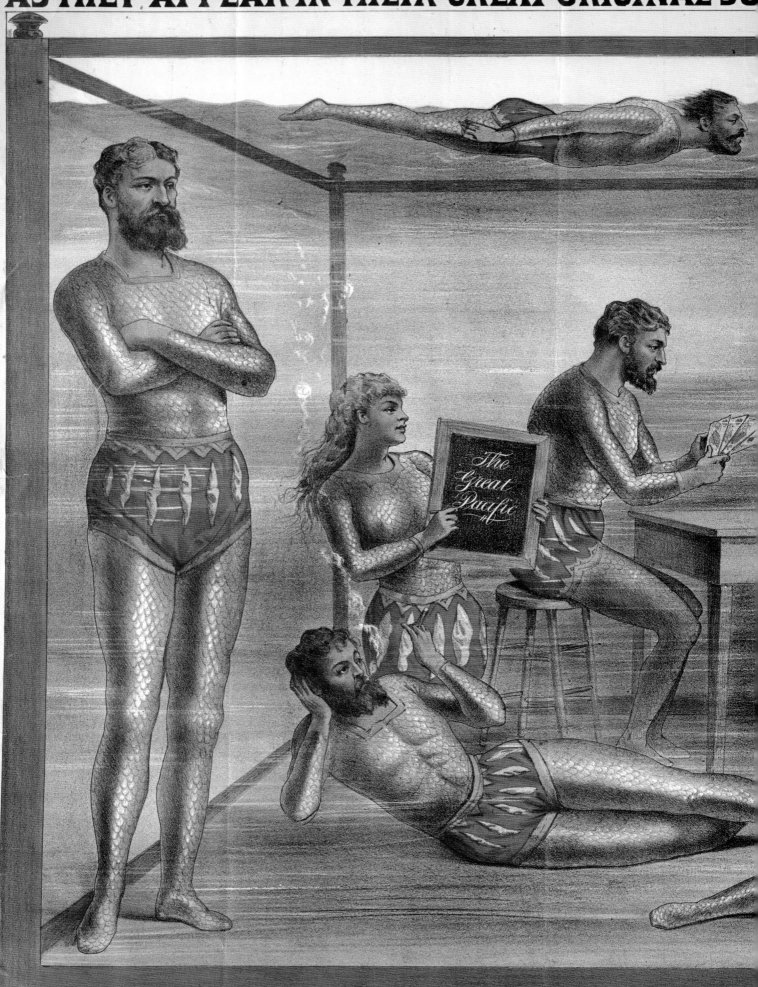

The Great Pacific

THE NEW GREAT PACI[FIC]

TENT CITY

❖ ◆ ❖

BACKSTAGE
AT THE
CIRCUS

Linda Granfield

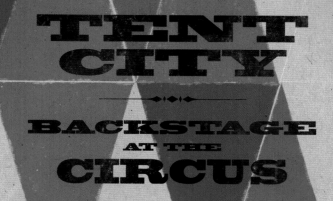

TENT CITY

BACKSTAGE AT THE CIRCUS

Linda Granfield

Dawn breaks in a Midwest American town, and the horizon is emblazoned with spectacular hues. Not the color-burst of a vibrant sunrise, mind you, but the jolt of primary colors popping off the side of a weathered barn. Dramatic images of acrobats, beasts, and faraway places punctuate an otherwise monotone landscape. The huge typography of the posters shout what is on the way—"Ringling Bros. Sublime Spectacle of the Arabian Nights"—with "May 29" printed larger than your tallest brother. The circus is coming to town!

opposite
1948 With no shower at hand, the Bogino Troupe, a celebrated Italian family of acrobats, devises a *fun way to get a shampoo* in the ubiquitous circus water bucket. Sinks and running water were not among the dressing tent amenities.

page 303
1953 Life on the circus lot had its own peculiar rules and traditions; for example, even the most glamorous circus stars, like beautiful *aerialist Pinito Del Oro*, had to deal with the mere two buckets of water that were allotted to each performer. This was life in their tent city, and performers loved it.

1945 Circus folks are fond of souvenir snapshots. Here, *Margaret and Dora Caudillo*,
two Mexican performers, pose with two uniden-
tified clowns for a souvenir of their tour with the
Cole Bros. circus. The clown on the right sports
a classic white-face clown makeup and costume.

If the advance men did their job well, many towns found themselves "sheeted
up," or plastered with huge posters announcing the circus' arrival. Two weeks in
advance of the show, local barns were covered overnight with billboard-sized posters
that heralded the excitement and commotion that was to descend upon the community. In the 19th century, billboards that we take for granted as part of our rural and
urban landscapes were rarely seen. The multiple paper "sheets" that made up the oversized circus posters were usually affixed to board fences and the sides of buildings
within sight of a well-traveled road. Where no sheds or barns were available, circuses
contracted with local carpenters to erect wooden walls (early billboards) to paste the
posters onto. The more surface area to cover the better. Shopkeepers displayed one-
sheet posters in their display windows, and newspaper ads were purchased to create

even more buzz. Farmers might have been paid for the use of their barns with free
tickets to the show, or posters might have been slapped on without their permission,
causing what was known as "poster nuisance."

While all circuses large and small put up posters and distributed hundreds of
handbills, the larger ones, like the Barnum and Ringling circuses, could afford to post
thousands of sheets in every town they visited. Printing companies like the Strobridge
Company of Cincinnati, Ohio, and the Courier Company of Buffalo, New York,
made fortunes from the multicolored images lithographed by stone or printed with
carved wooden blocks. By fine-tuning the execution of the printed sheets, using more
innovative machinery, and printing with improved, more vibrant inks, poster companies created disposable artworks that a century later have become highly collectible
art. The bold images used on the bright posters of, for instance, tigers leaping toward
the viewer came to epitomize the circus to fans across America. Ferocious beasts that
seemed to truly jump from the posters were part of the spirit of fearsomeness and
recklessness that would attract local audiences to the big top a few weeks later. Stories
about the circus and its performers would run in local newspapers, and later on radio
stations, and add to the frenzy of publicity.

The news that "the circus is coming!" caused excitement in town but also meant
that job opportunities were on the horizon. When wagons or trains delivered circus

1950 *Clown Bumpsy Anthony* gives a playful
spanking to fellow performer Helen Dobbs,
an image that wouldn't have made it beyond the
intimate confines of the back lot.

1949 The circus played twice daily, in the afternoon and evening. Since the circus train was usually not stationed nearby, Ringling Bros. and Barnum & Bailey *performers relaxed on the back lot* between shows.

equipment to the lot, it took more than the owner's employees to raise the canvas tents, which included those needed to house the animals, the sideshow, the performers (if they were not living in train cars, rented hotel accommodations, or, later, trailers), the souvenir and food booths, and, of course, the mighty big top. The acreage covered by canvas was sometimes larger than today's football field. Local roustabouts were temporarily hired to help circus employees put up and later take down the tents.

A Magic City of Canvas

While the number of tents depended upon the size of the circus, the basic construction of the tents was similar. The huge center poles traveled with the circus on specially built extralong wagons. Circus elephants were not just performers; their brute strength helped unroll the massive heaps of canvas and move the tent poles. Ropes were attached to various sections of the canvas tent and poles, and then attached to stakes. Finally, the canvas roof was raised by a bale ring around the center poles. Bleachers were erected, chairs unfolded, animals unloaded from the wagons or trains and exercised and fed. All this construction and attention to many details was done typically with extraordinary precision and speed, and often under the gaze of hundreds of townspeople who would gather to watch the building of the lot. No ticket was needed for this, and circus owners knew that the rubbernecks or "gawks" who watched the tents go up at 5 A.M. would most likely want to get inside them come showtime. If the townspeople were willing to arrive in the damp predawn darkness to watch and wait—and they were—that was fine as long as they stayed out of the way!

On smaller overland shows, townspeople got their first glimpse of the circus "family" as they passed through town on their way to the show lot, having previously stopped outside of town, washed, and changed into their pageant wardrobe. On big railroad circuses, however, the circus performers were usually first introduced to each town during the parade. Before advances in mass communication, both were important ways to announce the arrival of the show. Dressed in their costume finery, sitting upon their colorful wagons or bedecked horses, the performers paraded down the main street. There was no better advertisement for the circus' visit than this incredible parade of people and animals previously only imagined. Shops were often closed for the duration of the parade; no profits could be made when potential customers were busy gaping at the spectacle, standing three-deep on the wooden sidewalk outside the store. The storekeeper no doubt also wanted to see the parade. Gorgeous showgirls in richly ornamented howdahs sat atop huge elephants. Bandwagons and a calliope, the famous "steam piano," were pulled by horses adorned with plumes. Camels and zebras brought glimpses of the exotic. So magnificent was the spectacle that some people followed the parade right out into the nearby field, right up to the ticket wagon, and, later, right into the big top.

All in the Family

After the parade made its way to the show lot, the performers dispersed to the back lot to get ready, practice, eat, and hang out with other performers until the first of usually two performances of the day began. For all the apparent glamour, they also had to take care of daily life. Ripped costumes had to be stitched, hair had to be tinted, broken saddles and ladders had to be repaired. Babies had to be fed, laundry washed and pressed, and older children had to be homeschooled in the usual subjects as well as in the circus arts if they were going to carry on with a family tradition. Children in the circus family might literally "learn the ropes" from anyone in the backyard who had the needed skills. Children also worked as performers, typically as acrobats and jugglers. They fed animals that might be part of their family's act, cleaned equipment, learned to sew and mend costumes, or read newspapers to illiterate staff members. While some observers argued that many of the children's efforts were actually child labor, others acknowledged that the children were engaged, as their parents had been before them, in a family trade.

As in any large family that lives and travels together for so many months, there could be problems carrying on with daily life. The lack of privacy in the wagons and

1903 "The big thrill for me was the over-whelming sense of belonging, of being part of this puzzling, physically talented extended family, a *tenacious tribe of semigypsies*." (Bill Ballantine, *Clown Alley*, 1982)

tents, the constant touring, rained-out performances, and even the occasional flea infestation brought stress with sometimes little relief. Although foreign languages continued to be spoken by the performers, circus lingo, the language particular to circus life and its many elements, brought some cohesiveness. This shared communication had evolved throughout circus history and at times baffled locals who might be as unfamiliar with the lingo as with a foreign language.

Sightseeing in local towns was not barred, but many companies such as Ringling Bros. had rules of behavior that disallowed fraternization with the local men or women. That, of course, didn't mean that assignations weren't furtively made. While it was rare for them to take place between local men and show women, showmen sometimes enjoyed the attention of local women interested in a little adventure or romance but who didn't want to tarnish their local reputations. They also might meet with prostitutes attracted to the potential business of a large, traveling male population. When fraternization between a "towner" and a trouper was discovered, some kind of demerit or justice might be meted out by the circus owner or by the family member who served as community leader on the lot.

Since the performers spent all day, every day with the same people, both in the circus ring and in the backyard, a natural outcome was the sequence of "matching" (circus lingo for courtship and marriage) and "hatching" (having children). The mar-

riages often joined two families who had performed in circuses for generations in Europe before their subsequent immigration to the United States, and these unions created yet another generation of performers who would be trained since infancy on the circus back lot. Circus dynasties such as the Cristiani family, riders and acrobats who appeared with many circuses in the 20th century, portrayed a circus ancestry that dated back to early 19th-century Italy.

How They Really Lived

A local newspaper reporter strolling on assignment through the backyard of the circus might have found the blacksmith putting new shoes on a pinto. Or a painter dabbing fresh paint on chipped wagons. He may have been sprayed by the fellow filling hundreds of buckets with fresh water, each bucket personalized with the name of a performer. With no running water in the tents and trailers, the dented buckets for personal use were refilled constantly from a town tap, or for overland shows from a nearby stream, and were used to wash clothes. Circus performers spent their free time playing chess, card games, or baseball, or going fishing, sightseeing, relaxing, or taking a coveted bath in a local hotel, sunbathing, and practicing new and old routines. While officially no gambling was allowed, candid snapshots and performer interviews prove such forbidden activities also took place.

1955 For decades the American circus world's chaplain was the legendary Father Ed Sullivan, seen here on the back lot playfully chasing the devil (in the person of a costumed performer). Circus folks are *often religious and almost always superstitious*.

1900s At the turn of the 20th century, *equestri-enne Miss Laurence and her assistant* wait behind the curtain to enter the ring. They are being entertained by two performers in a giraffe outfit, ready to do what was known as a "jargo," a clown act performed in an animal costume.

pages 308–309
1955 *"A world of its own,* the circus…it has its births and deaths and marriages, its pains and joys… But to us…it has one thing more. There is a fraternity there, that we of the circus who have ventured in the Outside World, do not find in that strange place." (Josephine DeMott Robinson, *The Circus Lady,* 1936)

CIRCUS DAY AROUND THE CLOCK
When Your Town Is A One-Day Stand

"The First" or "The Squadron," the first of the four, long Ringling Bros and Barnum & Bailey circus trains to arrive in your town, starts to unload its cargo—menagerie cages and cookhouse wagons and trucks.

Truck hauled wagons, containing cookhouse and dining equipment, and rolling motor ranges complete trip from "runs" (unloading crossings) and reach show lot.

Cookhouse and dining tents are raised—"Hotel Ringling." 174 men preparing breakfast. Second train arrives at runs.

"Ham and eggs! Hotcakes!" Breakfast! "Come and get it!" Horse tents in the air.

Third train steams onto siding. Stakes are driven for menagerie, big top, sideshows, dressing and shop tents. Wagons rolling on lot.

Poles for big top, menagerie and other tents raised. Unloading canvas from wagons starts.

Crews start lacing canvas middle-pieces and round-ends together—"making canvas." Fourth train arrives—maybe. No hurry with it—mostly staff and performers. (Brass and Art.)

Great tents rise—massive mushrooms, with horses and elephants hauling aloft the peaks adding to the conceit of fantastic fungi. Thump: row upon row of trunks are spotted in the dressing rooms of performers.

10

Cages spotted and trimmed by working elephants in vast menagerie tent. Sideshow banner lines ranged along midway; sideshow interior stages installed; ringbanks, stages, aerial riggings placed in big top; doctor's tent erected; blacksmith and shop tents set up.

Grandstands and bleachers erected in big top, chairs aligned tier by tier by waves of men. Orderly chaos resolves into quiet and symmetry in steel, cordage and canvas. "The flag's up" for lunch.

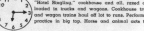

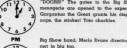

Sideshow talkers orate its opening. Ticket wagons on midway raise windows for Big Show patrons. Tented refectories serve soft drinks and hot dogs to throngs. Circus Day!

"DOORS!" The gates to the Big Show via the menagerie are opened to the expectant crowds. Gargantua the Great grunts his displeasure and naps, the stinker! Toto chuckles.

Big Show band, Merle Evans directing, gives concert in big top.

The performance of The Greatest Show On Earth begins—at 2:15.

Dinner is served, with special eating preview for sideshow artists at 3:00. They must be ready for "big show come-out." All others off duty, including performers, start as per schedule.

Matinee performance over. All others eat now.

"Hotel Ringling," cookhouse and all, razed and loaded in trucks and wagons. Cookhouse truck and wagon trains haul off lot to runs. Performers practice in big top. Horse and animal acts too.

Cookhouse trucks, rolling ranges and wagons loaded on "First" at runs.

(Continued on next page)

11

above and opposite
1946 The Ringling Bros. and Barnum & Bailey program featured this four-page spread detailing the daily routine of **setting up the gigantic tent city**, from the arrival of the first trains at 4 A.M. to the departure of the last train at 2 A.M. the following night.

Conditions inside railroad-car sleeping quarters would have made even the sturdiest circus employee opt for time outside on a fair-weather day. Workmen's berths or bunks were often stacked three-high and could be stifling hot or damp. Performer's accommodations varied with their status, ranging from two-high bunks to a stateroom depending on their contract, and each performer had their own trunk, which was unloaded into the dressing room each day. Bathroom facilities in the backyard consisted of those omnipresent water buckets and pit toilets.

Preparing food for a traveling circus was a huge undertaking for those who worked in the cookhouse tent. In the largest circuses, thousands of meals were served each day to performers, staff, and work crews. Hundreds of loaves of bread, pounds of ham, thousands of eggs, and dozens of gallons of milk were consumed at one breakfast alone. If the circus was in town for only one day, as was often the case, the cookhouse staff had to have the dining top and cookhouse taken down, packed in crates and barrels, moved miles away to the next site, and put up again between dinner and the next morning's breakfast. The cookhouse manager had to be a master in scheduling, purchasing, and coordination. Depending on the size of the circus outfit, additional kitchen help was sometimes needed, and local boys were hired to peel potatoes, shell peas, set the tables, or scour pots, all for the magnificent payment of a free ticket to the show.

A flag fluttering from the top of the dining tent announced when a meal was being served. Inside the dining tent were tables made of planks and trestles for easy assembly. Waiters served the performers at their tables depending on the size of the circus, while other circuses served the food buffet-style. Early photographs of the circus sitting down to a meal show performers wearing lots of clothing; the men wear ties, vests, and jackets, and sometimes straw boater hats. The women are draped in long wool skirts and shirtwaists, even on a hot summer's day. In the dining top, the circus mirrored the way the rest of society would have dined: properly dressed, hair coiffed, faces shaved, and tables set with care. Performers were largely not allowed to associate with nonperformers, and the two groups sat on separate sides of the dining tent. Work crews and lesser bosses were served on enameled tinware; the performers and circus officials were served meals on china. Even the length of the tables differed. Workers sat at long tables; performers sat at short ones.

In the early days of the circus, huge hot griddles were kept heated for hours, cooking thousands of pancakes for breakfast. Wood and charcoal-burning stoves were used to stew, fry, or boil tons of meat and vegetables. As traveling ovens were introduced, hundreds of loaves of bread and pies kept the temperatures high and the pace of preparations hot. And after the circus family was fed, the dishes had to be washed (electricity was generally available starting in the 1910s, and dishwashing machines appeared only in the 1930s), every pot and pan scoured and packed away, and every tablecloth packed, wet or dry, clean or soiled. The cookhouse and dining tops came down, and the crates were replaced on the wagons to be transported yet again to the

1950 *Water buckets*, each bearing the name of a performer, were the most common object seen on the back lot. Performers could refill their allocated two buckets whenever fresh water was available.

312

CHAPTER 7

PM — Main Entrance "doors" thrown open for night performance.

Big Show Band Concert.

PM — The Big Show night performance starts.

Menagerie cages and lead stock leaves menagerie tent.

Menagerie lowered, packed and loaded into wagons.

PM — Menagerie area cleared and menagerie cavalcade leaves for the runs. Sideshow dismantled.

Menagerie cages and wagons loaded on first railroad train.

PM — "The First," the first railroad train, with the cookhouse and dining departments and the menagerie, except the elephants, rolls out of town. Tomorrow's another circus day.

The night performance is over. The pundits and the crowds depart.

PM — The big top is filled with the thunder of a falling world, a world tumbling in regimented rhythm and sequence into rumbling wagons and trucks that roll from under acres of sagging and looping canvas. Small tents fade into the night.

Sideshow loaded at runs.

PM — The big top—a great, grey moth, flutters in gigantic, grotesque convulsions to the earth. Men swarm over it unlacing and rolling its flattened sections. Cranes swing the huge bales into wagons. Searchlights sweep the lot.

The big top and dressing room wagons, strung behind power trucks roll down the streets toward the runs.

AM — The big top pole wagon—the last off—leaves the lot, its crew gathering up the street corner guiding flares as it rumbles to the runs.

The second and the third trains are loading. The "Second" soon starts along the sidings to the main line and is away.

AM — All trains have departed, with the possible exception of the "Fourth," which with its load of big top stars and featured performers, its talent and its acumen, moves in dignity and majesty without unseemly haste.

TOMORROW IS ANOTHER DAY
ANOTHER CIRCUS DAY
IN ANOTHER TOWN

12

13

below
1947 **Circus elephants** were much more than gifted performers. During setup they could be seen all over the circus lot pushing heavy wagons, rolling huge canvas bales, transporting poles, and doing every possible task that fit their strength, agility, and intelligence.

next day's lot. The constant traveling during the circus season ended as fall set in and the performers returned to their homes and the animals to the circus' winter quarters. Except for the headlining performers, circus performers typically spent one or two years with the same circus. During the winter months, new acts were choreographed and new troupes scouted for the next year. Invitations from countries abroad meant opportunities for performers to travel the world.

The Romance, and Grit, of the Open Road

The apparent freedom to travel anywhere, to wander the country or the world, indeed, through life, trouble-free, and doing what one most enjoyed, be it swinging from a trapeze or feeding animals, was attractive to those who found society's restrictions more than they could bear. "Running away with the circus" could be a way to travel the country at a time when it wasn't possible, sidestep mainstream society, escape the grind of an office job or an isolated existence on a farm, or, in some cases, escape brutal child abuse, as was the case with legendary circus owner James A. Bailey. Those who did leave their past life and follow the circus out of town often found that circus life was far from glamorous. Backbreaking toil, living conditions, "laws" within the new community, endless travel on dirt roads or sooty rail lines, and perhaps in the end even homesickness could lead many a runaway back home. Other runaways embraced the new lifestyle and in time were accepted into the circus family for life, if they stayed that long. Runaways typically worked on the lot as canvas men, "candy butchers" selling sweets in the stands, waiters, or cage boys who cleaned the animal dens. Runaways who eventually became performers were less common, since this usually required a long-term apprenticeship.

The circus as a metaphor for both the trials and tribulations of life, as well as relief from them, can be seen in literature from the late 19th century. James Otis (1848–1912) discouraged young readers from even considering running away with the circus in his book *Toby Tyler, or Ten Weeks With a Circus*. Serialized in 1880–81, the novel follows young orphan Toby through 10 weeks of cruelty, pain, and some small doses of love while on the road with a circus. As in Tod Browning's film *Freaks* (1932), comfort is offered by the sideshow people. In the end, Toby returns to his uncle's home, having learned his lesson in this didactic tale. In this rendition, to run away with the circus meant to lose one's way, spiritually and morally.

The grueling work and the seemingly endless travel stopped during the winter months. Hired staff would man the winter quarters, and performers would return to

their homes, sometimes in the same city, especially in those where the circus had a prominent presence. In many cases, the winter quarters were at first located in northern states. Later, they were relocated to warmer climates in the West and South. There, performers looked for recuperation and rejuvenation. Back in their "hometowns" some performers sought temporary work in local theaters or vaudeville venues. Others looked for jobs in the town's shops or garages. The wagons or railroad cars were refurbished, the next season's show was planned. Seamstresses spent the winter months designing, sewing, and bejeweling the elaborate costumes. Children might be placed in city schools, and families could enjoy "real" beds in their seasonal rental homes. There was leisure time to paste last season's newspaper clippings and photographs into scrapbooks. Cities, like Sarasota, Florida, grew as circus performers returned for the winter, or to retire and reminisce, or, in the end, to die and be buried alongside their former fellow performers. And with the coming of spring, the burnished wagons and brightly painted railroad cars carried the circus performers, their talents, and their magic back onto the roads and rails crisscrossing America. Once again, it was time for another year's "sublime spectacle."

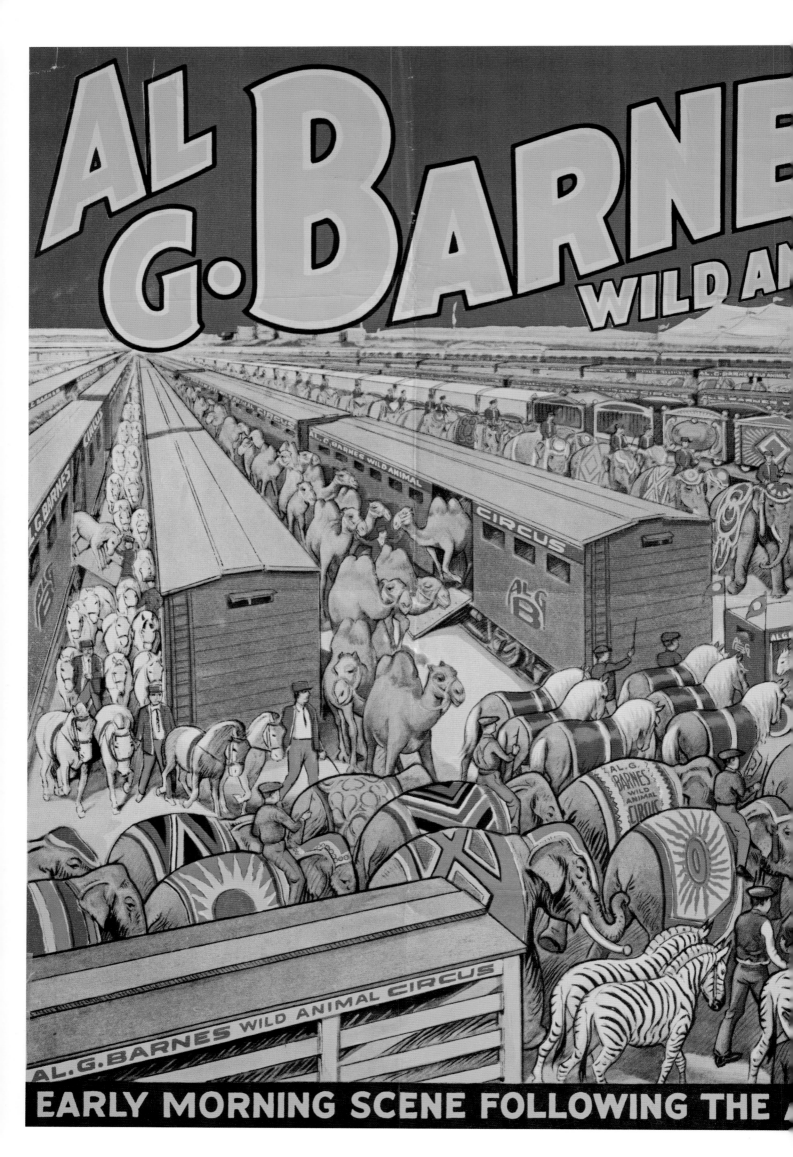

pages 314–315
1934 ***The arrival of circus trains*** was an attraction in itself, and circuses, like Al G. Barnes, used that image in the huge posters they plastered all over town and on surrounding barns whose farmers were then rewarded with complimentary tickets.

right and center
1937 and 1952 Boys and girls got up early to head to the railroad yard and watch the unloading of the ***zoo on wheels*** that was the circus train. For the few who couldn't afford a ticket to the show, this scene was the next best thing.

below
1948 A huge crowd is awaiting the uncharacteristically late arrival of the Cole Bros. circus train in Delavan, Wisconsin. ***Circus Day has already begun***, and everyone is there to enjoy it from start to finish, especially since this part is free of charge.

1949 The systems and equipments used to load and unload the circus trains had been perfected by W. C. Coup, Barnum's partner, in 1872, and had not changed much by 1949, when the Cole Bros. circus unloaded its *colorful 1903 wagon, America,* remodeled to house a calliope.

1923 The golden age of the circus was assured in 1872 when P. T. Barnum announced boldly that his show would *travel entirely by railroad.* This would radically change circus economics, making it a phenomenon and the largest entertainment industry the world had ever seen.

1915 To the crowd gathered on the rail yards, the emergence of the first animal from the circus' boxcars felt like all of ***Africa, India, and Asia had landed*** in one's hometown.

1959 The circus was created by horsemen in 1770 in England. More than 150 years later, in 1959, any self-respecting circus had high-quality equine performers. Ringling Bros. and Barnum & Bailey's ***horses were numerous and beautiful*** and a sight to behold to any who witnessed the unloading of the circus train.

opposite
1959 Seeing the elephants, perennial audience favorites, appearing from their stock cars was the ***most anticipated moment for the crowd*** who'd come to watch. This, more than anything else, meant that the circus was in town at last.

opposite

1946 The important "king pole" is up. Hundreds of men repeated the ritual every morning: hammering stakes, erecting giant poles, hauling up vast expanses of canvas, all with amazing precision and efficiency. For many *African American laborers* who had a hard time finding jobs in a racially divided country, the circus remained an important employer. But the work was far from easy.

1902 "*Thousands of stakes* are driven into the ground by gangs of sledge-hammer drivers, who will surround a stake and with unerring aim and in perfect cadence drive it many feet into the solid ground in less time than it takes to read this description," (Barnum & Bailey, *Realm: A Magazine of Marvels*, 1903)

1956 Unfolding the *gigantic big top canvas* required an army of workers, many of whom were hired for the day from the town's available workforce. Teenagers helped, too, with menial work in exchange for complimentary passes.

1915 *"76,000 yards of canvas* are made into the world's largest big top…with its cordage, weighs 19 tons, three times that when wet. There are 73 miles of rope in the Big Show's tents and, reduced to a single strand, it would more than encircle the globe." (Ringling Bros. and Barnum & Bailey program, 1949)

1943 The raising of the *big top's center poles* was always a spectacular sight and the first sign that the giant city of canvas was at last taking shape. Between the six poles of the Ringling Bros. and Barnum & Bailey tent, the show would unfold on three rings and two stages and seat 12,000 to 14,000 spectators.

322

above
1950 *High-wire legend Harold Alzana*
checks the cables and stakes that hold his high
wire under the big top. The paper cups, at right,
were put on the stakes so that others wouldn't
trip accidentally. Performers always checked their
rigging after it was first set up and again before
each of the two daily shows. Their lives often
depended on it.

below
1948 The swift and amazingly efficient setup
of the giant city ***attracted huge crowds*** to the
lot, who watched the fascinating preshow free
of charge, as perhaps they had watched that
unloading of the circus train and would have
watched, in the old days, the street parade.

pages 326–327

1896 "To construct and dismantle this metropolis of amusement, to give *over 300 performances in 150 cities*…these are a miracle to me. The exploits of Hannibal, Alexander, and Napoleon…would be nothing but weekend runs for present-day tent showmen." (Dexter Fellows, *This Way to the Big Top*, 1936)

1915 Erecting the giant city of canvas was the same every day, fast and complex, ready for showtime within hours. It was *a true miracle of efficiency*. The big top was the largest tent, fronted by the vast menagerie tent through which the audience entered. The line of sideshow banners can be seen, bottom right, in front of the sideshow tent, leading to the circus' main entrance. Flanking the big top were the dressing tents, the wardrobe tent, Clown Alley, smaller department tents, and the huge dining tent, bottom left.

1906 The bleachers have been installed, the intricate rigging of aerial apparatuses is done, the lights are up, and sawdust has been laid in the rings. Tonight, after the show, *everything will disappear in just a few hours*.

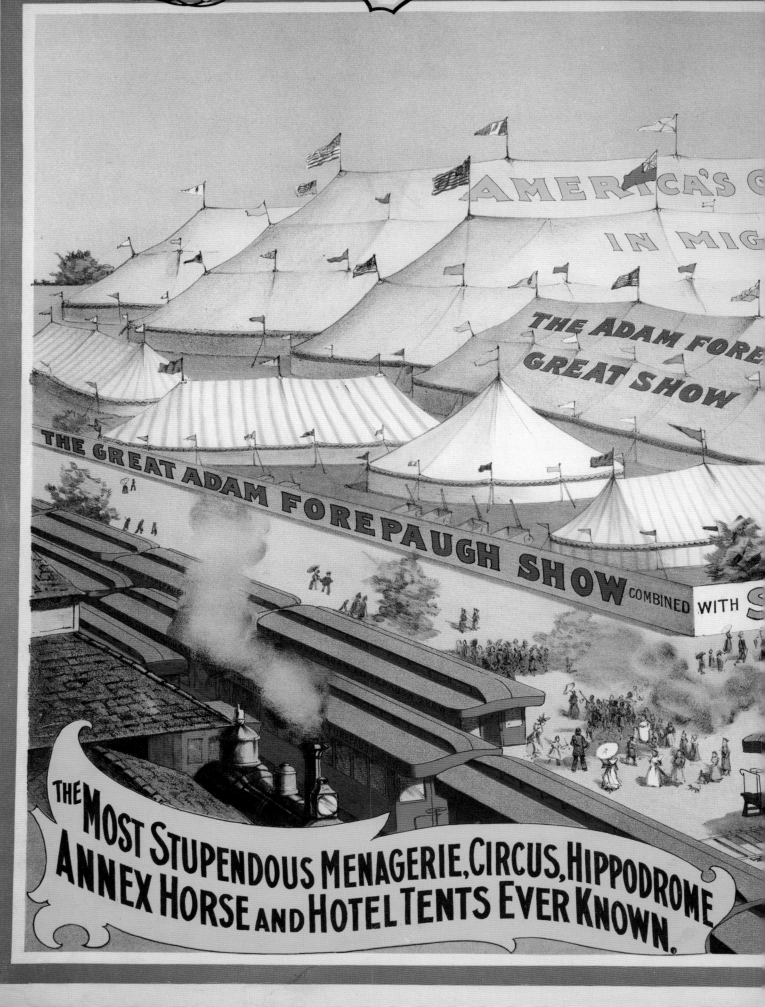

pages 328–329
1942 These showgirls, who just participated in the Ringling Bros. and Barnum & Bailey's "Ballet of the Elephants" (choreographed by George Balanchine to an Igor Stravinsky score), ***rush to the dressing tent*** to change costumes for the next pageant.

opposite
1949 Another snapshot that will end up in this performer's scrapbook after the end of the season: posing, ready to enter the big top, in front of circus props with a ***Band-Aid on her leg*** due to a recent, but small, injury.

1953 Glamour is found under the big top, not on the back lot. In the heat of a summer day, ***showgirl Toni Scott*** rests her tired feet in her water bucket and fans herself while waiting in the dressing tent for her next cue.

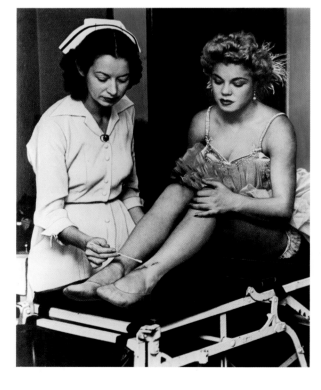

1950s Circus is by nature a hazardous occupation. Ringling Bros. and Barnum & Bailey had a doctor and sometimes a nurse on staff, too, shown here attending to a performer who had injured herself. In spite of the number of people put at risk daily in the circus, ***accidents were quite rare***.

1949 The back lot is a ***training ground*** for acrobats between shows. A trick that didn't go well during the last performance, a new act, or a simple warm-up is worked out on any space available between the big top and the dressing tents.

1950 A ***tumbling run*** on the tender grass of the back lot can be a warm-up, a way to relax one's nerves, or sometimes a competition between acrobats just for the fun of it. For most of them, tumbling was the foundation of their apprenticeship.

1902 During showtime, traffic on the back lot was similar to that of a big city: heavy and dangerous. When a ***herd of galloping horses*** left the big top, you'd better pay attention and keep your distance from the traffic area.

above
1940s Free time was a rare commodity on the circus lot, but performers could find time to relax between shows. ***Playing chess was a favorite*** pastime among men, as well as card playing, soccer, or baseball, and going fishing if a body of water was nearby.

below
1940 Like everybody else in the outside world, circus performers celebrated holidays. On July 4, 1940, a ***pie-eating contest*** was launched on the Ringling Bros. and Barnum & Bailey back lot.

center
1957 Helen Wallenda, like all circus performers, spent much of her life between the train and the dressing tent, with visits to the dining tent and, of course, performing under the big top. The back lot was her true home, however, where throwing a party meant ***cooking a welcome barbecue*** for fellow performers.

1951 Many circus children have been raised—and trained—on the circus back lot. Here, at a party with circus friends in the shadow of the big top, *famed equestrian Alberto Zoppé* engages in a balancing act with his son Tino in a pose so classic that it can be found in the scrapbooks of many performers—and parents.

1926 Although aerialist Lillian Leitzel didn't have children of her own, she considered all circus children her extended family, and they were always welcome in her private dressing tent. Here Dolly Jahn, the daughter of perch-pole balancer Hans Jahn, *plays on the warm-up Roman rings* of the circus superstar.

pages 336–337
1954 The dressing tent was home to a circus woman who knew how to use it for all its worth—including *stretching laundry lines* between its ropes on a washing day.

opposite
1954 To take a full bath in a *real bathtub was a luxury* that circus performers could afford only during a long stand or on a Sunday if the circus was not moving: They had to rent a hotel room with a bath for the occasion. For this lucky circus toddler, a water bucket did the trick.

above
1920s To circus *children raised on the back lot*, this is what a shower meant: two water buckets and a sprinkle of cold water on a sunny day on the back lot.

below
1944 For circus children, the back lot was everything—a backyard, a playground, a laundry room, a shower room, or a training place—and they felt *a keen sense of community*. The circus was their extended family.

left
1900s In major circuses executives and top performers had their own ***dining car on the circus train***, replete with waiters and a trained chef. On special occasions, the chef even issued fancy printed menus heralding the specials of the day.

below
1935 In ***the dining tent*** performers and administrative staff ate at separate tables. Within the performers' space, there was also a class system: The higher the status, the shorter the table. Short tables were reserved for performers and management, who were expected to dress appropriately.

1941 An iconic figure of the Ringling Bros. and Barnum & Bailey circus, *clown Lou Jacob puffs on a cigar of his own brand*, with one of the legendary Cristiani bareback riders. Clowns were fond of oversized props, which could be spotted easily in the vast big top.

right
1902 The last meal was served between 4 and 5:30 P.M., before the evening show. Then the dining tents were struck down, and all the cooking equipment, including these *oversized coffee pots*, were packed in the dining department wagons that were then loaded on the first circus train to arrive in the next town.

RINGLING-BARNUM COOK HOUSE
FOURTH OF JULY ———— 1935
FITCHBURG, MASS.

pages 346–347

1954 The spec *Dreamland* is ready to go and the ***showgirls put on their monkey outfits***. "The Circus is a village, if you will, situated on the border between Real and Make-Believe.… It is a will-o'-the-wisp sort of village, here today and gone tomorrow." ("The Secret of its Charm," excerpt from the *San Francisco Chronicle*, Ringling Bros. and Barnum & Bailey program, 1951)

1920s It is ***not easy being a clown***. Clowns and showgirls were the performers who spent the most time in the ring. Sitting on his trunk in Clown Alley, this one takes advantage of a rare idle moment to take a quick nap.

opposite

1940s This contortionist, photographed by ***design legends Charles and Ray Eames*** on their trip to the circus, has finished his act and is relaxing near the ring entrance. Contortionists favored vertically striped costumes, which enhanced the lines of their bodies when they folded themselves like human pretzels.

1954 Ringling Bros. and Barnum & Bailey ***clown Charlie Bell is putting on his makeup in the open***, a rare occurrence since clowns typically made up away from prying eyes in the privacy of Clown Alley. It was washing day for some performers whose pink leotards are drying in the background.

SECONDS FROM

DEATH

RISKING

LIFE & LIMB

FOR THE CROWD

Dominique Jando

ZAZEL.

ZAZEL, the HUMAM PROJECTILE

SECONDS
FROM
DEATH
RISKING
LIFE & LIMB
FOR THE CROWD

Dominique Jando

Before Evel Knievel or reality television shows began offering dangerous and spectacular stunts, the circus offered daredevilry on a scale never seen before. Above all, the circus offered a version of the daredevil that was up close and personal. It was a direct, live experience and deeply human—emulated today in contemporary action films, television, and the world of cartoon superheroes, yet only in two dimensions. In the circus there was no possible staging or trickery, and one couldn't help but empathize with the daredevils. Their (and, therefore, our) triumphant victory over "daring the devil" during their performances was cause for celebration. To be sure, circus performers play with extremes: precarious balance, dizzying heights, extraordinary displays of strength and agility, and lurking, if not always apparent, danger. In essence, the circus is about overcoming our limitations, doing the seemingly impossible—from a simple somersault to a seven-person pyramid on a high wire. But daredevils, who are generally the final punctuation of the circus performance, present the audience with the ultimate thrill: watching someone truly overcome a life-threatening challenge.

opposite,
1881 Born Rosa Richter, *Zazel was one of the very first human cannonballs.* She was catapulted from a cannon to a trapeze. Introduced to American audiences by P. T. Barnum's *Greatest Show on Earth* in 1880, her breathtaking Eagle Swoop was a worldwide sensation.

page 349
1949 *Sylvana Zacchini* was a member of the American circus' royal family of daredevils. Seeing her shot from a giant cannon was an awe-inspiring and alarming vision, yet her daring certainly attracted audiences to the big top.

Victory of Life Over Death

Danger, even if it's a matter of perception, is also what attracts audiences to the big top. Whatever the level of artistry of a performance, and notwithstanding the fact that a vast majority of circus performers try to keep genuine risks in check, true circus daredevils do not play with danger, they defy it. Although performing daredevils prepare their stunts carefully, true danger is what defines their act. Their goal, however, is to end the act unscathed and work the next season. And this is ultimately what their audiences want to see—victory of life over death, proof of our ability to survive the most challenging circumstances. In this way the daredevil, and by extension the circus, is a modern incarnation of ceremonial rituals of survival and resurrection. Daredevils offer their own version of these rituals, albeit as entertainment.

In the 18th and 19th centuries, equestrian acts, which were mostly acrobats on horseback, formed the core of early circus performances, and these performers were the daredevils of their day. It was truly awesome to see someone stand on one foot, posing like Mercury, on the back of a galloping horse. But long before equestrians began mesmerizing early circus audiences with their extraordinary stunts in the 1770s, the first performing daredevils were ropedancers who performed high above the crowds of the great medieval fairs. By the end of the 18th century, those who constantly pushed the limits of their ropewalking audacity acquired unprecedented fame in their communities—perhaps not coincidentally about the time when the word "daredevil" appeared in common English usage. Long before the famous Wallendas staged their seven-person high-wire pyramid in American circuses in the 1950s and '60s, ropewalkers' stunts riveted audiences. In 1859 the legendary Jean-François Emile Gravelet, better known as Blondin, was the first person ever to walk over the gorge of Niagara Falls on a 3-inch-thick, quarter-mile-long rope, stretched 160 feet above the water. He repeated the stunt several times, sometimes blindfolded or pushing a wheelbarrow, and even once carrying his fearless (or suicidal) manager on his back. Not in a position to compete with the extravagant stunts of Blondin and his numerous imitators, the ropedancers and wire walkers of circus and variety shows had to devise elaborate stunts of their own, more adapted to the constraints of their performance space.

Circuses also imported daredevils from fairgrounds where, by the mid-19th century, traveling showmen began to appear as they had for centuries in Europe. These acts were sometimes crude: Alois Peters, advertised in show programs and posters as "the Man Who Hangs Himself," dove from a high platform with a long rope fastened around his neck in a hangman's noose. To the amazement of the audience, he ended his jump dangling from his rope, still alive, except on the fateful occasion when the noose slipped and Peters hung himself. The danger of most daredevil acts is unfortunately all too real, and what should be a celebration of survival can sometimes—and, thankfully, rarely—become a tragedy.

Breakneck Speeds & High-Hurdle Heights

We have all jolted awake at night after feeling a free fall in our dreams. In the circus, daredevils transform the free-fall nightmare into a sensational act where the frightening fall ends in a safe landing. Daredevils like Alois Peters used this well-known feeling to confront the fears of audiences, who hope that, like in good dreams, the fall will be interrupted by a safe landing. Time and again, the free fall has been used by daredevils. A classic free-fall stunt is a dive from a high platform, landing after a somersault or two on a small crash mat, or plunging headfirst into a narrow water basin, both of which look to the audience like targets too narrow to be reached. To the diver, this was not an illusion either. The smallness of the target, combined with the height of the plunge, presented a genuine risk. One of the most bizarre stunts in the free-fall category was the performer Desperado's "terrible" Leap for Life, in which the daredevil jumped from a platform in a "terrific descent of 80 feet through space, landing upon his chest on a skid placed at an angle of 50 degrees," as promoted in a 1909 Barnum & Bailey poster.

During the Industrial Revolution in the 19th century, daredevils began devising new stunts using mechanical devices. One of the first of these stunts was the spectacular human cannonball, an act that never ceased bewildering crowds and is as popular today as it was when it first appeared in America on the Yankee Robinson show in 1875. The original catapulting system, whose concept was still at the core of the giant cannons used in the 20th century by the legendary Zacchinis, was devised by the colorful character Guillermo Antonio Farini. Born in Canada as the less exotic-sounding William Leonard Hunt, "Signor Farini" was himself a daredevil. Like Blondin, he had crossed the Niagara gorge on a tightrope, once adding his own personal touch to the stunt by carrying a washing machine strapped on his back—one of the first product placements in show business. He had a brilliant career as a ropewalker and daredevil in circuses and vaudeville houses all over Canada and the United States and later as a celebrated flying trapeze artist with his young adopted son, Samuel, known as "El Niño." When Farini retired from performing, he patented a catapulting contraption

that could send his son flying several feet in the air to catch a trapeze. It was a rather crude device placed directly on the stage floor; there was no cannon to dramatize the effect. A handsome boy, "El Niño" Farini performed his vertical flight through the air as none other than the graceful and elegant "Mademoiselle Lulu," described in the press as "the eighth wonder of the world." Lulu was a sensation in Paris before mesmerizing New York audiences in 1873. Farini knew, like any circus pressman worth his salt, that a death-defying stunt always looked much more dramatic if performed by a beautiful young woman.

Defying the Laws of Gravity

In show business, the success of others has always been a source of inspiration. Two years later another acrobat, George Loyal, who hailed from an old French circus dynasty and worked in American circuses, adapted Farini's catapulting system and installed it inside a giant cannon barrel, becoming the first human cannonball. To be shot from the mouth of a cannon instantly became the ultimate act of daredevilry. A cannon symbolized danger, destruction, and death, and when combined with a living person formed an awe-inspiring and alarming vision. Loyal improved on the Farinis's spectacle with Ella Zuila, "the Ethereal Queen," a genuine female acrobat who was propelled 60 feet from the cannon to a trapeze, just like Lulu Farini but with the stunning addition of smoke effects and a powder-inducted thundering "Boom!" Farini didn't hesitate to answer this challenge with a bigger barrel, at first suspended in the air, from which the beautiful Zazel, British-born Rosa Richter, was catapulted to a trapeze bar suspended high above the ground. She then landed in a safety net. This breathtaking daredevil act was known as the Eagle Swoop and became a worldwide sensation. P. T. Barnum introduced the thrilling Zazel to American audiences in 1880, and she was as popular as she had been in Europe.

Zazel's fame paved the way for many imitators, some of whom introduced interesting variations to the stunt, such as Alar, "the Human Arrow," who replaced the cannon barrel with a gigantic crossbow. Alar was catapulted from it in a "terrific and sensational flight through the air, piercing a target 80 feet from the bow," claimed a 1896 Barnum & Bailey poster. After passing through the bull's eye of the paper target, she caught the hands of a catcher hanging from a trapeze. For once, circus press agents were at a loss for words: The 1896 Barnum & Bailey posters deemed the act "terrific and sensational," although to circus crowds it was certainly much more than that. The woman lying powerless on the oversized crossbow seemed like a mythological, sacrificial creature. When she suddenly took flight, one felt that she was bound for heaven.

By the 1890s, however, the human cannonball vogue had dissipated. It was replaced by another stunt more attuned to the new fad of its day: bicycle riding. Daredevils, always in search of a new, more exciting stunt, came up with the Looping the Loop stunt on a bicycle. It proved such a hit that, as soon as the automobile entered everyday life, it was put to the loop-the-loop test too. In the bicycle stunt, a giant track went from an elevated platform to the ground and curled back up into a complete loop before returning to the floor. The bicycling daredevil started from the plat-

1930 Before Evel Knievel or extreme reality television shows, the circus offered live daredevilry on a scale never seen before. *Former trapeze artist Wilno* was inspired to create a cannonball act in the late 1920s after meeting one of its originators, the legendary Zazel.

form high up above the ring, gaining speed in the descent, and then rode up and around the 360-degrees loop before reaching the sawdust.

A Frightful Flight With Fate

Whatever the real or apparent danger of a stunt, there is always another daredevil to make it even more dangerous. This is the true spirit of daredevilry. The Ancilottis, an old family of Italian acrobats, performed the bicycle stunt at the turn of the 20th century with Barnum & Bailey, using a loop whose top section had been taken out. As a result, at the apex of his looping, Ugo Ancillotti made a jump in space, head down and wheels up, between the two remaining sections of the loop track. The Ancillottis brought yet another improvement to the stunt, "a fearful frolic and frightful flight with Fate," as described in the circus courier with the colorful alliterations of which circus press agents were so fond. It was "a hazardous dual achievement, so full and fraught with peril as to fascinate, enthrall, astound and please all spectators. Approaching each other from widely separate starting points, the artistes meet and are seen flying in space in the same direction, one upside down, when striking opposite sections of the apparatus they ride safely away in opposite directions, thus presenting a double paradox." In actuality, the two-person stunt was considerably shorter and much simpler and more spectacular than the "paradox" described so floridly.

Looping the Loop in an automobile required an even bigger and more complex piece of equipment. This act was first performed in 1905 on the Barnum & Bailey show by its pioneer, "the fearless, young and fascinating Parisian" Mauricia de Tiers, whose original *Bilboquet Humain* (human cup-and-ball) stunt had been an unprecedented sensation at the Casino de Paris and all over Europe. In her stunt in America, Mademoiselle de Tiers performed in her *auto bolide* (meteor car) a "dreadful, headlong leap, loop, and topsy turvy somersault," as described by the Barnum & Bailey program. Her little car slid down a railed ramp that turned it upside down at its curling end, at which point her vehicle was released free into a full somersault and landed on its four wheels on another ramp that led it to the ground. It was an extraordinary stunt in more than one aspect: It was spectacular, it was modern, and it was performed by a thoroughly modern, "liberated" woman. In time, to keep the crowds in awe, somersaulting cars would graduate to double and triple somersaults.

In the circus, daredevils also used bicycles in combination with other dangerous contraptions like the Wall of Death. A circular wooden track, it was made of

separate planks placed on a double railing so that the audience could see through it. When the bicyclist reached a sufficient speed to keep running on the track, the basket was sometimes hauled up far above the ring, revealing a terrifying hole through which the daredevil could fall if he ever lost his momentum. Other times, to make the effect more dramatic the "basket" had a bottom, which suddenly opened when the contraption had reached an alarming height under the big top. It was a nerve-racking vision, and the act required a bicyclist with amazing strength and stamina, not to mention courage. In time the bicycle was replaced with a motorcycle, and the act evolved into the modern Globe of Death, a meshed, metallic sphere in which two or more motorcyclists ride in all directions at dizzying speeds trying not to collide. On the old fairgrounds, the Wall of Death even involved crude automobiles as well as motorcycles.

In the 1920s the good old human cannonball made a spectacular comeback. A former bicycle-and-automobile circus daredevil, German-born Paul Leinert had rediscovered the forgotten thrills of Farini's and Loyal's cannons. But Leinert had one built that was even more impressive than the smaller versions of his predecessors, and he revived the attraction in Europe with great success. The cannon from which he hurled himself was bigger, louder, and more powerful—perfect ingredients for a great thrill act—than any of the cannons ever seen in the circus. Modern technology could make the act much more spectacular than it ever was, and human cannonballs blossomed again all over the circus world. Soon after, Cliff Aeros, another famous German daredevil, was running three such acts in America in various circuses between 1926 and 1929.

So the human cannonball was back with a bang, and this time was here to stay. One of the most famous of them, "the Great Wilno," born Otto Wiedrich in Dresden, Germany, had been a watchmaker before becoming a trapeze artist and finally a daredevil. By 1929, inspired by a meeting with the legendary and by then retired Zazel, Wilno was performing with considerable success under American big tops with a giant cannon, which he eventually mounted on a truck, making the huge contraption faster to set up and transport. In 1930 even Fred "Fearless" Gregg, who had acquired a certain degree of fame looping the loop with his little car, switched for a cannon he had bought from Cliff Aeros. Many others followed, like Luis Raluy, who had two people shot simultaneously from his cannon, supposedly doubling the thrill for his audiences.

5901-23

The Most Famous Name in Daredevilry

The most legendary name in human cannonball daredevilry is of course Zacchini. Like Wilno, Ildebrando Zacchini, the first-generation owner of a small Italian family circus, had been inspired by Zazel. And like Wilno, he, too, had envisioned a much bigger cannon. His son, Edmondo, who had a degree in mechanical engineering, designed and built a gigantic contraption, which he mounted on a truck and used for the first time in 1922. By 1926 they had built a bigger, more powerful cannon, which sent Vittorio, Edmondo's brother, to a distance of 100 feet and a height of 50 feet. The stunt took this circus favorite to a whole new level. Edmondo had two other brothers, Hugo and Bruno, who duplicated the act. In 1929 John Ringling brought Hugo and Bruno to America, and the rest of the family soon followed them. The many children of the Zacchini brothers entered the business, and by the 1950s one could see all over America a fearless Zacchini or two shot from the mouth of a giant cannon with a bang and a cloud of smoke. Performing with the circus and fairgrounds across the country, the Zacchini family had become America's greatest thrill suppliers, turned into living legends by journalists following the lead of the ever-

efficient American circus press agents. The Zacchini name became synonymous with circus daredevilry.

Why do daredevils like Lulu Farini, Zazel, Mauricia de Tiers, Desperado, "the Great Wilno", the Wallendas, and the Zacchinis fascinate us? In the circus, daredevils are creatures of flesh and blood, defying death right in front of us. In this their aptitude for overcoming the most terrifying situations is a far more visceral and potent experience than the action-hero feats of the silver screen, television, or comic books. Those are fun and fascinating for sure, but they don't operate on our human scale. In the circus, audiences can see themselves in these amazing performers. By living the thrill of the daredevil, every member of the audience experiences a vicarious triumph. "I don't know exactly what the circus gave me," reflected the Russian novelist and playwright Maxim Gorky, "except that I saw people risking their lives with grace for the entertainment of their fellow men; yet I think that's enough." His reflections go to the heart of the circus: "Everything I saw in the ring blended into something triumphant, where skill and strength confidentially celebrated their victory over mortal danger."

1900s A group of Barnum & Bailey's acrobats present *a humorous backstage take on the human cannonball* stunt using a clown-gag prop. True circus daredevils do not play with danger: They defy it.

above
ca. 1959 The *Italian daredevil Hugo Zacchini* came to America in 1929 with a giant cannon built by his brother Edmondo. His spectacular stunts and savvy press agents made him a sensation. This photograph is from his performance in *The Big Circus* (1959).

left and below
1930s Fred "Fearless" Gregg engineered a ***double Looping the Loop*** stunt with an automobile, adding an extra thrill to an already popular act. He sent two cars down a ramp, at the end of which one car was propelled into a somersault while the other passed underneath. The drivers, his wife, Bette, and his brother-in-law, Henry Le Grave, only had to sit still in the vehicles. The stunt was a prowess of engineering. Bette Gregg can be seen performing the stunt for the last time in the movie *Pennies From Heaven* (1936), starring Bing Crosby.

1938 With time, to keep the crowds in awe, single-somersaulting cars would graduate to double or triple somersaults, as did those of *"the Great Florenzo"* who faced death "twice daily" with the Cole Bros. circus.

1930s Daredevils like *the "Fearless" Greggs* performed on fairgrounds such as this one in Long Beach, California. The Greggs also played circuses such as the Gollmar Bros. during the early 1900s. In both cases, their stunts attracted large crowds.

THE ADAM FOREPAUGH AND SELLS BROTHERS
AMERICA'S GREATEST SHOWS CONSOLIDATED

UPON AN ORDINARY ROAD BICYCLE,
DASHING DOWN A GIANT STAIRWAY FROM THE
MADISON SQUARE GARDEN ROOF TO THE GROUND
BELOW. A SHEER DESCENT OF OVER ONE HUNDRED FEET

KILPATRICK'S FAMOUS RIDE

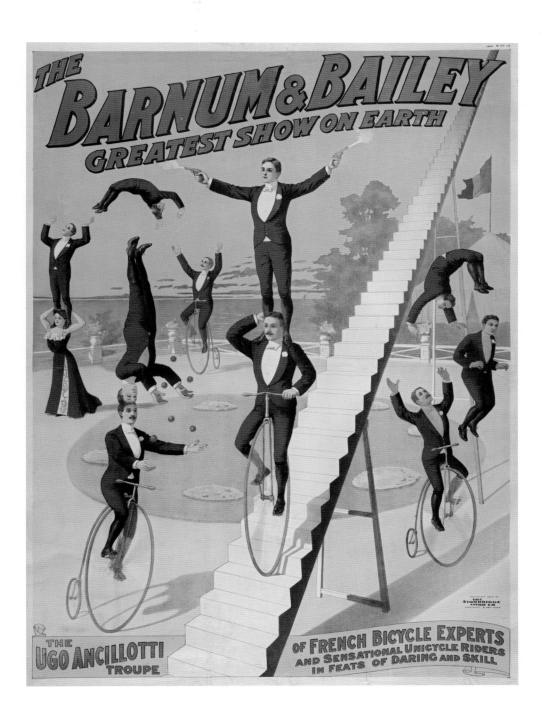

1901 Audiences wanted to see daredevils flirt with death, but ultimately rise above it, as seen in this photograph of *Max "Dare Devil" Schreyer* at an amusement park. The daredevil, and by extension the circus, is a modern incarnation of rituals of survival and resurrection.

The Great Adam Forepaugh and Sells Bros. Enormous Shows United

Tremendous, Thrilling, Fire-Show Spectacle of Fighting The Flames. 8 Big Bewildering Circuses in 3 Big Rings, on 3 Mammoth Stages. Gigantic Greco-Roman Arenic Eclipse, Presenting More than Three Hundred Artists and Performers and Showing an Additional Canopied Entablature of Earthward Suspended and Skyward Projecting Dare-Devil Aerial Sensations Climaxed by the Blood-Chilling TRIP TO THE MOON.

THE ABSOLUTE HAZARD OF ALL HAZARDOUS DEATH-DEFYING-FEATS,

THE TERRIBLE TRIP TO THE MOON

AN AWFUL HOLDING OF LIFE AS A PAWN.

REACHING THE CRESCENT OR DASHING TO DEATH.

Presenting a Giant Show so Big as to Make of All Others Mere Side Shows, so Vast in Size as to Defy the World to Produce One, Half its Equal.

ABSOLUTELY THE SENSATION OF ALL SENSATIONS.

TREMENDOUS All-Embracing, OMNI-ARK MENAGERIE Of All The World's Wild Animal Life.

PRESENTING EVERY MORNING AT 10 O'CLOCK THE MOST COLOSSAL GORGEOUS

BIG FREE STREET PARADE

EVER SEEN BY HUMAN EYES, INAUGURATING ABSOLUTELY THE GREATEST SHOW ON EARTH.

TWO COMPLETE EXHIBITIONS DAILY, AT 2 AND 8 P. M. DOORS OPEN ONE HOUR EARLIER. ONE 50-CENT TICKET ADMITS TO EVERYTHING. CHILDREN UNDER 12 YEARS OF AGE, HALF-PRICE, SPECIAL LOW RATE EXCURSIONS ON ALL RAILROADS

1890s Forepaugh & Sells Bros. presented *"the terrible Trip to the Moon,"* in which the daredevil dashed down a ramp, let go of his bicycle, and flew up into a moon-shaped net. It was, said the poster, "an awful holding of life as a pawn; reaching the crescent or dashing to death."

right and below
right and below
1904 *Looping the Gap,* presented by Maurice Ancillotti with Barnum & Bailey, was an improvement on the Looping the Loop stunt on a bicycle. A section of the looping track had been removed, which meant that the daredevil jumped through space with head down and wheels up. The Ancillottis, who were remarkable bicycle acrobats, were also the most successful bicycling stuntmen at the turn of the 20th century. They consistently imagined new, increasingly daring stunts, which kept them performing for many years.

1900s *Diavolo's Looping the Loop contraption* was a huge and complicated setup that was rigged before the show and stayed there. Here it is shown outside, but it was also possible to set it up under the vast expanse of the American big top, allowing daredevils to flourish there.

1905 The *Ancillottis's double-bicycle stunt* was described in the 1905 Barnum & Bailey program as "a hazardous dual achievement, so full and fraught with peril as to fascinate, enthrall, astound and please all spectators."

opposite
1904 Performing his Looping the Loop bicycle stunt with the Forepaugh & Sells Bros. circus, *Diavolo, the "danger deriding, death defying, desperate daredevil,"* chose not only to dare the devil but to be the devil with his costume.

1902 S. N° 92

ING RACES BETWEEN FROM TWO TO SEVEN RIDERS ON AN OPEN FENCE TRACK ONLY
ER PITCHED AT AN ACUTE ANGLE OF 70°. ALSO MARVELOUS TRICK & FANCY RIDING.

pages 364–365

1902 *The Gaynell Troupe* was billed as the "7 Wild Wheel Whirl Wonders" and raced via bicycles on a wooden track, 5 feet high and 20 feet in diameter, inclined at a steep angle.

1900s *Alexander Patty hopped on his head* down a flight of stairs on the Ringling Bros. back lot to the amazement of a crowd who'd gathered to witness this unusual, and rather painful, acrobatic stunt free of charge.

1908 Circus advertising liked to improve upon acts such as *Alexander Patty's upside-down acrobatics.* Compare this poster to the actual stunt, above, performed by a much less elegant Patty.

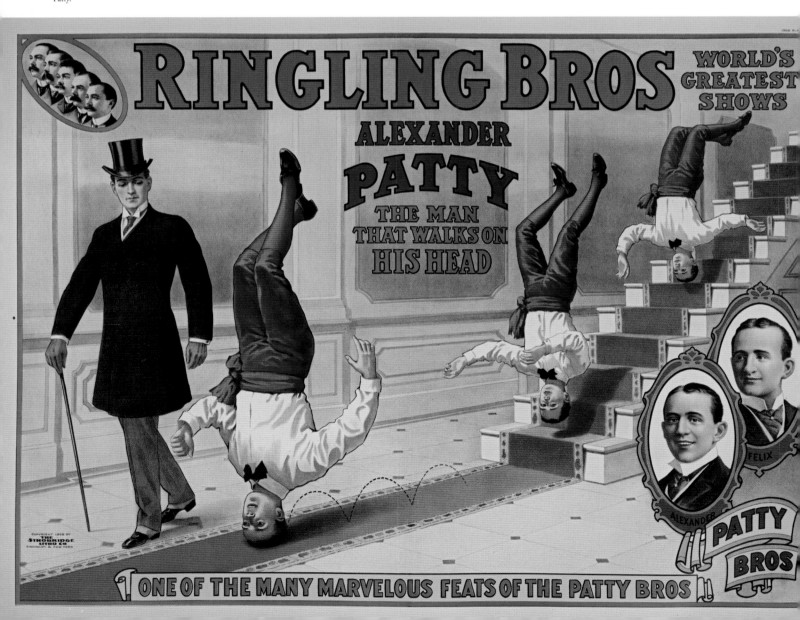

1900s Fire was often used by daredevils. A classic example was a *free fall with the performer's overalls aflame* that ended by plunging into a small water basin or water-filled pit. Some performers even added fire to the basin by coating the water's surface with a layer of gasoline.

1900s "*High diving horses* are the latest novelty in the line of animal performers.... During the seconds that elapse between the dive and the striking of the water, the spectators stand breathless with astonishment and repressed excitement.... The horses seem to take the feat without a bit of fear and jump without any urging." (*Mexia Evening Ledger*, September 15, 1899)

opposite
1882 The worldwide success of the daring **Zazel, "the Human Projectile,"** was so wide-spread that her act appeared in children's books such as *The Children's Circus and Menagerie Picture Book*, published jointly in New York and London in 1882.

right
1881 **The Eagle Swoop,** Zazel's breathtaking flight from a cannon to a trapeze, made her an instant international celebrity. Her "startling performance…literally hurled her from the jaws of death into the arms of fame," claimed the Lincoln, Nebraska, *Evening News* in 1895.

pages 370–371
1888 In the early 1880s, the Barnum & London circus advertised several female daredevils as human cannonballs performing a **Dive for Life**. The thrill of watching a woman perform death-defying stunts was more exciting for turn-of-the-century audiences than watching men.

left
1877 Zazel's original catapulting system had been devised by the colorful character Guillermo Antonio Farini, a former daredevil who, like Blondin, crossed Niagara Falls on a tightrope. **Zazel's first cannon** was suspended in the air, as seen in this 1877 photograph. Farini is watching Zazel, bottom right.

center
1881 **George Loyal** was the first daredevil to conceal Farini's original catapult in a cannon barrel in 1875. He improved the spectacle with his wife, Ella Zuila, "the Ethereal Queen," who dangled from a trapeze, catching him at the end of his 60-foot flight. They also added smoke effects and a gunpowder "Boom!"

To MY DEAR FRIEND
FRANK J. WALTER
FROM
Hugo Zacchini
S. R 1948

right
1940s Human cannonball ***Bruno Zacchini***
is surrounded by a crowd of young admirers.
The Zacchini family performed with circuses
and fairgrounds across the country and become
America's greatest thrill suppliers long before
Evel Knievel.

right
1933 The giant cannon used by Hugo Zacchini (here on the Ringling Bros. and Barnum & Bailey back lot) had been **designed by his brother Edmondo,** who had a degree in mechanical engineering. It could send any of the Zacchini brothers (Hugo, Bruno, Vittorio) to a distance of 100 feet at a height of 50 feet.

opposite
1948 John Ringling brought **Hugo Zacchini** to the U. S. in 1929, and the rest of the family soon followed. The many Zacchini children entered the business, and by the 1950s one could find a fearless Zacchini or two being shot from the mouths of giant cannons all over America.

1929 When Hugo Zacchini came from Italy to perform in 1929, the circus advertised his act using a **classic war cannon** instead of the slick state-of-the-art, motorized silver cannon he actually used. The poster artist likely had not yet seen the new cannon.

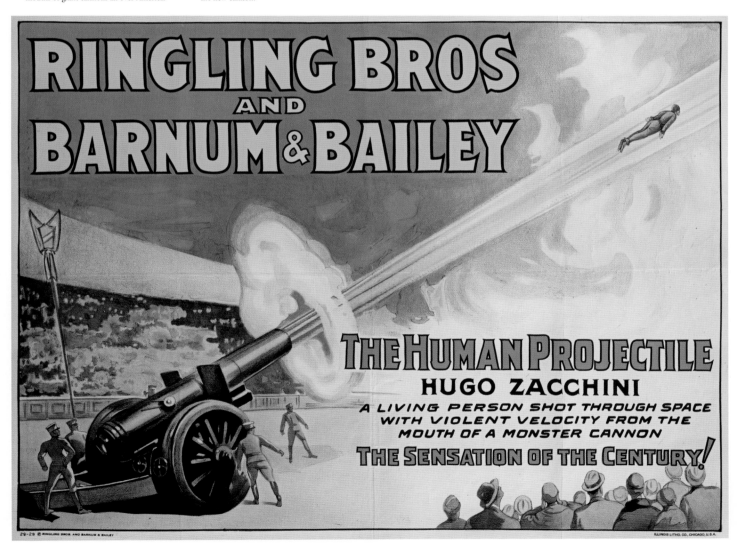

1949 "When [the Zacchinis] are *fired from the mouth of a cannon* within four fifths of a second…the limit in thrills seems to have been reached. If not, then man has not yet conceived the ultimate breathtaker." (*The Fitchburg Sentinel*, June 28, 1935)

below
1949 The Zacchinis improved on the human cannonball stunt by having *two persons shot simultaneously* from the mouth of one cannon. To make the stunt even more exciting, Zacchini sisters Duina, left, and Egle performed it together.

opposite
1940s "Everything I saw in the ring blended into something triumphant, where skill and strength confidently celebrated their *victory over mortal danger*." (Maxim Gorky quoted by A. Lebedeva, *Maxim Gorky's Impressions of the Circus,* 1967)

pages 376–377
1914 Kar-Mi performed a new version of this classic stunt with a unique twist inspired by sword swallowing. Instead of being the projectile, Kar-Mi was the barrel: With a stripped-down gun barrel slid partially down his throat, he *shot buckshot from his mouth* to a target that rested on the head of a fearless, blindfolded partner—the true daredevil.

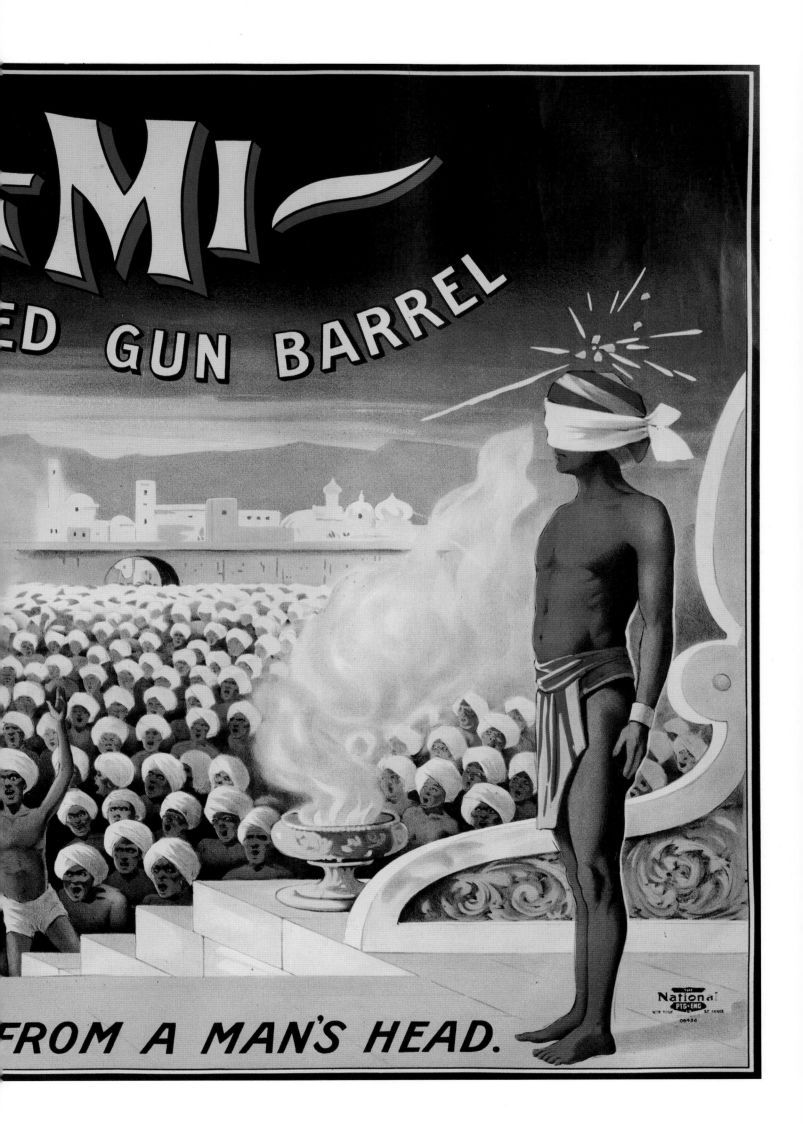

ADDITIONAL
POSTER CREDITS

Posters below appear as details in the book.

INTRODUCTION
SOMETHING WICKED THIS WAY COMES

"Lu Lu the Flying Artist," W. C. Coup circus, 1881 (pp. 2–3).
The John & Mable Ringling Museum of Art, Tibbals Digital Collection.

CHAPTER 2
WONDERS OF THE WORLD AWAIT YOU

"The Marvels of Many Nations," W. W. Cole's circus, 1881 (p. 69)

CHAPTER 3
VENUSES OF THE AGE: THE FEMALE PERFORMER EMANCIPATED

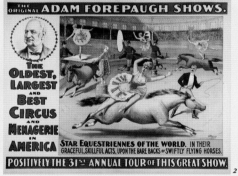

1–5: Miss Linda Jeal, P. T. Barnum's circus, 1879 (pp. 130–131); "Star Equestriennes of the World," Adam Forepaugh circus, 1894 (p. 132);
Lottie Aymar, "Europe's Greatest Rider," Barnum & Bailey, 1889 (p. 134); Mademoiselle Zoe, "Queen of the Air," Barnum & London, 1885
(pp. 142–143); Carlotta, "Lady with Teeth of Steel," Van Amburgh, Chas. Reiche & Bros. circus, 1880s (pp. 156–157).
The John & Mable Ringling Museum of Art, Tibbals Digital Collection.

CHAPTER 4
STRANGE BEASTS FROM FOREIGN LANDS

1–2: "The Realistic Jungle Menagerie," Barnum & Bailey, 1897 (pp. 164–165); Blacaman,
"Hindu Animal Hypnotist," Hagenbeck-Wallace circus, 1938 (pp. 198–199).
The John & Mable Ringling Museum of Art, Tibbals Digital Collection.

CHAPTER 5
CIRCUS ACTS: CONTROLLED MAYHEM TO DAZZLE AND DELIGHT

1: "The 4 Cornella Brothers, America's Best Acrobats," Barnum & Bailey, 1891 (p. 206)
The John & Mable Ringling Museum of Art, Tibbals Digital Collection.

CHAPTER 6
EATING FIRE, THROWING KNIVES: FREAKS & WONDERS OF THE SIDESHOW

  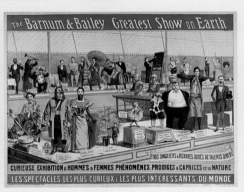

1: "The Human Salamander," Barnum & Bailey, 1889 (p. 245). *Circus World Museum, Baraboo, WI.*
2–3: Thauma, Barnum & Bailey, 1889 (p. 252); "Curieuse Exhibition d'Hommes et Femmes,"
Barnum & Bailey, 1902 (pp. 264–265). *The John & Mable Ringling Museum of Art, Tibbals Digital Collection.*

CHAPTER 8
SECONDS FROM DEATH: RISKING
LIFE & LIMB FOR THE CROWD

1: Zazel, "the Human Projectile," John B. Doris circus, 1881 (p. 350), *Circus World Museum, Baraboo, WI.*

INDEX

Page numbers in **bold** refer to illustrations.

Chapters are used as subsets for longer entries. The chapters are:
Introduction: Something Wicked This Way Comes
Chapter 1: Worldwide Roots of Circus, Invention, Performance, and Play
Chapter 2: Wonders of the World Await You
Chapter 3: Venuses of the Age: Female Performers Emancipated
Chapter 4: Strange Beasts from Foreign Lands
Chapter 5: Circus Acts: Controlled Mayhem to Dazzle and Delight
Chapter 6: Eating Fire, Throwing Knives: Freaks & Wonders of the Sideshow
Chapter 7: Tent City: Backstage at the Circus
Chapter 8: Seconds from Death: Risking Life & Limb for the Crowd

A

Adam Forepaugh & Sells Bros. circus, 57, 143, **186, 218–219, 233, 326–327, 358**, 360, **360**, 362, **363, 364–365**
Adam Forepaugh circus, 16, **18–19**, 25, 75, **75**, 132, **132**, 155, **369, 378, 379**. *See also* Adam Forepaugh & Sells Bros. circus
Adgie, Mademoiselle, 196, **196**
Adler, Felix, 24, **24**
Aeros, Cliff, 354
Africa, 68, 72, 94, 103, 163, 166, 318
Agra, Zalumma, 274
Aladdin, 72
Aladdin and His Wonderful Lamp (spectacle), 72
Alar ("the Human Arrow"), 353
Alexander, 324
Alfonso ("the Human Ostrich"), **264**
Al G. Barnes circus, 70, **116**, 188, **188–189, 314–315**, 317
Alpaugh, Colleen, 226, **227**
Alzana, Harold, 226, **228–229**, 230, **231**, 323, **323**
"Ambassadors from Mars, the." *See* Muse, George and Willie
America (spectacle), **148**
American Museum, 42, 60, **60**, 68, 72, 249, 267, 274, **274**
American Revolution (spectacle), **75**
Ancillotti, Maurice, 361, **361**
Ancillotti, Mrs., 232, **232**
Ancillotti, Ugo ("the Great Ancillotti"), 354, 359, **359**
Ancillotti family, 354, 359, 361, 362, **362**
Anthony, Bumpsy. *See* Hulme, George
Antiquae urbis splendor (book), 43, **43**
Antony, Mark, 74, 88
Arabian Nights, 81, 305
Arcaris, Kate, **1**, 16
Arcaris, Signor, **1**, 16
Arrigosi Sisters, 115
Arthur, King, 73
Arwood family, 179, **179**
Astley, Patty, 112,
Astley, Philip, 44, 47–48, 57, 58, 72, 112, 162, 207
Astley's Amphitheatre, 47, 58, **58**
Astley's Riding School, 44, 47, 112
Atwell, Harry A. (photographer), **26** bottom, 94, **94**, 99, **99, 115, 147** top left, **150, 196** top and center, **216** top right, **224** top, **225** top and bottom, **240, 246, 268** top, **281** top
Aymar, Lottie, 134, **134**
"Aztec Children, the." *See* Maximo and Bartola

B

Baba, 68, 162
Baba, Ali, 73
Bailey, Hachaliah, 68, 163
Bailey, James A., 25, 313
Balanchine, George, 30, 330
Balkis, 90
Ballantine, Bill, 236, 237, 249, 310
Ballet of the Elephants (spectacle), 330
Bambi (film), 166
Bara, Theda, 67, 73, 84
Barbette. *See* Broodway, Van der Clyde
Barnello, Signor. *See* Barnwell, Edward A.
Barnes, Harold, 226, **226**
Barnum, P.T. (Phineas Taylor)
Introduction, 25, 26
Chapter 1, 47–48, 107, 108, 60, **60**, 61
Chapter 2, 68, 72
Chapter 3, 133
Chapter 4, 163, 166, 167, 169
Chapter 6, 248, 251, 267, **267**, 268, 291, 292
Chapter 7, 317
Chapter 8, 351, 353
Barnum & Bailey circus. *See also* Barnum & London; P.T. Barnum's circus; Ringling Bros. and Barnum & Bailey
Introduction, 25, **28, 31**
Chapter 2, **66**, 67, 73, 74, **74**, 75, **75, 76–77, 78–79**, 80, 80, 81, **81**, 83, **86–67**, 90, **90, 92–93**, 94, 99, **99**
Chapter 3, **112**, 113, 115, **120–29, 126, 134** bottom, 141, **141**, 144, 152, **153, 155**
Chapter 4, 162, **164–165**, 168, **168, 176, 176**, 177, **178**, 184, 185, **185, 189, 192–193**, 196, **196**
Chapter 5, **206, 214–215, 222**, 223, 226, 232, **238**
Chapter 6, **245**, 247, **252**, 253, **264–265**, 268, **268** bottom, 270, 274, 278, **278**, 283, 286, 292, 295, **296–297**, 298, **298, 299**
Chapter 7, **310**
Chapter 8, 352, **352**, 353, 354, 355, 356, **359**, 361, **361**, 362, **362**
Appendix **378, 379**
Barnum & London circus, 25, **142–143, 151, 167**, 267, **267**, 369, **370–371, 378**. *See also* Barnum & Bailey; P.T. Barnum's circus; Ringling Bros. and Barnum & Bailey
Barnwell, Edward A. ("the Human Volcano" or "Signor Barnello"), 249, 286, **286**
Bartik, Ottokar, 80
Bary, Howard Y., 166, **166**
Battle of Summit Springs. *See* Summit Springs
Beatty, Clyde, **82**, 83, 166, 195, **195**, 197, **197**, 204
Beeson, Herbert "Berta," 147, **147**
Belford Troupe, 232, **232**
Belgian Congo, 72
Bell, Charlie, 345, **345**
Ben-Hur (spectacle), 70, **70**
Ben-Hur: A Tale of the Christ (book), 70
Bennett Sisters, 152, **152**
Bentley circus. *See* Charles A. Bentley circus
Bet, 68, 95
Bibrowski, Stefan. *See* Lionel, "the Lion-Faced Boy"
Bilboquet Humain (act), 354
Birth of the Rainbow (spectacle)
Blacaman, **160**, 161, 197, **198–199**
"Blind Girl from Mars, the." *See* Green, Elizabeth
Blondin (Jean-François Emile Gravelet), 352, 353, **353**, 369
Blue Beard's Chamber, 295, **296–297**
Blue Cloud, 103
Boden, Zelda, **65**, 67, 80, **80, 670**
Bogino Troupe, **304**, 305
Book of the Thousand Nights and a Night, The, 75
Booptee, 282, **282**
Boston, 48
Boulevard du Crime, 47
Boulevard du Temple, 47
Bowen, Eli, 248, **248**
"Boxing Fat Sisters, the." *See* Carlson, Dorothy and Florence
Bradna, Ella, 116
Bradna, Fred, 116, 135, 179, 208, 230
Brady, Mathew (photographer), 267, **267**, 268, **268**
Brides and the Beasts (spectacle), 81, **81**
Brilloff, Rudolf, 47
Broadbent, Betty, 251, 290, **290**
Broadway (theater), 30, 60, 67, 74, 75, 90, 293
Broodway, Van der Clyde ("Barbette"), 147
Brooklyn, 250
Brown, Joshua Purdy, 48
Browning, Tod, 253, 293, 313
Bruce, Vera, 210
Brunn, Francis, 208, **240**, 241, **241**
Brunn, Lottie, **201**, 203
Buck, Frank, 73
Buffalo Bill. *See* Cody, William F.
Buffalo Bill's Wild West, 75, **104**, 105, **105, 106–107**
Bunker, Chang and Eng, 253, 293, **293**
Burton, Sir Richard, 72
Butler, Roland, 72, 133, **133**

C

"Camel Girl, the." *See* Harper, Ella
Capa, Cornell (photographer), 230, **231**
Caratha, Grand Turk Mahomed, 48, **50–51**
Carlisle, Richard Risley, 220
Carlos, Charles, 177, **177**
Carlotta, Miss, 155, **156–157**
Carlson, Dorothy and Florence ("Half Ton Twins" or "Boxing Fat Sisters"), 262, **262**
Carlson Sisters. *See* Carlson, Dorothy and Florence
Carnegie, Andrew, 22
Caroli family, 44
Castello, Dan, 25, 48, 72
Caudillo, Dora, 306, **306**
Caudillo, Margaret, 306, **306**
Chained for Life (film), 293
Chang and Eng. *See* Bunker, Chang and Eng
Chang Tu Sing ("the Chinese Goliath"), **266**, 267
Chaplin, Charlie, 27
Charles 1st, monkey, **168**, 169
Charles V, Holy Roman emperor, 47
Charles IX, king of France, 44
Charles A. Bentley circus, **209**
Charmaine, Miss, 155, **155**
Chiarini family, 44
Children's Circus and Menagerie Picture Book, The, **159**, 161, 369
China, 42, 73, 99, 267
Ching-Ling-He Troupe, **78–79**
Christy Bros. circus, **163**
Ciniselli family, 44
Circus Day, 26, **26**, 30, **30**, 68, **68**, 72, 169, **312–313**, 316, **316**
Circus Maximus, 44, 47
Circus Serenade (spectacle), 90, **93**
Cirque Olympique, 47, 54, 162
Clark, Vera, 128, **128**
Clark, William, 24
Clarke, Ernest, 223, **223**
Clarke, Ernestine, 222, **222**, 122, **122**
Clarkonians, 223
Clausen family, **182–183**, 185
Clemens, Dick, 197, **197**
Cleopatra, 74, 75, 88
Cleopatra (film), 67, 73, 84
Cleopatra, Queen of Egypt (spectacle), 75, **86–87**, 88, 204
Clifford, Mademoiselle, 283, **283**
Clown Alley, 236, **236–237**, 324, 345, **345**
Coco, 58, **58**, 162
Cocteau, Jean, 147
Codona, Alfredo, 26, 210, 224, **224**
Coffey, James W. ("the Skeleton Dude"), **265**
Cole, Harry, 102, **102**
Cole & Rogers circus, 195, **195**
Cole Bros. circus, 16, **133, 197**, 212, **212–213**, 226, **226**, 277, 278, 306, 316, **316**, 317, **317**, 357, **357**
Coliseum, 43, **43**
Colleano, Con (Cornelius Sullivan), 208, 226, **226, 227**
Colleano, Winnie, 116
Columbine, 47
Columbus and the Discovery of America (spectacle), **74**, 75
Concello, Antoinette ("Toni"), 116, 126, **127**, 207, **207**, 210, , **220**, 225, **225**
Concello, Arthur, 207, **207**, 210
Coney Island, **258** (top & bottom). *See also* World Circus Side Show
Confessions of Felix Krull, Confidence Man (book), 113
Cooper & Bailey circus, **32–33**
Corbin, Myrtle ("the Four-Legged Woman"), 294, **294**, 295
Cordon Troupe, **100–101**, 102
Cornella Brothers, **206**, 207
Corsicana (Texas), 28, **28**
Costentenus, Georges ("Captain Costentenus" or "the Tattooed Prince"), 291, **291**
Coup, W.C. (William Cameron), 25, 48, 72, 163, 317
Courier Company, **130–131**, 306
Court, Alfred, 166
Covent Garden, 48, 57
Cripe, Jack, 291, **291**
Cristiani, Corky, **109**, 111
Cristiani, Marian, 241, **241**
Cristiani family, 44, 111, 207, 310, **342–343**
Crosby, Bing, 356
Cybele, 42

D

Dailey Bros. circus, **25**, 209
DaMann family, 104, **218–219**, 220
Dann, Harry, 238, **239**
Darwin, Charles, 248
"Darwin's Missing Link." *See* Krao
Davenport Troupe, 226, **226**
Davis family, **276**, 277
De Bach, Christophe, 75, 85, 95
De Burgh, Emma, 290, **290**
Deisler, Juanita "Neets," 224, **224**
De La Fontaine, Jean, 54
Delavan (Wisconsin), 316
Delkano ("King of Fire"), 286, **286**
Del Oro, Pinito, **21**, 23, 116, 148, **149, 303**, 305
DeMarlo, 128, **128**
De Morgues, Jacques Le Moyne, 41
Denier, Tony, 57, **57**
Depression. *See* Great Depression
Desperado, 352, 355
De Tiers, Mauricia, 354, 355
Diavolo, 362, **362, 363**
Dibdin, Charles, 47
Dietrich, Marlene, 126
Dionysus, 42
Disher, Maurice Willson, 44
Disney, Walt, 28, 166, 238
Disneyland, 147
Divine, Miss, 73, **73**
Dixon, Samuel J., 352, **353**
Dobbs, Helen, 306, **306**
"Dog-Faced Boy, the." *See* Jo-Jo
Doll family, 260, **260–261**
Dolly Dimple. *See* Geyer, Celesta
Downie Bros.'s circus, **258**
Dracula (film), 253
Dreamland (Coney Island), **262**
Dreamland (spectacle), **346–347**
Dumbo (film), 30

E

Eames, Charles and Ray, 345
Earle, Jack (Jacob Ehrlich), 268, **268**
Earl family, 217, **217**
Eck, Johnny, 253
Egypt, 41, 42, 75, 81, 83, 88, 90
Ehrlich, Jacob. *See* Earle, Jack
Eisman, Nieman, 262, **263**, 286, **288–289**
Eko and Iko. *See* Muse, George and Willie
"Electric Girl," 283, **283**
"El Niño." *See* Farini, Samuel
England, 42, 28, 107, 112, 132, 267, 293, 318
Ernesto Sisters, 144, **144**
Europe
Chapter 1, 42, 44, 47, 48, 57
Chapter 2, 70, 72
Chapter 3, 112, 222, 225, 134, 144, 147
Chapter 4, 163, 168
Chapter 5, 204, 210
Chapter 6, 267, 277
Chapter 7, 310
Chapter 8, 352, 353, 354
Evans, Walker, 258, **258**

F

Fairbanks, Douglas, 73, 210
Famous Robinson circus, **217**
Farini, Krao ("the Missing Link"), 248
Farini, Lulu, 353, 355
Farini, Samuel ("El Niño"), 352–353
Farini, Signor Guillermo Antonio. *See* Hunt, William Leonard
Favetier, Natal, **190**, 191
Fellig, Arthur. *See* Weegee
Fellows, Dexter, 324
Ferroni family, 44
Fields, W.C., 28
Flying Randolls, 224
Folies Bergère, 90, 113
Ford, Henry, 27
Ford Model T, 27
Forepaugh-Sells circus. *See* Adam Forepaugh & Sells Bros. circus
"Four-Legged Woman, the." *See* Corbin, Myrtle
Fox, Norma ("La Norma"), 223, **223**
Franconi, Antonio, 47, 207
Franconi, Henri, 47
Franconi, Henri Narcisse, 47
Franconi, Laurent, 47
Franconi family, 44, 47, 58, **58, 59**, 162
Frank A. Robbins circus, **118–119**
Fratellini family, 44
Freaks (film), 253, 293, 313
Freeland, Forrest, **114**, 115
French Revolution, 47, 48
Funambuli, 41, 209

G

Gable, Clark, 30
Gabrielle, Mademoiselle ("the Living Half Woman"), 298, **299**
Gangler's Novelty circus, 185, **185**
Gardner, Frank "Cheerful," 208
Gargantua, 166, 191, **191**
Gaynell Troupe, **364–365**
Gebel-Williams, Gunther, 166
Genders, Gracie, 225, **225**
Gentry Bros. and James Patterson circus, **194**
George III, King, 112
Geraldo Troupe, 224, **224**
Germany, 47, 73, 102, 169, 185, 203, 209, 354
Geyer, Celesta (née Herrmann, "Dolly Dimple" or "Jolly Dolly"), 262, **263**
"Giraffe-Neck Women," 72, 96, **96**, 99, **99**
Glasier, Frederick Whitman (photographer)
Chapter 2, **65, 72, 73, 80, 81, 84** top, **96, 102, 103** top and bottom, **104, 105**
Chapter 3, **113, 126, 128, 135** bottom, **138** bottom, **144, 148** bottom left and right, **155**
Chapter 4, **177**
Chapter 5, **232** bottom, **233** top
Chapter 6, **268** bottom
Chapter 7, **311, 317, 340** top
Chapter 8, **359, 366, 367** top and bottom
Appendix **670**
Goliath, 267
Gollmar Bros. circus, 357
Gorky, Maxim, 355, 375
Gravelet, Jean-François Emile. *See* Blondin
"Great Ancillotti, the." *See* Ancillotti, Ugo
Great Cantilever Bridge, 352
Great Depression, 28, 30
Greatest Show on Earth. *See* Barnum & Bailey; Barnum & London; P.T. Barnum's circus; Ringling Bros. and Barnum & Bailey
"Great Florenzo, the," 357, **357**
Great Pacific circus, **300–301**
Great Roman Hippodrome, 48
Great Wallace circus, **256–257**
"Great Wilno, the." *See* Wiedrich, Otto
Green, Elizabeth ("Betty," "Blind Girl from Mars," or "Koo Koo"), 260, **261**
Gregg, Bette, 356, **356**, 357, **357**
Gregg, Fred ("Fearless"), 354, 356, **356**, 357, **357**
Griebling, Otto, 212, **212**
Griffin, Charles E., 283, **283**
Griffith, D.W., 73
Griffith, J., 112
Griffith, Mrs., 112
Grimaldi, Joseph ("Joey"), **56**, 57, **57**, 179
Grunatho Sisters, 141, **141**
Gryifith, Margaret Vergh, 108, **108**

H

Hagenbeck, Carl, 169
Hagenbeck, Gottfried, 169
Hagenbeck firm, 73, 169
Hagenbeck-Wallace circus, **82–83**, 83, 98, 226, **226, 198–199**, 234, 563, **379**
"Half-Ton Twins, the." *See* Carlson, Dorothy and Florence
Han Dynasty, 41, 42, 73
Hanneford, Edwin, Jr. ("Poodles"), 83, **83**
Hanneford, Gracie, 115, **115**
Hannibal, 324
Hanson, Fred, **10**, 16
Harlequin and Mother Goose (pantomime), **56, 57**
Hartford (Connecticut), 30, 31
Hayes, John ("the Tattooed Man"), **264**
Hemingway, Ernest, 67
Henri IV, King, 44
Hepburn, Katharine, 126
Herbert, Dorothy, 128, **128, 129**, 133, **133**
Hicks, Clyde ("Tiny"), **246**, 247
Hilton, Daisy and Violet, 293, **293**
Hippodrome de l'Étoile, 47
"Hirsute Wonder, the." *See* Unzie
Hobart's circus, **378**
Hodgini, Harriet, 26
Hollywood, 30, 84, 90, 111, 115, 116, 126, 150, 253, 268
Horompo, Paul, 238, **238**
Howerton, Clarence ("Major Mite"), **246**, 247, 268, **268**
Howes, Nathan, 68
Howes, Seth B., 47
Howes & Cushing circus, **62–63**
Hughes, Charles, 47, 48, 207
Hugo the Giant, 269, **269**
Hulme, George ("Bumpsy Anthony"), 306, **306**
"Human Arrow, the." *See* Alar
"Human Pin Cushion, the." *See* Kongee, Leo
Human Salamander, **245**, 247
"Human Volcano, the." *See* Barnwell, Edward A.
Humpty Dumpty (pantomime), 57, **57**
Hunt, William Leonard ("Signor Guillermo Antonio

CREDITS, AUTHORS' BIOGRAPHIES, ACKNOWLEDGEMENTS

CREDITS

Key: t: top; c: center; b: bottom; l: left; r: right.
Gary Bart Photo Archive, Beverly Hills, California: 132 b., 156 t., 182 t., 206 t., 278 b., 291 t. l., 374 t. r., 374 b., 375, 393, 416 b., 447, 461, 462 t., 463 t., 466 t., 468 b., 488 b., 493 b., 506 b., 519 t. l., 568 t., 603 t. l., 603 b., 610, 619, 623 b. **Bridgeman Art Library,** London: 67. **Circus World Museum,** Baraboo, Wisconsin: 12, 27 b. r., 28 b., 30 b., 32 b., 38 t., 52 t. r., 52 c., 58–59, 62 t. r., 64–65, 122 t., 122 c., 122 b., 123, 130–31 t., 130 b., 138–39, 140, 144 b., 164 b., 166–67, 169 t., 175 b., 178 t., 181 b., 195 t., 200, 205, 208–209, 214, 216 t., 222 t., 225 b., 246 t., 250 t., 253 t., 258, 259 t. l., 259 c. r., 264 b., 265 t., 267 b., 268 t., 268 c., 268 b., 270, 283, 294, 300 b., 306 b., 307 t. l., 308 b., 312 t., 322 t., 335 t., 335 b., 336–37, 338 b., 342 t. r., 342 t. l., 350 b., 362 b., 363, 364, 366 t., 372, 377, 380–81, 384 t. r., 384–85, 391 b. l., 391 b. r., 392 c., 398 t., 399 t., 399 b., 406 t., 406 b., 412 t., 414 b., 419 c., 422, 429, 430, 432–33 t., 432 b., 437, 445 t., 445 b., 446 t. r., 450, 454, 455 t., 456, 458–59, 460 b., 463 b., 467, 468 t. l., 469 b., 473 b., 474 t., 475, 477 t., 477 b., 478 b., 479, 484, 485 b., 486 t., 487 t., 489 t., 490 t., 492, 493 t., 494, 495 t., 495 c., 495 b. l., 496, 498 b., 499, 502–503, 504 t. l., 504 b., 505 b. r., 506 t., 512 t. r., 512 b., 515, 516–17, 518, 530 t., 532 t., 533 t., 539 b., 544–45, 545 b., 546 b., 555 t., 558–59, 562 c., 563 b., 571 b., 574 t., 574 b., 575 b., 577 t., 577 b., 579 b., 583 t., 587 t., 593 t., 594 c., 600, 605 t., 605 b., 616, 618 b., 626 t., 626 b., 627 t., 628 t., 628 b., 629, 633, 635 b., 649 c., 649 b., 650–51, 652 t., 652 b., 653 t., 655 t., 655 b., 656. **Noel Daniel Collection,** Los Angeles, California: 53 b., 259 b., 303 b., 385 t. r., 469 t., 511 b., 514 b. l., 640 b., 641 t. **D. B. Denholtz Archive,** Fort Myers, Florida: 180 t. l., 180 t. r., 433 b., 443 b., 444 t., 444 b., 446 t. l., 446 b., 455 b., 487 b., 497 b., 514 t., 514 b. r., 519 t. r. **Dan DePalma Collection,** Laguna Niguel, California: 33 t., 143 b., 538 b., 614, 640 t. **George Eastman House,** Rochester, New York: 415. **Getty Images,** Hulton Archive, Weegee (Arthur Fellig)/International Center of Photography: 60 b., 61 b., 285 t., 356 b., 654 b. **Getty Images,** Time & Life Pictures, Cornell Capa: 307 t. r., 409, 654 t. **Steve Gossard Collection,** Bloomington, Illinois: 260, 390 t., 400. **Larry Gottheim, Be-hold, Inc.,** Yonkers, New York: 47 t., 226 b. **Ken Harck Collection,** Bollingbrook, Illinois: 154. **Harry Ransom Humanities Research Center,** the University of Texas at Austin: 1, 87, 110–11, 293, 468 t. r., 485 t., 497 t., 500 t., 501 (detail), 603 t. r. **Jim Heimann Collection,** Los Angeles, California: 416–17. **Illinois State University, Milner Library, Special Collections,** Normal, Illinois: 26 b., 29 b., 54–55, 71 b., 82, 83 t. l., 83 t. c., 83 t. r., 83 c., 83 b., 90, 93 t., 105 b., 108 b. l., 108 b. r., 115 t., 115 c. r., 115 l., 162–63, 168 b., 170–71, 188 t., 261 t., 339, 350 t., 402 t., 442 b., 448–49, 462 c. l., 462 c. r., 482 t., 482 b. l., 482 b. r., 488 c., 504 t. r., 505 b. l., 559 t., 563 t., 569 b. **Illinois State University, Milner Library, Special Collections,** Normal, Illinois: Sverre O. Braathen, photographer: 8–9, 23, 27 b. l., 28 t., 31, 36, 39 t., 41 t., 42–43, 45, 46, 47 b., 48–49, 50, 56 t., 56 b., 57, 147, 152 t., 157, 162 t., 165, 172 t., 190–91, 199, 203 t., 210, 213, 217 b., 225 t., 227, 231, 232–33, 239, 244 b., 245 b., 257, 263, 266, 285 t., 298, 308 t., 309 b., 310 t., 318–19, 334, 338 t., 347, 354, 355 b., 356 t., 367, 373, 391 t., 397 t., 398 b. r., 401 b., 404–405, 408 t., 408 c., 408 b., 420 t. l., 423 t., 423 b., 438–39, 452, 491, 523, 526 t., 527, 528–29, 532 b., 533 b., 536, 537 b., 538 t., 541 b., 542, 547, 550 t., 551 t., 553, 555 b., 556 b., 557 t., 572 b. l., 573 t., 575 t., 576, 578 t., 579 t., 583 b., 584 t., 584 b., 585 b., 590–91, 596–97, 599, 657 t., 657 b., 662. **P. Jacob & C. William, TOHU Cité des Arts du Cirque,** Montréal, Canada: 68, 70, 71 t., 72, 73, 74, 75, 76, 84, 85, 86, 92, 93 b., 94 t., 96, 97 t., 97 b., 98 t., 98 b., 99 b., 100–101, 102, 103, 104, 105 t. l., 109, 110 t., 116 t., 116 b., 117, 118 c. l., 118 c., 118 c. r., 118 b. l., 118 b. c., 118 b. r., 119 t., 119 b., 120 t., 120 c., 353 b., 402 b., 513. **Dominique Jando Collection,** San Francisco, California: 116 c., 118 t., 120 b., 121 b. l., 121 b. r. **Collection of Ricky Jay,** Los Angeles, California: 94 b., 95, 99 t., 105 t. r., 106 b. l., 106 b. r., 107, 108 t., 111 t., 112, 113 t., 113 c., 113 b. **The John & Mable Ringling Museum of Art,** Sarasota, Florida: 80, 291 b., 321 t., 327, 365 b., 390 l., 489 b., 511 t., 586–87. **The John & Mable Ringling Museum of Art, Glasier Glass Plate Negative Collection,** Sarasota, Florida: 60 t., 127, 134, 135 b., 142, 150, 153 t., 153 b., 160 b., 161 b., 164 t., 174 t. l., 174 t. r., 180 b., 182 b., 192 t., 193 t., 193 b. l., 193 b. r., 194 t., 195 b., 203 b., 212 l., 237 t., 237 b., 238 b., 240 b., 247 b., 250 b., 256 b., 262 b. l., 262 b. r., 267 t., 271 t., 313 b., 376 b., 412 b., 413 t., 419 t., 419 b., 474 b., 488 t., 531, 551 b., 573 b., 586 t., 612, 645 t., 646 t., 646 b., 670. **The John & Mable Ringling Museum of Art, Tibbals Digital Collection,** Sarasota, Florida: 2–3, 20–21, 27 t., 32 t., 34–35, 40 t., 40 b., 41 b., 44 b., 124–25, 131 b., 132 t., 135 t., 136 t., 136 b., 137 b., 143 t., 144 t., 145 b., 146, 148–49, 152 b., 155 t., 155 b., 156 b., 158–59, 160 t., 160 c., 161 t., 168 t., 172 b., 174 b., 176–77, 178 b., 179, 181 t., 183, 184–86, 187, 192 b., 194 b., 196–97, 202, 207, 212 r., 215, 217 t., 218–19, 224, 226 t., 228–29, 234–35, 237 c., 238 t., 240 t., 242–43, 244 t., 246 b., 247 t., 251, 252, 253 b., 254–55, 256 t., 259 t. c., 261 b., 262 t., 264 t., 265 b., 269, 271 b., 272–73, 276, 278 t., 279, 280–81, 284, 288, 292 t., 295, 301, 303 t., 304–305, 307 b., 310 b., 312 b., 313 t., 316–17, 320, 321 b., 322 c., 322 b., 323, 324–25, 326 b., 332–33, 340, 341 b., 342 b., 343 t., 343 b., 344–45, 351, 352, 355 c., 362 t., 368–69, 376 t., 378–79, 382 b., 383, 384 t. l., 385 t. l., 386–87, 389, 392 t., 392 b., 396, 397 b., 403, 407, 413 b., 414 t., 420 b., 426–27, 436, 453, 470–71, 472, 480–81, 490 b., 498 t., 508–510, 519 b. 520–21, 539 t., 541 t., 548–49, 550 t., 552 t., 556 t., 560–61, 562 b., 566 t., 572 t., 585 t., 585 c., 588 t., 602, 604, 606, 608 t., 608 b., 609 t., 609 b., 611 t. l., 611 t. r., 613, 617 t., 617 b., 618 c., 623 t., 624–25, 627 t., 631 t., 632 t., 632 b., 635 t., 636 b., 637, 638–39, 642–44, 645 b., 647, 649 t., 653 b., 658 t., 659. **The Library of Congress,** Washington, DC: 4–5 (*Look* Magazine Collection, Stanley Kubrick, photographer), 44 t., 188 b., 248–49, 296–97, 302, 306 t., 314, 328–31, 365 t., 374 t. l., 394–95, 410–11, 424 t. (© 2007 EAMES OFFICE LLC), 440, 476, 592 (© 2007 EAMES OFFICE LLC), 620–21, 622, 630, 631 b., 634. **The Lisette Model Foundation, Inc.** (1983). Used by permission. Collection International Center of Photography: New York: 348, 357. **The Metropolitan Museum of Art,** New York: 460 t. (Walker Evans Archive, 1994 (1994.253.39.1) © Walker Evans Archive, The Metropolitan Museum of Art, New York), 460 c. (Walker Evans Archive, 1994 (1994.253.39.3) © Walker Evans Archive, The Metropolitan Museum of Art). **National Museum of American History,** Washington, DC, Glen Fishback Photographs and Papers, Archives Center, Behring Center, Smithsonian Institution: 53 t., 61 t., 62 b., 63, 315 t., 315 b., 370, 388 b., 425, 546 t., 588 b. **National Portrait Gallery,** London: 114. **National Portrait Gallery, Smithsonian Institution,** Washington, DC: 473 t. l., 473 t. r., 474 c. **Collection of The New-York Historical Society,** New York: 204 (detail, 79798T), 477 l. (79794T), 512 l., (79797T), 658 b. (79795T). **Collections of The New York Public Library,** Astor, Lenox, and Tilden Foundations, New York: 121 t. (Courtesy of Dominique Jando). **Pfening Archives,** Columbus, Ohio: 6–7, 241, 358–59. **Princeton University Library,** Department of Rare Books and Special Collections, Princeton, New Jersey: 434 b., 486 b. l. **Réunion des Musées Nationaux / Art Resource,** New York: 106 t. **Robert F. Sabia Collection,** Williamsburg, Virginia: 24, 62 t. l., 128, 137 t., 245 t., 282 l., 282 r., 290, 291 t. r., 292 b., 300 t., 326 t., 388 t., 478 t., 526 b., 540 t., 540 b., 557 b., 566 b., 572 b. r., 641 b. **Robert F. Sabia Collection,** Williamsburg, Virginia; William Day and Jim Hoye, photographers: 10, 19, 26 t., 29 t., 33 b., 38 b., 39 b., 52 t. l., 52 b., 133, 145 t., 169 b., 173, 175 t., 206 b., 216 b., 220, 222 l., 223, 230 t., 236, 309 t., 311, 360, 366 b., 398 b. l., 401 t., 418, 420 t. r., 421, 424 b., 435, 457, 462 b., 524, 530 b., 534, 537 t., 550 c., 552 b., 554, 562 t., 563 c., 564–65, 567, 568 b., 569 t., 570, 571 t., 578 b., 580–81, 582, 584 c., 589 t., 593 b., 594 t. r., 594 b. **Jim Secreto Photography,** Clarkston, Michigan: 442–43, 505. **Smithsonian American Art Museum,** Washington, DC / Art Resource, New York: 505 t. **Toronto Public Library,** Osborne Collection of Early Children's Books, Toronto, Canada: 275 (detail), 648. **Peter Turner Collection,** Edmonton, Alberta, Canada: 286–87, 341 t., 382 t., 434 t., 464–65, 466 b., 483, 486 b. r., 500 b., 636 t. **Winter Works on Paper,** New York: 353 t., 417 b. **Wisconsin Historical Society,** Madison, Wisconsin: 589 b. (WHS image ID 23003). **Witte Museum, Hertzberg Circus Collection,** San Antonio, Texas: 77, 78–79, 88–89.

Any credit omissions are unintentional and appropriate credit will be given in future editions if any holders of copyright contact the publisher.

ABOUT THE CONTRIBUTORS

Fred Dahlinger, Jr., is a circus historian and the author of several books on the American circus. Dahlinger was the historical consultant on this project, using the extensive archive of publications and unique primary source material he has compiled over the past 40 years on the technology, art forms, music, and management of circuses and outdoor amusement.

Linda Granfield is a widely published author whose book *Circus: An Album* (2001) won six awards, including a place on the "Best of the Best" list by Chicago Public Library. Known for her clear and accessible writing, Granfield has penned many young adult publications as well as adult nonfiction books.

Dominique Jando has written five books and numerous articles on American and European circuses. He was associate artistic director of New York's Big Apple Circus from 1983 to 2002, and creative director and director of the San Francisco School of Circus Arts from 2003 to 2004. He is cofounder of Paris' annual world-famous circus arts competition, the Festival Mondial du Cirque de Demain.

ABOUT THE EDITOR

Noel Daniel is a book editor based in Los Angeles. After graduating from Princeton University, she studied in Berlin on a Fulbright Scholarship. She received a Master's in London and was the director of a photography art gallery before becoming a book editor.

ACKNOWLEDGEMENTS

From the editor: I would like to first thank Dominique Jando, Fred Dahlinger, Jr., and Andy Disl, my "circus family" for the duration of this project. They set out on this adventure with me, offering indefatigable support and guidance, sharing the love of the material, and experiencing with me a thousand small moments of joy in the rigorous but beautiful process of pulling together this story about a long-neglected part of American cultural history. For his additional research and friendship, special thanks to Robert F. Sabia, who was part of the project from the beginning, and to Linda Granfield for her work ethic and enthusiasm. I am grateful also to Benedikt Taschen for putting this show on the road, for appreciating the research and energy that went into it, and for his generous enthusiasm about the subject.

My deep appreciation for their time and energy behind the scenes to Erin E. Foley of the Circus World Museum, Steve Gossard and Teresa Lynn Thomason of the Milner Library Special Collections, Illinois State University, Jennifer Lemmer Posey and Deborah Walk of the Circus Museum at the John & Mable Ringling Museum of Art, and Andy W. Kraushaar of the Wisconsin Historical Society.

Many thanks to Stan Ackert, Helen Adair, Andy Adams, Doug Adrianson, Alex and Bruce Bacon, Josh Baker, Tony Bannon, Erin Barnett, Gary Bart, Miles Barth, Kim Beckwith, Jennifer Belt, Christiane Bonneau, Ellsworth H. Brown, Anke Burger, Ann Charback, Pierre Charrier, Tina Ciborowius, Kathe Conley, Pete Cristiani, Tom and Margery Daniel, Perry Daniel, Janet M. Davis, Joel Dein, Ken DellaPenta, Eames Demetrios, David Denholtz, Raffaele De Ritis, Sheri Dolfen, Lucia Eames, C. W. Eldridge, Cheryl Elzy, Kenneth Feld of Feld Entertainment, Mia Fineman, Stephen T. Flint, Steve Freese, Carl Fuldner, Amy Fulkerson, Barbara Galasso, Lizanne Garrett, Christopher George, Frank Goerhardt, Larry Gotheim, Liz Gray, Charles Greene, Judith L. Griffin, David Haberstich, Francoise Hack, Annie Hambly, Christian Hamel, Ken Harck, Jan Harlan, Michaele Haynes, Jim Heimann, David Hertsgaard, Dana Holst, Pascal Jacob, Ricky Jay, Robert Johnson, Nancy Marie Kauth, Karen Kevorkian, Denise King, Florian Kobler, David Kotin, Kora Krines, Christiane Kubrick, Dennis Letbetter, Eric W. McConnell, John H. McConnell, Sammy P. McGivney, Leslie McGrath, Hugh Milstein, Jason Mitchell, Kathrin Murr, Kristen Neveu, Amelia Klem Osterud, Elena Panova, AnnaLee Pauls, Kay Peterson, Fred Pfening, Jr., Fred Pfening III, John F. Polacsek, Michelle Butnick Press, Dave Price, Rick Purdue, Jill Reichenbach, Richard J. Reynolds III, Emily Roisman, Jeffrey Rosenheim, Christophe Rousseau, Susan Sabia, Philippe Safavi, Jim Secreto, Laura Sedlmayr, Fran Seegull, Anna Skinner, Morgan Slade, William L. Slout, Donald Stacey, Jenn Stamm, Al W. Stencell, Joe R. Struble, Lauren Taschen, Heidi Taylor, James Taylor, Stuart L. Thayer, Michelle Thomas, Philip Thurston, Howard C. Tibbals, Helen Trompeteler, Jan Todd, Peter Turner, Brian Wallis, Cara Walsh, Rick Watson, Steffen Wedepohl, Veronica Weller, Nina Wiener, Christian William, David Winter, Julie Zeftel, Marco Zivny, Tino Wallenda Zoppé.

I would also like to thank the legions of talented, humorous, mischievous circus wordsmiths and press agents who ushered in the modern era of press and publicity, who whetted the appetite of millions to see the circus. Their color, along with vintage circus song titles, inspired the endpapers, the chapter titles, and the chapters' paragraph headers. Finally, to all the performers, crew, and circus owners who dedicated so much of themselves to the circus, and who profoundly changed the way we experience popular culture.

IMPRINT

© 2012 TASCHEN GmbH
Hohenzollernring 53, D–50672 Köln
www.taschen.com
Original edition: 2008 TASCHEN GmbH

This 2012 edition published by Metro Books by arrangement with TASCHEN GmbH.

Design: Sense/Net Art Direction, Andy Disl and Birgit Reber, Cologne
Editorial coordination: Florian Kobler, Kathrin Murr, Cologne
Production: Morgan Slade, Los Angeles; Tina Ciborowius, Cologne
German translation: Anke Burger, Berlin
French translation: Philippe Safavi, Paris

ISBN 978–1–4351–4239–8
Printed in China

2 4 6 8 10 9 7 5 3 1

p. 662
Contortionist, Cole Bros. circus, 1949. *Illinois State University, Milner Library, Special Collections.*

p. 670 (detail p. 127)
Zelda Boden, photographed by F. W. Glasier, 1910s. *The John & Mable Ringling Museum of Art, Glasier Glass Plate Negative Collection.*